ROUGH
GUIDES

T0082390

POCKET **ROUGH GUIDE**
COPENHAGEN

written and researched by
TARANEH GHAJAR JERVEN
this edition updatcd by
ANTHON JACKSON

CONTENTS

Introduction   4

When to visit.. 5
What's new 6
Where to... 7
Bruges at a glance 8
Ghent at a glance... 10
Things not to miss... 12

Places   27

The Markt... 28
The Burg... 36
South of the Markt.. 46
North and East of the Markt... 70
Damme 88
Central Ghent.. 94
Southern and eastern Ghent... 118

Accommodation   129

Essentials   137

Arrival 138
Getting around... 139
Directory A–Z 141
Festivals and events 146
Chronology... 148
Language 150
Glossary.. 155
Small print.. 156

BRUGES AND GHENT

Passing through Bruges in 1820, William Wordsworth declared that this was where he discovered 'a deeper peace than in deserts found'. Indeed, Wordsworth was one of the first Victorians to fall in love with a city whose charms continue to enthral its many visitors: Bruges's slender canals are flanked by an enchanting ensemble of ancient buildings, punctuated with a string of excellent museums, principally the Groeninge Museum with its world-class collection of early Flemish paintings. Neighbouring Ghent boasts its share of handsome medieval buildings, too, and also possesses one of the artistic wonders of the medieval world – the *Adoration of the Mystic Lamb* altarpiece by Jan van Eyck. Nonetheless, the atmosphere here is markedly different from that in Bruges: the tourist industry supplements but does not dominate the local economy. Ghent is, first and foremost, a vibrant Flemish city.

Ghent's beautiful old town

For the modern palate, Bruges's blend of antique architectural styles, from tiny brick cottages to gracious classical mansions, is a welcome relief and retreat. It certainly brings out the romance in many of its visitors – stay here long enough and you can't help but be amazed by the number of couples wandering its canals hand-in-hand, cheek-to-cheek. Neither does it matter much that a large part of Bruges is not quite what it seems: many buildings have been carefully constructed to resemble their medieval predecessors. Bruges has spent time and money preserving its image, rendering almost everything new in various versions of medieval style, and the result is one of Europe's most beautiful city centres. On the other hand, Ghent is a vital, bustling metropolis whose booming restaurant and bar scene wends its way across a charming cityscape, comprising a network of narrow canals overseen by dozens of antique red-brick houses. If Bruges is a tourist industry with a town attached, Ghent is the reverse – a proudly Flemish city with a population of around 470,000, Belgium's third-largest conurbation.

Bruges and Ghent share a similar history. Both prospered as lynchpins of the cloth trade, turning high-quality English wool into clothing that was exported

A guild house in Ghent

all over the world. It was an immensely profitable business that made Bruges, particularly, a focus of international trade. Through the city's harbours, Flemish cloth was exchanged for hogs from Denmark, spices from Venice, hides from Ireland, wax from Russia and furs from Bulgaria. However, despite (or perhaps because of) this lucrative state of affairs, Bruges and Ghent were dogged by war. The weavers and merchants of both cities were dependent on the goodwill of the kings of England for their wool

When to visit

Bruges and Ghent are all-year destinations. Give or take the vagaries of climate change, both cities enjoy a fairly standard temperate climate, with warm, if mild, summers and cold winters without much snow. The warmest months are usually June, July and August (averaging 18°C); the coldest, December and January (averaging 2°C), when short daylight hours and weak sunlight can make the weather seem colder (and wetter) than it is. Rain is always possible, especially in summer, which has more rainfall than autumn or winter. Warm days in April, May and early June, when the light has the clarity of springtime, are especially appealing, especially in Bruges, before summertime tourists arrive in full force. If you're planning a short visit, it's worth noting that many of the cities' museums are closed one day a week.

What's new

In the past few years, Ghent has emerged as a gastronomic pace setter, witnessing the opening of a string of inventive, much-vaunted restaurants – *Roots* (see page 116) and *De Lieve* (see page 115) are two cases in point. Bruges trades on its continuity, but the city's main concert hall, the Concertgebouw (see page 147), has made sterling efforts to open itself to casual visitors and now offers an enjoyable programme of guided tours.

supply, but their feudal overlords, the counts of Flanders and their successors, the dukes of Burgundy, were vassals of the rival kings of France. Consequently, whenever France and England were at war – which was often – both cities found themselves in a precarious position.

The Habsburgs swallowed Flanders – including Bruges and Ghent – into their empire in 1482, and the sour relations between the new rulers and the Flemings led to the decline of the two cities. Economically and politically marooned, Bruges was especially hard hit and withered away, its houses deserted, its canals empty and its money spirited away by the departing merchants. Some four centuries later, Georges Rodenbach's novel *Bruges-la-Morte* alerted well-heeled Europeans to the town's aged, quiet charms, and Bruges attracted its first wave of tourists. Many of them – especially the British – settled here and came to play a leading role in preserving the city's architectural heritage. Ghent, meanwhile, fared somewhat better, struggling on as a minor port and trading depot until its fortunes were revived by the development of a cotton-spinning industry in the early nineteenth century. Within forty years, Ghent was jam-packed with factories producing all manner of industrial goods. Although the city has moved on from its industrial base, it remains economically buoyant and is Belgium's third-largest metropolis.

The Concertgebouw, the main concert hall in Bruges

Where to...

Shop

The holy trinity of Belgian shopping is chocolates, beer and lace. Bruges and Ghent have a platoon of chain and family–run chocolate shops, and neither is there any shortage of beer stores. Lace is somewhat different: in Bruges, it's sold in shops all around the city, but they mostly only stock imported, machine-made pieces – the only real exception is 't Apostelientje – while in Ghent, there isn't much evidence of lace at all. If you're after international chain stores, you'll find plenty of outlets, especially in Ghent. Most are on the three main pedestrianised shopping streets: **Langemunt** and **Veldstraat** in Ghent and **Noordzandstraat** in Bruges.
OUR FAVOURITES: Bruges: Reisboekhandel see page 34; The Chocolate Line see page 65; 't Apostelientje see page 86. Ghent: Tierenteyn see page 113; Himschoot see page 113; Music Mania see page 126.

Eat

As you might expect of a major tourist destination, Bruges has many restaurants, but many are aimed squarely at outsiders, meaning standards can be patchy, especially on and around the Markt. That said, the city does possess a good supply of first-rate places to eat, which are well worth seeking out. Ghent's restaurant scene is arguably more reliable (with fewer tourists), and the city has an enviable reputation for its pace-setting restaurants. They range from top-draw, Michelin-starred places with an international menu to more local haunts, which characteristically offer traditional Flemish cuisine with a twist.
OUR FAVOURITES: Bruges: De Schaar see page 68; Christophe see page 67. Ghent: Maison Elza see page 116; De Lieve see page 115.

Drink

With every justification, Belgium is famous for its beers and bars. In both Bruges and Ghent, the hallmark bars are small and dark affairs dotted around the city centre rather than concentrated in a particular spot, with decor that varies from the simple to the cluttered and intense. All the best bars have beer menus, with some running to several hundred brews, mostly bottled but a few on tap. Many also sell *jenever*, which is similar to gin, made from grain spirit and flavoured with juniper berries. There are two main types – the young (*jonge*) and the smoother old (*oude*), but both are served ice cold in shot glasses.
OUR FAVOURITES: Bruges: De Garre see page 45; L'Estaminet see page 69. Ghent: 't Dreupelkot see page 116; Dulle Griet see page 117.

Go out

Frankly, you don't visit Bruges for its nightlife, though the city's festivals and special events (see page 146) boost a relatively modest scene. In Ghent, the most boisterous part of the city is the student quarter on and around Overpoortstraat, where there are many heaving late-night bars and clubs.
OUR FAVOURITES: Bruges: Bar Rose Red 69. Ghent: Vooruit see page 127; Decadence see page 127.

WHERE TO...

Bruges at a glance

North and east of the Markt p.70.
The areas north and east of the centre are home to an especially beguiling collection of handsome streetscapes, with graceful mansions and intimate brick houses draped along a lattice of slender canals, crisscrossed by dinky little stone bridges.

The Markt p.28.
At the centre of Bruges, this handsome cobbled square was long the commercial heart of the city and it's still home to one of the city's most striking medieval landmarks, the Belfort, whose distinctive lantern tower pierces the city's skyline.

South of the Markt p.46.
The streets south of the Markt are where you'll find Bruges' biggest cultural attraction: the superb Groeninge Museum, which boasts one of the world's finest collections of early Flemish paintings, including works by Jan van Eyck and Hieronymus Bosch. The area is also home to several other key sights, from the medieval Onze Lieve Vrouwekerk and the St-Janshospitaalmuseum, through to the whitewashed cottages of the Begijnhof and the Minnewater, the so-called "Lake of Love".

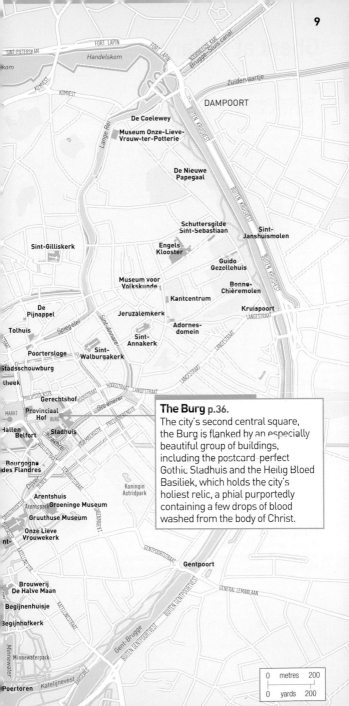

FORT LAPIN
SINT-PIETERSKAAI
Handelskom
NOORDWEESE KAI
Brugge-Sluis canal
Zuidervaartje
DAMPOORT

KOMVEST
Lange Rei
BUITEN KRUISVEST

De Coelewey
Museum Onze-Lieve-
Vrouw-ter-Potterie

De Nieuwe
Papegaal

Schuttersgilde
Sint-Sebastiaan
Sint-
Janshuismolen

Sint-Gilliskerk
Engels
Klooster

Guido
Gezellehuis

Museum voor
Volkskunde
Bonne-
Chièremolen

Kantcentrum
Kruispoort
LANGESTRAAT

De
Pijnappel
Jeruzalemkerk

Spiegelrei
Adornes-
domein

Tolhuis
Sint-
Annakerk

Poortersloge
Sint-
Walburgakerk

LANGESTRAAT

Stadsschouwburg
theek

PHILIPSTOCKSTR.
HOOGSTRAAT LANGESTRAAT

Gerechtshof
Greenerei

Provinciaal
Hof
BURG
PREDIKHERENREI

MARKT

Hallen
Belfort
Stadhuis

HOOGSTRAAT

The Burg p.36.

The city's second central square,
the Burg is flanked by an especially
beautiful group of buildings,
including the postcard-perfect
Gothic Stadhuis and the Heilig Bloed
Basiliek, which holds the city's
holiest relic, a phial purportedly
containing a few drops of blood
washed from the body of Christ.

Bourgogne
des Flandres

Dijver DIJVER

Koningin
Astridpark

Arentshuis
Arentspark Groeninge Museum
Gruuthuse Museum

Onze Lieve
Vrouwekerk
nt-

GENTPOORTSTRAAT
Gentpoort

GENERAAL LEMANLAAN

Brouwerij
De Halve Maan

Begijnenhuisje

Begijnhofkerk

Gent-Brugge
BUITEN GENTPOORTVEST

Minnewaterpark

Minnewater
Katelijnevest
BOECHUT

Poertoren

| 0 | metres | 200 |
| 0 | yards | 200 |

Ghent at a glance

Central Ghent p.94.
Ghent's ancient centre holds a glorious set of
Gothic buildings, including the stirring
St-Baafskathedraal (also home to the
remarkable Adoration of the Mystic Lamb by
Jan van Eyck), St Niklaaskerk, the medieval
guild houses of the Graslei, and a forbidding
castle, Het Gravensteen.

Het
Gravensteen

REKELINGESTRAAT

Leie

Oude
Vismijn

Design
Museum

Groo
Vleesh

Sint-
Niklaaskerk

Sint-
Michielskerk

Het
Pand

Museum Arnold
Vander Haeghen

Hôtel d'H
Steenhu

PAPEGAAISTRAAT

ANNONCIADENSTR

SER VANDERVELDESTR

ZONNESTRAAT

Conce
Hande

Gerechtshof

Opera
Ghent

BERNARD SPAELAAN

MARTELAARSLAN
MARTELAARSLAAN

NEDERKOUTER

Coupure

Leie

MARTELAARSLAAN

GEROLD BRITANNIELAAN

GODSHUIZENLAAN

De
Bijloke

STAM

Leie

KORTRIJKSEPOORTSTRAAT

Damme p.88.
A popular day-trip from Bruges, the pretty
little village of Damme perches beside a canal
7km to the northeast of the city; it's best reached
by bicycle.

LIZERLAAN

CHARLES DE KERCHOVELAAN

Damme

Bruges

Citadelpark

| 0 | miles | 8 |

| 0 | kilometres | 10 |

S.M.A.K.
(Stedelijk Museum
voor Actuele Kunst)

Ghent

STEENDAM

STEENDAM

Sint-Jacobskerk

SINT-JACOBSNIEUWSTRAAT

uis

dshal
Lakenhalle

Sint-Baafskathedraal

Geeraard de
Duivelsteen

VLAANDERENSTRAAT

BRABANTDAM

RK 1

BRABANTDAM

KUIPERSKAAI

VLAANDERENSTRAAT

Vooruit

FRANKLIN ROOSEVELTLAAN

GRAAF VAN VLAANDERENPLEIN

ZUIDSTATIONSTRAAT

ZUIDPARKLAAN

FRANKLIN ROOSEVELTLAAN

Lei

DAMPOORTSTRAAT

HOOFDBRUG KAAI

HAGELANDKAAI

DOK-ZUID

OKTROOIPLEIN

Lei

Sint-Baafsabdij

Coyendanspark

KASTEELLAAN

KASTEELLAAN

KASTEELLAAN

KEIZER KARELSTRAAT

KEIZER KARELSTRAAT

SINT-ANNA

NIEUWBRUGSTR

LANGE VIOLETTESTRAAT

LANGE VIOLETTESTRAAT

BRUSSELSEPOORTSTRAAT

Koning
Albertpark

Sint-Pietersabdij

Kunsthal

Muinkpark

Southern and eastern Ghent p.118.
Ghent's two leading fine art museums –
historic works at MSK and contemporary
art at S.M.A.K. – are located a couple of
kilometres south of the centre, not far
from the main train station.

MSK
useum voor
one Kunsten)

CITADELLAAN

CITADELLAAN

| 0 | metres | 200 |
| 0 | yards | 200 |

15

Things not to miss

It's not possible to see everything that Bruges and Ghent have to offer in one trip – and we don't suggest you try. A selective taste of their highlights follows – from eye-catching architecture to exquisite art.

> ### St-Walburgakerk, Bruges
> **See page 75**
> This fluent Baroque extravagance, built for the Jesuits in the seventeenth century, is perhaps the most charming of all the parish churches in Bruges.

< ### Onze-Lieve-Vrouwekerk, Bruges
See page 54
This intriguing medieval church is home to a Michelangelo Madonna and two superbly crafted medieval sarcophagi in the choir.

∨ ### Het Gravensteen, Ghent
See page 104
Ghent's stern and forbidding castle, Het Gravensteen, has long cast a steely eye over the city centre.

< **Adoration of the Mystic Lamb, Ghent**
See page 110
In Ghent's St-Baafskathedraal, Jan van Eyck's visionary painting celebrates the Lamb of God, the symbol of Christ's sacrifice.

∨ **Kantcentrum, Bruges**
See page 78
The Kantcentrum (Lace Centre) exhibits a small but exquisite collection of antique lace and hosts informal demonstrations of traditional lace-making.

< Minnewater, Bruges
See page 64
The so-called 'Lake of Love' is one
of the city's most romantic spots
and attracts canoodlers.

∨ S.M.A.K., Ghent
See page 119
Ghent's premier contemporary art
gallery features an adventurous
programme of temporary
exhibitions.

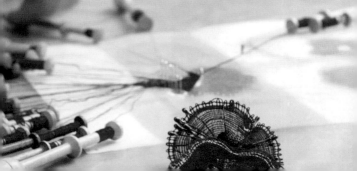

∧ **Chocolate Line, Bruges**
See page 65
Most chocolate shops in
Bruges are chains, but this one
isn't – and the chocolates are
mouthwateringly divine.

< **St-Baafskathedraal, Ghent**
See page 94
At the heart of Ghent, St-
Baafskathedraal is one of
Belgium's finest and most
distinguished Gothic churches.

∧ The Belfort, Bruges
See page 35
One of Belgium's most distinctive landmarks, the soaring lantern tower of the Belfort (belfry), pierces the skyline of central Bruges.

∨ Groeninge Museum, Bruges
See page 49
In the process of being remodelled, this remains the city's leading art museum, internationally famous for its outstanding collection of early Flemish paintings from van Eyck onwards.

∧ **St-Janshospitaal, Bruges**
See page 56
This former medieval hospital is now a museum housing a delightful sample of the paintings of Hans Memling.

< **MSK, Ghent**
See page 103
This outstanding art gallery displays an excellent collection of Belgian art from the Flemish Primitives to Magritte and Ensor.

< **St-Baafsabdij, Ghent**
See page 124
Off the beaten track, the rambling ruins of this charming, mostly medieval abbey are well worth the detour.

∨ **Heilig Bloed Basiliek, Bruges**
See page 36
The city's most important shrine, home to the much-venerated phial of the Holy Blood, its contents reputedly washed from the body of the crucified Christ.

Day One in Bruges

The Burg. See page 36. Begin in the heart of Bruges. Few squares in Europe can match the architectural delights of the Burg, home to both the Stadhuis and the Basilica of the Holy Blood, one of the holiest shrines of medieval Christendom.

Rozenhoedkaai. See page 34. Bruges is remarkably picturesque, but check the view back towards the Belfort from the Rozenhoedkaai (the Quay of the Rosary), as it's gorgeous.

The Markt. See page 28. The Markt is a charming central square, its cobblestones shadowed by the Belfort (belfry). If you have the energy, climb its distinctive lantern tower for views across the city.

Heilig Bloed Basiliek

🍴 **Lunch**. See page 34. Of all the cafés near the Markt, *Lb DbB* is the pick. It's a neat little place serving delicious salads at competitive prices.

Groeninge Museum. See page 49. Allow at least a few hours to explore the city's premier fine art gallery and brush up on your knowledge of early Flemish art. Here you'll encounter all the great masters, from Gerard David to Jan van Eyck.

Onze-Lieve-Vrouwekerk. See page 54. Few would say this historic church is pretty, but it is fascinating – from its grave frescoes and Renaissance mausoleums to its delicately carved Michelangelo sculpture.

View from the Rozenhoedkaai

🍴 **Dinner**. See page 68. Escape the more crowded parts of the city and stroll out to *De Schaar*, an infinitely cosy canal-side restaurant.

Drink. See page 69. Later, drop by *L'Estaminet* to sample those famed Belgian beers.

Groeninge Museum

Day Two in Bruges

St-Janshospitaalmuseum. See page 57. One of the most talented early Flemish painters was Hans Memling and this museum, which once sheltered the sick of mind, body and soul, holds an exquisite selection of his work.

St-Salvatorskathedraal. See page 60. This is the most important church in Bruges and home to a set of tapestries and the matching paintings from which they were copied – a rarity indeed.

🍴 **Lunch**. See page 86. Take a break in style at *Blackbird*, an agreeable café with a menu that's strong on all things healthy.

A painting in St-Salvatorskathedraal

Spiegelrei canal. See page 74. Stroll the easy sweep of the Spiegelrei, one of the most graceful canals in Bruges, its blue-black waters flanked by handsome old mansions redolent of Bruges' late medieval heyday.

St-Walburgakerk. See page 75. The very Catholic citizens of Bruges have punctuated their city with lovely churches. This is one of the most striking with its flowing Baroque facade.

The Adornesdomein. See page 76. Learn about the roller-coaster life and times of one of Bruges' most important medieval families and check out their unusual church, the Jeruzalemkerk.

The Spiegelrei canal

Kantcentrum. See page 78. Admire the intricate lacework of the women of Bruges.

🍴 **Dinner**. See page 86. Dine at the excellent *Sans Cravate*, which serves traditional Franco-Flemish cuisine in a sixteenth-century townhouse on Langestraat.

Drink. See page 87. Continue to *Café Vlissinghe*, one of the oldest bars in Bruges.

An exhibition at the Adornesdomein

Day One in Ghent

St-Baafskathedraal. See page 94. The obvious place to start an exploration of Ghent is the cathedral, home to the city's greatest artistic treasure: the *Adoration of the Mystic Lamb*.

St-Niklaaskerk. See page 99. Admire the peaked roofs, arching buttresses and pencil-thin turrets of St-Niklaaskerk – the most visually arresting of all Ghent's churches.

The Graslei. See page 102. Head for Tussen Bruggen, once the main harbour, and work your way along the decorated series of medieval guild houses.

Design Museum. See page 103. A hymn of praise to Belgian decorative and applied arts, this fascinating museum displays period rooms at the front and all manner of artefacts beyond; don't miss the Art Nouveau furniture.

Lunch. See page 116. Take lunch at the idiosyncratic *Maison Elza*, where, if the weather holds, you can eat out on the pontoon at the back.

Het Gravensteen. See page 104. Sullen and stern, the cold stone walls of Ghent's castle dominate this part of the city centre. Inside, there's a series of exhibitions about the medieval city.

Huis van Alijn. See page 106. Get to grips with the traditional culture of Flanders, from funerary rights and religious processions to celebrations and street games.

Dinner. See page 115. Ghent has an excellent restaurant scene: head for *De Lieve* to sample traditional Flemish food.

Drinks. See page 117. Round off the evening with a few beers – the *Het Waterhuis aan de Bierkant* will do very nicely.

The vaulted nave in St-Baafskathedraal

Medieval guild houses on the Graslei

The Design Museum

Day Two in Ghent

MSK. See page 122. Art lovers will want to make a beeline for this excellent museum, which holds a prestigious collection of Belgian art from the Flemish Primitives to Paul Delvaux and René Magritte.

S.M.A.K. See page 119. Not for the artistically squeamish, perhaps, but this capacious museum has a reputation for its adventurous, sometimes shocking exhibitions of contemporary art, featuring works from every corner of the globe.

Citadelpark. See page 119. Ghent is oh-so-very flat, so the wooded hillocks of this large park come as a pleasant change – and its assorted fountains, grottoes and statues are an agreeable surprise.

Lunch. See page 123. *Vooruit* may not be a gourmet paradise, but it is the city's cultural centre, especially for Ghent's university students. Its barn-like café-bar serves filling snacks and light meals at affordable prices.

St-Baafsabdij. See page 124. Well off the beaten track, the evocative ruins of this ancient abbey are genuinely delightful and incorporate an ivy-covered Gothic cloister and all manner of finely carved architectural bits and bobs: gargoyles, terracotta panels, capitals, columns and so forth.

Dinner. See page 127. *Martino* is Ghent at its liveliest, a busy, bustling diner with first-rate steaks and burgers. The house speciality is the 'Martino' comprising raw beef with mustard, Tabasco, tomato and anchovy.

A gallery at MSK

Citadelpark

St-Baafsabdij

Art in Bruges

Bruges is a small city, but it's big on medieval art. The top galleries attract most of the attention, but the parish churches and smaller museums are worth seeking out.

St-Jakobskerk. See page 70. The walls of this handsome church display more than eighty paintings gifted by the city's merchants. The pick is two finely executed triptychs dating from the late fifteenth century.

St-Walburgakerk. See page 75. The Jesuits of the seventeenth century had a Counter-Reformation point to make when they built St-Walburgakerk, a Baroque extravagance complete with Pieter Claeissens the Younger's triptych celebrating Philip the Good, count of Flanders.

Detail from a painting at St-Jakobskerk

St-Annakerk. See page 76. With its slender brick tower, this dinky little church may look restrained from the outside, but the interior holds a huge and gaudy *Last Judgement* by the itinerant artist Hendrik Herregouts.

Lunch. See page 87. No argument; *Café Vlissinghe* is one of the most charming café-bars in Bruges, all wood-panelling and long tables. The food is simple Flemish fare at competitive prices.

The altar at St-Walburgakerk

Museum Onze-Lieve-Vrouw ter Potterie. See page 82. This intimate museum occupies a one-time medieval hospital. The old sick room displays a charming assortment of medieval religious paintings, most memorably a striking panel painting of *St Michael triumphing over the Devil*.

Dinner. See page 86. Stay on the northern side of the city centre for an excellent meal at *Locàle by Kok au Vin*.

Museum Onze-Lieve-Vrouw ter Potterie

A drinker's day in Bruges

The key to enjoying and exploring Bruges's delightful bars is to pace yourself – and pay close attention to the alcohol percentage on the beer bottle or draft pump.

Bourgogne des Flandres. See page 43. Make a leisurely start with this brewery tour, which introduces the brewing process. Afterward, you'll get a bottle of their classic red-brown beer to quaff.

De Garre. See page 45. Down a **narrow** alley, this ancient tavern is an absolute delight with a wide-ranging beer menu, plus jazz and classical music.

🍴 **Lunch.** See page 44. Just off the Burg, the friendly *Bar Rose Red* does a good line in light lunches – including plates of cheese and charcuterie, all in amenable surroundings.

Bar Rose Red. See page 45. This smart little place has the full range of Trappist beers from all six of Belgium's monkish breweries: Achel, Chimay, Orval, Rochefort, Westmalle and Westvleteren.

Grand Café Craenenburg. See page 34. One of the few café-bars on the Markt to retain a local clientele, the *Craenenburg* has the flavour of old Flanders with its antique benches and mullion windows.

The Bottle Shop. See page 44. Every Belgian beer you can think of and then some is on sale here at this bright and cheerful shop; there is a wide selection of *jenever*, too.

🍴 **Dinner.** See page 45. Arguably the best seafood restaurant in town, *De Visscherie* is smart, expensive and enjoyable; the sole and the mussels are house specialities.

Bourgogne des Flandres brewery

Grand Café Craenenburg

The Bottle Shop

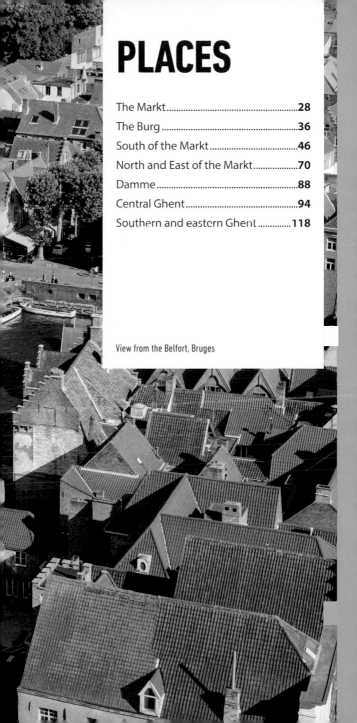

PLACES

The Markt..**28**

The Burg..**36**

South of the Markt.....................................**46**

North and East of the Markt...................**70**

Damme..**88**

Central Ghent...**94**

Southern and eastern Ghent..............**118**

View from the Belfort, Bruges

The Markt

To the surprise of many first-time visitors, Bruges is not the perfectly preserved medieval city described by much tourist literature but rather a clever, frequently seamless combination of medieval original and nineteenth- and even twentieth-century additions. This is especially true of the city's principal square, the Markt, an airy open space fringed by pavement cafés where horse-drawn buggies clatter over the square's cobbles, and tourists mill around in their droves. It's overlooked to the south by the imposing Belfort (belfry), long the city's proudest landmark, while the north and west sides of the Markt are flanked by a charming ensemble of biscuit-tin buildings whose mellow ruddy-brown brick culminates in a string of gables, each slightly different from its neighbour. This isn't, however, a planned confection but a sympathetic rehashing of what went before. Finally, the Markt's east side is all neo-Gothic, with the thunderous facade of the old provincial government building announced by a brace of stone lions.

Biscuit-tin buildings on the Markt

Monument to Pieter de Coninck and Jan Breydel

MAP P.30, POCKET MAP C5
Markt.

The burghers of nineteenth-century Bruges were keen to put something suitably civic in the middle of the Markt and the result is the conspicuous **monument** to Pieter de Coninck of the guild of weavers, and Jan Breydel, dean of the guild of butchers. Standing close together, they clutch the hilt of the same sword; their faces turned to the south in slightly absurd poses of heroic determination – a far cry from the gory events that first made them local heroes. At dawn on Friday, 18 May 1302, in what was later called the **Bruges Matins**, their force of rebellious Flemings crept into the city and massacred the unsuspecting French garrison, putting to the sword anyone who

Monument to Pieter de Coninck and Jan Breydel

couldn't correctly pronounce the Flemish shibboleth *schild en vriend* (meaning 'shield and friend'). Later the same year, the two guildsmen went on to lead the city's contingent in the Flemish army that defeated the French at the Battle of the Golden Spurs – no surprise, then, that the monument takes its cue from the battle rather than the massacre. Curiously enough, the statue was unveiled twice: in July 1887, a local committee pulled back the drapes to celebrate Coninck and Breydel as Flemings, while in August of the same year, the city council organised an official opening when King Leopold II honoured them as Belgians.

Provinciaal Hof

MAP P.30, POCKET MAP C5
Markt 3. No public access.

Hogging the eastern side of the Markt is the former provincial government building, the **Provinciaal Hof**, a fancy if over-large neo-Gothic edifice whose assorted spires, balustrades and

The Museum Card

The **Museum Card**, valid for three days, covers entry to all the main museums and costs €33 (18–25-year-olds €25; 13–17-year-olds €17; ⓦ museabrugge.be/en). Thirteen municipal museums are covered, including the Belfort, the Stadhuis, the Groeninge, the Gruuthuse, Onze-Lieve-Vrouwekerk and St-Janshospitaalmuseum. Depending on exactly which museums you visit, the pass can offer a significant saving compared to buying individual tickets. Sites not covered by the pass include St-Salvatorskathedraal and gimmicky new attractions like the **Historium** on the Markt, where you can don virtual reality goggles to 'visit' medieval Bruges. Museum passes can be bought at any participating museum and from the tourist office (see page 145); note that most museums close one day a week, often on Mondays.

Provinciaal Hof

dormer windows took forty years to complete. They were finally finished in 1921. The smaller building immediately to the left is also neo-Gothic, added in the 1920s and complete with twin arcaded galleries.

Grand Café Craenenburg

MAP P.30, POCKET MAP C5
Markt 16.

Today, the **Grand Café Craenenburg** (see page 34) occupies a relatively undistinguished modern building on the corner of St-Amandsstraat, but this was the site of the eponymous medieval mansion in which the guildsmen of Bruges imprisoned the Habsburg heir, Archduke Maximilian, for three months in 1488. The reason for their difference of opinion was the archduke's efforts to limit the city's privileges, but whatever the justice of their cause, the guildsmen made a big mistake. Maximilian made all sorts of promises to escape their clutches, but a few weeks after his release, his father, Emperor

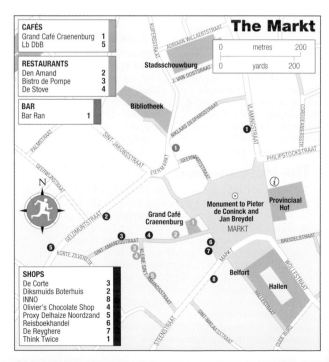

CAFÉS	
Grand Café Craenenburg	1
Lb DbB	5

RESTAURANTS	
Den Amand	2
Bistro de Pompe	3
De Stove	4

BAR	
Bar Ran	1

SHOPS	
De Corte	3
Diksmuids Boterhuis	2
INNO	8
Olivier's Chocolate Shop	4
Proxy Delhaize Noordzand	5
Reisboekhandel	6
De Reyghere	7
Think Twice	1

The Markt

Stadsschouwburg

Bibliotheek

Monument to Pieter de Coninck and Jan Breydel

MARKT

Provinciaal Hof

Grand Café Craenenburg

Belfort

Hallen

The bells, the bells

Bruges still employs a full-time bell-ringer and you're likely to spot them fiddling around in the **Belfort's Carillon Room** (see page 32) as s/he prepares for one of the city's regular **carillon concerts**. As in other Flemish cities, **bells** were first used in Bruges in the fourteenth century as a means of regulating the working day, and as such, reflected the development of a wage economy – employers were keen to keep tabs on their employees. Bells also served as a sort of public address system with everyone understanding the signals: pealing bells, for example, announced good news; tolling bells summoned the city to the Markt; and a rapid sequence of bells warned of danger. By the early fifteenth century, a short peal of bells marked the hour, and from this developed the carillon (*beiaard*), with Bruges installing its present version in the middle of the eighteenth century.

Frederick III, turned up with an army to take imperial revenge, with a bit of hanging here and a bit of burning there. Maximilian became emperor in 1493 and never forgave Bruges, failing to honour his promises and doing his considerable best to push trade north to its great rival, Antwerp.

Belfort

MAP P.30, POCKET MAP C6
Markt 7 ⓦ museabrugge.be/en. Entry via the Hallen (see page 32). Charge.

Filling out the south side of the Markt, the mighty **Belfort** (belfry) was long a potent symbol of civic pride and municipal independence, its distinctive octagonal lantern visible for miles across the surrounding polders. The Belfort was begun in the thirteenth century when the town was at its richest and most extravagant. However, it has had a blighted history, starting when the original wooden version was struck by lightning and burnt to the ground in 1280. Its brick replacement, with today's blind arcading, turrets and towers, received its octagonal stone lantern and a second wooden spire in the 1480s, but this spire didn't last long either, being lost to a thunderstorm a few years later. Undeterred, the Flemings promptly added a third

spire, though when this went up in smoke in 1741, the locals gave up, settling for the present structure with the addition of a stone parapet in 1822. It's a pity they didn't have another go, if only to sabotage Longfellow's metre in his dire but oft-quoted poem 'The Belfry of Bruges': 'In the market place of Bruges / Stands the Belfry old and brown / Thrice consumed and thrice rebuilt' and so on. Few

Belfort

The Carillon Chamber at the top of the Belfort

would say the Belfort is good-looking – it's large and somewhat clumsy – but it does have a certain ungainly charm. However, this was lost on G.K. Chesterton, who described it as 'an unnaturally long-necked animal, like a giraffe'.

Inside, the **belfry staircase** begins innocuously enough but gets steeper and much narrower as it nears the top. On the way up, it passes several mildly interesting chambers, starting with the **Treasury Room**, where the town charters and money chest were locked for safekeeping. Here also is an iron trumpet with which a watchman could warn the town of a fire outbreak – though given the size of the instrument, it's hard to believe this was very effective. Further up is the **Carillon Chamber**, a small and intimate cubby hole, where you can observe the slow turning of the large spiked drum that controls the 47 bells of the municipal carillon (see page 31); the largest bell weighs no less than 6 tonnes. A few stairs up from here and you emerge onto the **roof**, which offers fabulous views, especially in the late afternoon when the warm colours of the city are at their deepest.

Hallen

MAP P.30, POCKET MAP C6
Markt 7. Free.

The **Hallen** at the foot of the belfry is a much-restored thirteenth-century edifice with an austere style and structure modelled on the Lakenhalle in Ieper (see page 99). In the middle, overlooked by a long line of former warehouses, is a rectangular courtyard, which initially served as the city's principal market, its cobblestones once crammed with merchants and their wares, trading anything and everything from gloves, carpets, clerical hats and clogs through to fruits and spices. The entrance to the belfry (see page 31) is on the north side of the courtyard, up a flight of steps, while other parts of the Hallen are used for exhibitions geared up for the passing tourist trade. Incidentally, the gloomy set of arches to the rear of the Hallen, beyond the courtyard, was once the preserve of the money-changers, who had to deal with a bewildering variety of currencies in coins that might be clipped or debased as the issuers regularly varied the content. Developing a reliable banking industry was vital to the prosperity of medieval Bruges.

Shops

De Corte

MAP P.30, POCKET MAP C5

St-Amandsstraat 28

Ⓦ vulpennenbrugge.be.

Smart little shop in a handy location selling a premium selection of pens, notebooks, inks, bags and Swiss army knives. The Montblanc pens, one of the shop's specialities, attract well-heeled customers.

Diksmuids Boterhuis

MAP P.30, POCKET MAP C5

Gcldmuntstraat 23

Ⓦ diksmuidsboterhuis.be.

One of the few traditional food shops to have survived in central Bruges, this Aladdin's cave of a place specialises in cooked meats, bread, butter and Belgian cheeses, of which it has an outstanding selection. Friendly service, too.

INNO

MAP P.30, POCKET MAP C6

Steenstraat 13 Ⓦ inno.be.

The best department store in the city centre spread over four large floors. The ground floor sells watches, perfume, make-up, bags and lingerie, while the other floors are devoted mainly to good-quality clothes for both men and women.

Olivier's Chocolate Shop

MAP P.30, POCKET MAP C5

St-Amandsstraat 14

Ⓦ olivierschocolate.be.

Bruges has accumulated a small army of specialist chocolate shops in recent years, but this family-owned concern has won rave reviews for the quality of its chocolate. The shop is in a central location and sells the (slightly) larger and more traditional types of Belgian chocolate.

Proxy Delhaize Noordzand

MAP P.30, POCKET MAP B5

Noordzandstraat 4 Ⓦ delhaize.be.

Ordinary shops and stores have all but vanished from central Bruges, but there are a couple of smallish supermarkets – and this is perhaps the best: nothing fancy, but a reliable selection of fresh veg, cooked meats and so forth are on offer.

Diksmuids Boterhuis

Reisboekhandel

MAP P.30, POCKET MAP C5
Markt 12 ⓦ dereyghere.be.
Travel specialist with a wide
selection of travel guides, many
in English, plus road and city
maps. The shop also sells hiking
and cycling maps of Bruges and
its surroundings, and stocks
travel-related, English-language
magazines. Up the stairs, above
it is its sister shop, *De Reyghere*
(see below).

De Reyghere

MAP P.30, POCKET MAP C6
Markt 12 ⓦ dereyghere.be.
Founded more than one hundred
years ago, De Reyghere is a local
institution and a meeting place for
every book lover in town. The shop
stocks a wide range of domestic
and foreign literature, art and
reference books and is good for
international press.

Think Twice

MAP P.30, POCKET MAP C5
Vlamingstraat 25 ⓦ thinktwice-
secondhand.be.
Part of a well-intentioned chain of
Belgian stores – there are fifteen
in total – in which second-hand

clothes are collected, sorted and
re-sold at budget prices. This outlet
sells mostly women's wear.

Cafés

Grand Café Craenenburg

MAP P.30, POCKET MAP C5
Markt 16 ⓦ craenenburg.be.
Unlike the Markt's other tourist-
dominated café-restaurants, this
traditional place still attracts a
loyal, local clientele. With its
leather and wood panelling,
antique benches and mullion
windows, the *Craenenburg* has the
flavour of old Flanders. Although
the daytime-only food is routine
(mains average €20), it has a good
range of beers, including a locally
produced, tangy brown ale called
Brugse Tripel. €€

Lb DbB

MAP P.30, POCKET MAP C6
Kleine St-Amandsstraat 5
ⓦ debelegdeboterham.be.
This bright and breezy little place,
in attractively renovated premises
down a narrow lane, has a stalwart
local following for its substantial,
delicious salads. The service is

Think Twice

De Stove

prompt and friendly too. By some measure, it's the best place to eat in the vicinity of the Markt. €

Restaurants

Den Amand

MAP P.30, POCKET MAP C5
St-Amandsstraat 4
Ⓦ denamand.be.
This small and informal, family-run restaurant offers an inventive range of dishes combining Flemish, Italian and Asian cuisines. Mains from the limited but well-chosen menu – for instance, brill in coconut milk – average a reasonable €25. It's a small place, so book a few hours in advance. €€

Bistro de Pompe

MAP P.30, POCKET MAP C6
Kleine St-Amandsstraat 2 Ⓣ 050 69 26 86
In the old pump house, this first-rate restaurant may be in one of the busiest parts of the city, but it offers excellent Flemish cuisine – try, for example, the rabbit with prunes. Eat outside on the pavement

terrace or inside, where the décor is attractively folksy. €€

De Stove

MAP P.30, POCKET MAP C6
Kleine St-Amandsstraat 4
Ⓦ restaurantdestove.be.
Small and cosy Franco-Belgian restaurant that's recommended by just about everyone in town. The menu is carefully constructed, with fish and meat dishes given equal prominence: try the stew of pork cheeks or the stuffed courgette. Reservations essential. €€€

Bar

Bar Ran

MAP P.30, POCKET MAP C5
Kuipersstraat 4 Ⓦ barranbrugge.com.
Probably the best cocktail bar in the city, locally run and with an amiable, neighbourhood vibe. The décor is great too, though managing to stay on one of the stools can be tricky. The cocktails are fabulous – for something different, try the King Kong Milk Punch.

The Burg

Named after the ninth-century fortress built here by Baldwin Iron Arm, the first count of Flanders, the Burg is the city's architectural showpiece. It's a handsome square, no mistake, whose southern edge is flanked by an especially beguiling mix of late Gothic and Renaissance buildings, including Bruges's holy of holies, the Heilig Bloed Basiliek (Basilica of the Holy Blood). The fortress disappeared centuries ago, but the Burg long remained the centre of political and ecclesiastical power with the Stadhuis (Town Hall), which has survived, on one side and St-Donaaskathedraal, which hasn't, on the other. The French Revolutionary Army destroyed the cathedral in 1799. Although the foundations were laid bare a few years ago, they were promptly re-interred and now lie in front of and underneath the Crowne Plaza Hotel.

Heilig Bloed Basiliek

MAP P.38, POCKET MAP D6
Burg 13 ⓦ holyblood.com. Free, charge for the Treasury.

Once a celebrated place of pilgrimage, the **Heilig Bloed Basiliek** (Basilica of the Holy Blood) is named after the holy

Heilig Bloed Basiliek

relic that found its way here in the Middle Ages – a rock-crystal phial that purports to contain a few drops of blood and water washed from the body of Christ by Joseph of Arimathea (see page 37). The basilica is divided into two parts. Tucked away in the corner is the **lower chapel**, a shadowy, crypt-like affair originally built at the start of the twelfth century to shelter another relic, a piece of St Basil, one of the great figures of the early Greek Church. The chapel's heavy and simple Romanesque lines are decorated with just one relief, carved above an interior doorway and showing the baptism of Basil, in which a strange giant bird, representing the Holy Spirit, plunges into a pool of water.

Next door, approached up a low-vaulted, curving staircase, is the **upper chapel**, which was built just a few years later but has been renovated so frequently that it's impossible to make out the original structure – and it also suffers from an excess of kitsch nineteenth-century decoration. The chapel itself may be disappointing, but the large silver **tabernacle** that holds the phial of the Holy Blood is simply magnificent. It was the gift of Albert and Isabella of Spain in 1611. The Habsburg king, Philip II of Spain, had granted control of the Spanish Netherlands (now Belgium) to his daughter Isabella and her husband Albert in 1598, but they were imprudent rulers, exalting the Catholic faith – as per the tabernacle – while simultaneously persecuting those Protestants who remained in their fiefdom.

Beside the upper chapel is the tiny **Schatkamer** (Treasury), where pride of place goes to the ornate shrine that holds the holy phial during the Heilig-Bloedprocessie (Procession of the Holy Blood). Dating from 1617, it's a superb piece of work, the gold-and-silver, jewel-encrusted superstructure decorated with delicate religious scenes. The Treasury also contains

The main altar at the Heilig Bloed Basiliek

The holiest of holies: the Holy Blood

Local legend asserts that the phial of the **Heilig Bloed** (Holy Blood) was the gift of Diederik d'Alsace, a Flemish count who distinguished himself by his bravery during the Second Crusade and was thereafter given the relic by a grateful patriarch of Jerusalem in 1150. It is, however, somewhat more likely that the phial was acquired during the sacking of Constantinople in 1204 when the Crusaders ignored their collective job description and, instead of attacking the Muslim rulers of Palestine, slaughtered the Byzantines instead – hence the historical invention. Whatever the truth, after several weeks in Bruges, the relic was found to be dry, but thereafter the dried blood proceeded to liquefy every Friday at 6pm until 1325, a miracle attested to by all sorts of church dignitaries, including Pope Clement V. After 1325, the failure of the Holy Blood to liquefy prompted all kinds of conjecture – did it mean that Bruges had lost favour in the eyes of God? – but the phial, or more precisely its dried contents, remains an object of veneration today. It's sometimes available for visitors to touch under the supervision of a priest in the upper chapel, and on Ascension Day (mid-May), it's carried through the town in a colourful but solemn procession, the **Heilig-Bloedprocessie** (Procession of the Holy Blood; ⓦ bloedprocessiebrugge.be/en). The procession usually starts on Wollestraat at 2.30pm and then wends its way round the centre before finishing around 6pm. Grandstand tickets are sold online and at the main tourist office (see page 145) from 1 March.

an incidental collection of vestments, lesser reliquaries and a handful of late medieval paintings, most memorably a finely executed pair of panels by Pieter Pourbus depicting the 31 *Members of the Noble Brotherhood of the Precious Blood*. Born in Gouda, in The Netherlands, Pourbus (1523–84) moved to Bruges as a young man. He established a reputation for the quality of his portrait paintings, his closely observed figures very much in the Netherlandish tradition.

Less polished but equally charming is a naïve panel painting, *Scenes from the Life of St Barbara* by the Master of the St Barbara Legend. A hazy third-century figure, Barbara was supposedly imprisoned in a tower by her pagan father, who subsequently tortured and killed her on account of her Christian faith; the tower became Barbara's symbol and is shown here under construction. Finally, look out for the faded

Statue of Christ at the Heilig Bloed Basiliek

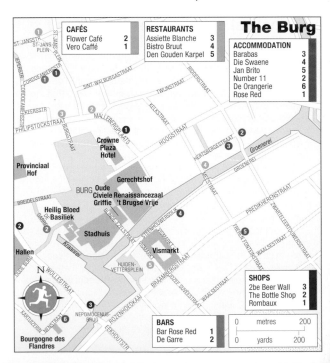

The Burg

CAFÉS
| Flower Café | 2 |
| Vero Caffé | 1 |

RESTAURANTS
Assiette Blanche	3
Bistro Bruut	4
Den Gouden Karpel	5

ACCOMMODATION
Barabas	3
Die Swaene	4
Jan Brito	5
Number 11	2
De Orangerie	6
Rose Red	1

SHOPS
2be Beer Wall	3
The Bottle Shop	2
Rombaux	1

BARS
| Bar Rose Red | 1 |
| De Garre | 2 |

| 0 | metres | 200 |
| 0 | yards | 200 |

strands of a seventeenth-century tapestry depicting St Augustine's funeral, the sea of helmeted heads, torches and pikes that surround the monks and abbots, very much a Catholic view of a muscular State supporting a holy Church.

Stadhuis

MAP P.38, POCKET MAP D6
Burg 12 ⓦ visitbruges.be. Charge, which includes the Renaissancezaal (see page 40).

The Stadhuis (Town Hall), just to the left of the basilica, has a beautiful sandstone façade of 1376, though its statues, mostly of the counts and countesses of Flanders, are modern replacements for those destroyed by the occupying French army in 1792. Inside, the high-ceilinged ground floor holds paintings of various royals and municipal bigwigs, including one of the Empress Maria Theresa with a delicate little foot poking out from her gown and another of Napoleon with the Bruges mayor, Baron de Croeser. The baron wears a nervous smile – but then he had good reason to: Napoleon had pledged to strip

all manner of privileges from the local oligarchy, though in the event the baron continued to prosper.

A flight of stairs clambers up from the ground floor to the magnificent Gothic Hall, dating from 1400 and the setting for the first meeting of the States General (parliamentary assembly) in 1464. The ceiling here has been restored in a vibrant mixture of maroon, dark brown, black and gold – dripping pendant arches like decorated stalactites. The ribs of the arches converge in twelve circular vault-keys, picturing scenes from the New Testament. These are hard to see without binoculars, but down below – and much easier to view – are the sixteen gilded corbels that support them, representing the months and the four elements, beginning in the left-hand corner beside the chimney with January (inscribed "Winter") and continuing clockwise right round the hall. The wall frescoes were commissioned in 1895 to illustrate the history of the town – or rather history as the council was keen to recall it. The largest scene, commemorating the victory over the French at the Battle

Stadhuis

Oude Civiele Griffie

has attracted all sorts of speculation (see page 43).

Renaissancezaal 't Brugse Vrije

MAP P.38, POCKET MAP D5
Burg 11A Ⓦ museabrugge.be/en. Charge, including the Stadhuis (see page 39).

Adjacent to the Oude Civiele Griffie, the **Landhuis van het Brugse Vrije** (Mansion of the Liberty of Bruges) is demure in comparison, but it boasts a distinguished history. Established in the Middle Ages, the Liberty of Bruges was a territorial subdivision of Flanders that enjoyed extensive delegated powers, controlling its finances and judiciary. A council of aldermen exercised power, and they demolished most of the original Gothic building in the early eighteenth century before Napoleon abolished them. Just one room has survived from the original structure, the Schepenkamer (Aldermen's Room), now known as the **Renaissancezaal 't Brugse Vrije** (Renaissance Hall of the Liberty of Bruges). Dominating the room is an enormous marble and oak chimneypiece, a superb example of Renaissance carving completed in 1531 to celebrate the defeat of the French at Pavia six years earlier and the advantageous Treaty of Cambrai that followed. A paean of praise to the Habsburgs, the work features Emperor Charles V and his Austrian and Spanish relatives. However, it's the trio of bulbous (and presumably uncomfortable) **codpieces** that catches the eye. The **alabaster frieze** running below the carvings was a caution for the Liberty's magistrates, who held their courts here. In four panels, it relates the then-familiar biblical story of **Susanna**, in which – in the first panel – two old men surprise her bathing in her garden and threaten to accuse her of adultery if she resists their advances. Susanna does just that, and the second panel shows her in court. In the third panel, Susanna is about to

of the Golden Spurs in 1302, has lots of knights hurrahing, though it's hard to take this seriously when you look at the dogs, one of which clearly has a mismatch between its body and head.

Adjoining the Gothic Hall is the Historische zaal (Historical Room), which features an intriguing audio-visual display exploring the city's relationship with the sea – and the endless cycle of dredging and embankment this has entailed.

Oude Civiele Griffie

MAP P.38, POCKET MAP D6
Burg 11. No public access.

Next door to the Stadhuis, the bright and cheery **Oude Civiele Griffie** (Old Civic Registry) was built to house the municipal records office in 1537, its elegant facade decorated with Renaissance columns and friezes. The gable features half a dozen gold-painted statues – three representations of civic virtues positioned slightly below Moses and Aaron with the blindfolded figure of Justice and her scales plonked right on the top. The building also spans the archway over **Blinde-Ezelstraat** (Blind Donkey Street), whose name

Grim tidings: the murder of Charles the Good

In 1127, **St-Donaaskathedraal** (see page 42) witnessed an event that shocked Western Europe when the count of Flanders, **Charles the Good** (1084–1127), was murdered while he was at prayer in the choir. A gifted and far-sighted ruler, Charles eschewed foreign entanglements in favour of domestic matters – unlike most of his predecessors – and improved the lot of the poor by ensuring a regular supply of food and controlling prices in times of shortage. These far-sighted policies and his piety earned Charles his sobriquet, but the count's attempts to curb his leading vassals brought him into conflict with the powerful Erembald clan. The Erembalds had no intention of submitting to Charles, so they assassinated him and took control of the city. Their success was, however, short-lived. Supporters of Charles rallied and the murderers took refuge in the tower of St Donatian's, from where they were winkled out and promptly dispatched. Shocked by the murder, one of Charles's clerks, a certain **Galbert of Bruges**, decided to write a detailed journal of the events that led up to the assassination and the bloody chaos that ensued. Unlike other contemporary source materials, the journal had no sponsor, which makes it a uniquely honest account of events, admittedly from the perspective of the count's entourage, with Galbert criticizing many of the city's leading figures, clergy and nobles alike. Galbert's journal provides a fascinating insight into twelfth-century Bruges. It's well-written too (in a wordy sort of way) – as in the account of Charles' death: 'when the count was praying ... then at last, after so many plans and oaths and pacts among themselves, those wretched traitors ... slew the count, who was struck down with swords and run through again and again'. The full text is reprinted in *The Murder of Charles the Good*, edited by James Bruce Ross.

The carved chimneypiece at the Renaissancezaal 't Brugse Vrije

Blinde-Ezelstraat

be put to death, but the magistrate, Daniel, interrogates the two men and uncovers their perjury. Susanna is acquitted, and the two men are stoned to death in the final scene.

Gerechtshof

MAP P.38, POCKET MAP D5
Burg 9. No public access.

At the eastern corner of the Burg is the Neoclassical **Gerechtshof** (Law Courts), a substantial sandstone complex surrounding a sizeable cobbled courtyard. It was built in the 1720s to streamline the administration of justice in Bruges and remained in use as a law court until 1984; it's now home to municipal offices. One of the most dramatic cases heard here was that of **Ludovicus Baekelandt**, a rough-and-tumble Fleming who joined the invading French army in 1794 and then deserted to become an outlaw preying on travellers from his forest hidey-hole. Baekelandt's activities made him something of a folk hero among his fellow Flemings, many of whom were deeply resentful of the French, but he and his gang

were caught in 1802 and brought to Bruges, where 24 of them were tried and guillotined in the Markt. A large and sullen crowd formed to watch.

St-Donaaskathedraal

MAP P.38, POCKET MAP D5
Burg.

On the corner of the Burg, the modern *Crowne Plaza* hotel marks the site of the east end of **St-Donaaskathedraal** (St Donatian's Cathedral), which was razed by the French army of occupation in 1799. By all accounts, the church was a splendid structure, a mighty Romanesque edifice dating from the tenth century with a lantern tower and a 16-sided ambulatory. To the French Revolutionary Army, however, it was a symbol of both religious superstition and of the reactionary city council, whose burghers had long held sway. Neither was the church's demolition a passing fancy: the French arrived with a team of demolition experts, who began by jacking up the church roof and inserting timber blocks in the gaps. They then set fire to the wood, so the building collapsed, leaving a pile of rubble that took decades to clear. The cathedral's foundations were uncovered in 1955 but were then reinterred and although there are vague plans to carry out another archaeological dig, nothing has happened yet.

The Vismarkt and around
MAP P.38, POCKET MAP D6

The arch beside the Stadhuis marks the start of **Blinde-Ezelstraat** (Blind Donkey Street), whose name has been the subject of much debate: one story suggests that donkeys coming along here were blindfolded in case they got spooked by the narrowness of the street, but it's more likely that the name refers to an old and long-gone tavern which sold the cheapest booze in town and whose clientele ended up as drunk as 'blind donkeys'. Whatever the truth, Blinde-Ezelstraat now leads south across the canal to the plain and sombre, early nineteenth-century Doric colonnades of the **Vismarkt** (Fish Market), though, with its handful of fish traders, this is but a shadow of its former self. There are no tanners in the huddle of picturesque houses that crimp the **Huidenvettersplein**, the square at the centre of the old tanners' quarter immediately to the west – a good job as the locals of yestercryear often complained about the stench. Tourists converge on this pint-sized square by the busload, holing up in its bars and restaurants and snapping away at the postcard-perfect views of the belfry from the adjacent **Rozenhoedkaai** – literally 'Rosary Quay', named after the amber and ivory rosaries that were a speciality of the craftsmen who worked here until the nineteenth century.

Nepomucenusbrug
MAP P.38, POCKET MAP D6

The **Nepomucenusbrug**, at the junction of Rozenhoedkaai and Wollestraat, sports a statue of the patron saint of bridges, St John Nepomuk. This fourteenth-century Bohemian priest earned his saintly spurs by purportedly being thrown bound and gagged into the River Vltava for refusing to reveal the confessional secrets of the queen to her husband, King Wenceslas IV. The bridge marks the start of the **Dijver**, which tracks along the canal as far as Nieuwstraat, passing the path to the first of the city's main museums, the Groeninge (see page 49).

Bourgogne des Flandres
MAP P.38, POCKET MAP C6
Kartuizerinnenstraat 6, off Wollestraat
Ⓦ bourgognedesflandres.be. Charge.

Pleased to have finally returned to Bruges, the **Bourgogne des Flandres brewery** occupies a pair of attractive brick buildings on a narrow side street just off Wollestraat. Guided tours (every half-hour, 45min) include a quick introduction to the brewing process, a gander at the equipment in the loft and, at the end of the tour, a bottle of the stuff to quaff. Bourgogne des Flandres is a classic red-brown beer blended with eight-month-old Lambic produced by the brewery's owners, the Brussels-based Timmermans Brewery.

Statue of St John of Nepomuk

2be Beer Wall

Shops

2be Beer Wall

MAP P.38, POCKET MAP D6
Wollestraat 53 ⓦ 2-be.biz/en.
Stroll through the old arch at the foot of Wollestraat and you are faced – quite literally – with a wall of Belgian beer bottles; take your pick and pay up. Alternatively, you can quaff your selection at the adjoining bar, which is short of creature comforts but does have a wide range of beers. Hence, it's a very popular tourist spot.

The Bottle Shop

MAP P.38, POCKET MAP C6
Wollestraat 13 ⓦ thebottleshop.be.
Just off the Markt, this bright and cheerful establishment stocks more than six hundred types of beer, oodles of whisky and *jenever* (gin), and all sorts of special glasses to drink them from. The Belgians have specific glasses for many of their beers.

Rombaux

MAP P.38, POCKET MAP D5
Mallebergplaats 13 ⓦ rombaux.be.
This establishment comprises two adjacent shops: one selling musical instruments, especially pianos and organs, the other with an enormous collection of CDs – and vinyl – covering every musical taste, including an excellent selection of jazz and classical music.

Cafés

The Flower Café

MAP P.38, POCKET MAP D5
Philipstockstraat 37 ⓣ 0478 34 37 01.
Firmly aimed at the tourist trade, this amiable café – and its lovely flowers – rustles up a delicious breakfast, including suitably buttery ham and cheese croissants, not to mention yogurt parfait with granola. Great coffee and fruit juice drinks too. €

Vero Caffé

MAP P.38, POCKET MAP C5
St-Jansplein 9 ⓣ 0484 76 41 10.
A simply decorated café with whitewashed brick walls where local hipsters and students rub shoulders to enjoy a perfect cup of coffee. There are home-baked cakes, too, but the tastiest disappear early. Its location on a quiet square is pleasantly removed from the hubbub of central Bruges. €

Restaurants

Assiette Blanche

MAP P.38, POCKET MAP C5

Philipstockstraat 23 ⓦ assietteblanche.be.
Slick and smart French restaurant decorated in a traditional – and very comforting – style. An enterprising menu features such pleasures as lamb couscous and cod fillet in a white wine sauce with mangetout – indeed, one of their specialities is their North Sea seafood. The main deal here is the set menu – three courses at €50, four at €62. Reservations are strongly recommended. €€€

Bistro Bruut

MAP P.38, POCKET MAP D5

Meestraat 9 ⓦ bistrobruut.be.
Head down a narrow, ancient side street close to the Burg and you'll find, overlooking a canal, this tastefully decorated bistro with a retro feel – love that black and white chequerboard floor! The chef chooses the menu – you choose the number of courses you want, up to a maximum of five or six. The menu elaborates on traditional Flemish cuisine, emphasising seasonal, organic ingredients. Try the lobster tartare with Brussels sprouts. It's pricey enough: at lunchtime, a six-course starter menu costs €70 but it is definitely worth it. Reservations are essential. €€€

Den Gouden Karpel

MAP P.38, POCKET MAP D6

Vismarkt 9 ⓦ vengoudenkarpel.be.
Since it opened, this seafood restaurant has garnered rave reviews for its simple and straightforward approach to both its wet fish and shell fish offerings. The restaurant itself comprises a handful of plain modern chairs and tables located behind the fish shop and counter. The restaurant menu varies depending on what fresh catches have been brought in. €€€

Bars

Bar Rose Red

MAP P.38, POCKET MAP C5

Cordoeaniersstraat 16 ⓦ rosered.be.
This intimate little lounge bar with red banquettes and an excellent selection of beers (seven on draught) is in a pretty handy location a couple of minutes' walk north of the Burg. The bar specialises in Trappist beers, selling – and this is very unusual – bottled beers from all six of Belgium's Trappist breweries: Achel, Chimay, Orval, Rochefort, Westmalle and Westvleteren. The bar is housed in an ancient building – hence the beamed ceiling – and there's a tiny courtyard out back.

De Garre

MAP P.38, POCKET MAP C6

De Garre 1 ⓦ degarre.be.
Down a narrow alley off Breidelstraat, between the Markt and the Burg, this cramped but infinitely charming and very ancient tavern (*estaminet*) has an outstanding range of Belgian beers and tasty snacks on offer, while the classical music playing in the background adds to the rather relaxing air.

De Garre

South of the Markt

The bustling area south of the Markt holds several of the city's key buildings and leading museums. The area is at its prettiest among the old lanes and alleys near the cathedral, St-Salvatorskathedraal, which claims to be the city's most satisfying church. However, the nearby Onze-Lieve-Vrouwekerk, with its brace of magnificent Renaissance tombs and Michelangelo marble, comes a close second. There is more cuteness in the huddle of whitewashed cottages of the Begijnhof and at the adjacent Minnewater, the so-called 'Lake of Love', a pleasant preamble to the ramparts beyond. As for the museums, St-Janshospitaal offers the exquisite medieval paintings of Hans Memling; the Gruuthuse is strong on applied art, especially tapestries and antique furniture; and the Groeninge Museum holds a simply superb, world-beating sample of early Flemish art. The Groeninge has always been a relatively modest museum for such a stunning collection and the city is currently building a new and lavish arts complex – BRUSK – on the Garenmarkt close by; at this stage, it's hard to know quite what will be displayed where when the new complex opens, but certainly, the new exhibition halls will extend over to the Groeninge. Work on BRUSK is scheduled to last until 2025.

The Arentshuis

Arentspark

MAP P.48, POCKET MAP C6-C7

A short stroll from the Burg, the **Arentshuis**, at Dijver 16, is a rather grand eighteenth-century mansion with a stately porticoed entrance. Formerly a museum, it stands in the north corner of the pocket-sized **Arentspark**, whose brace of forlorn stone columns are all that remain of the Waterhalle – an immense warehouse and covered harbour – that once straddled the most central of the city's canals but was demolished in 1787 after the canal was covered over. Also in the Arentspark is the tiniest of humpbacked bridges – **St-Bonifaciusbrug** – whose stonework is framed against a tumble of antique brick houses.

The humpbacked St-Bonifaciusbrug

One of Bruges's most picturesque (and photographed) spots, the bridge looks like the epitome of everything medieval, but it was only built in 1910. It takes its name from an eighth-century Anglo-Saxon missionary who Christianised the Germans and was stabbed to death by the more obdurate Frisians. Next to the far side of the bridge is a pensive, modern **statue** of Juan Luis Vives (1492–1540), a Spanish Jew and good friend of Erasmus who moved to Bruges in the early sixteenth century to avoid persecution. It was a wise decision: his family had converted to Christianity in Spain, but that failed to save them. His father was burnt at the stake in 1525, while his dead mother was dug up and her bones burned. Curiously, Vives also spent time at the court of Henry VIII, where his refusal to accept the legitimacy of the king's divorce from Catherine of Aragon cost him a stretch in prison.

The disappearance of Sir Frank Brangwyn

Born in Bruges to Welsh parents, **Sir Frank Brangwyn** (1867–1956) was apprenticed to William Morris in the early 1880s and became an official UK war artist in World War I. Over the ensuing decades, Brangwyn turned his hand to several different media, producing a raft of drawings, sketches and paintings that received mixed reviews – though, to be fair, his industrial drawings and sketches have a real sense of force and power. In contrast, it's his paintings that often slide into sentimentality. Brangwyn flitted between Britain and Belgium and in 1936, he donated a large sample of his work to his native town. For many years, these assorted works were displayed in the Arentshuis, but now this has closed as a museum, Brangwyn's work is in cold storage – perhaps for good.

Markets in Bruges

Bruges has a weekly food and flower market on the Markt and a more general food and clothes market on 't Zand. There's also a flea market along the Dijver and neighbouring Vismarkt, though there are more souvenir and craft stalls here than bric-a-brac places, and the tourist crowds mean that bargains are few and far between. If you're after a deal, you might consider popping over to the much larger flea market in Ghent (see page 101).

Gruuthuse Museum

MAP P.48, POCKET MAP C7

Dijver 17 ⓦ museabrugge.be. Charge.

The **Gruuthuse Museum** is located inside a rambling fifteenth-century mansion. The building is a fine example of civil and neo-Gothic architecture. It takes its name from the house owners' historical right to tax the *gruit*, the dried herb and flower mixture once added to barley during the beer-brewing process to improve the flavour. The last lord of the Gruuthuse died in 1492 and a century later,

Philip II of Spain snaffled up the mansion, only for one of his successors to give it to a loyal follower, who installed a charity pawnbroker here – the so-called 'Mount of Piety'. In 1875, the city of Bruges bought what was, by then, a dilapidated ruin and commissioned Louis Delacenserie to revamp and restore the place. It was a good choice, as Delacenserie specialised in restorations, and today's exterior is a seamless blend of the late-medieval original and the neo-Gothic. The mansion

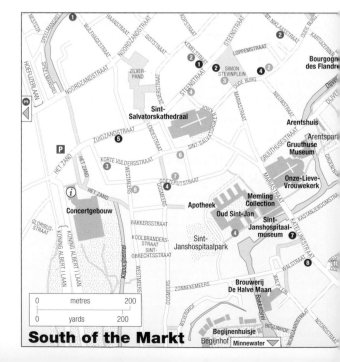

South of the Markt

was turned into a museum to hold a hotchpotch of Flemish fine, applied and decorative arts, mainly from the medieval and early modern periods. The museum's strongest suit is its superb collection of **tapestries**, primarily woven in Brussels or Bruges during the sixteenth and seventeenth centuries (see page 62). The museum's most famous artefact is, however, a polychromatic terracotta bust of a youthful Emperor Charles V. The house's most unusual feature is the oak-panelled **oratory** that juts out from the first floor to overlook the altar of the Onze-Lieve-Vrouwekerk next door (see page 54). The oratory allowed the lords of the *gruit* to worship without leaving home – a real social coup.

Groeninge Museum

MAP P.48, POCKET MAP D6–D7
Dijver 12 ⓦ museabrugge.be. Charge.

Gruuthuse Museum

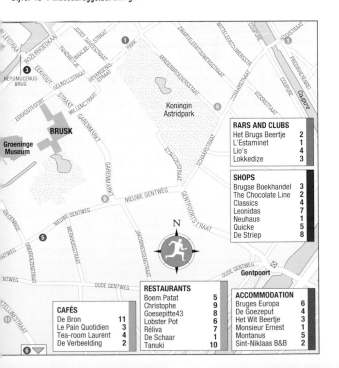

BARS AND CLUBS

Het Brugs Beertje	2
L'Estaminet	1
Lio's	4
Lokkedize	3

SHOPS

Brugse Boekhandel	3
The Chocolate Line	2
Classics	4
Leonidas	7
Neuhaus	1
Quicke	5
De Striep	8

RESTAURANTS

Boem Patat	5
Christophe	9
Goesepitte43	8
Lobster Pot	6
Réliva	7
De Schaar	1
Tanuki	10

ACCOMMODATION

Bruges Europa	6
De Goezeput	4
Het Wit Beertje	3
Monsieur Ernest	1
Montanus	5
Sint-Niklaas B&B	2

CAFÉS

De Bron	11
Le Pain Quotidien	3
Tea-room Laurent	4
De Verbeelding	2

Groeninge Museum

Medieval Flanders was one of Europe's most artistically productive parts, with each cloth town, especially Bruges and Ghent, trying to outdo its rivals with the quality of its religious art. Today, the works of these early Flemish painters, known as the **Flemish Primitives**, are highly prized and an exquisite sample is displayed in the **Groeninge Museum** in Bruges. **Jan van Eyck** is generally regarded as the first of the Flemish Primitives and has even been credited with the invention of oil painting itself – though it seems more likely that he simply perfected a new technique by thinning his paint with (then newly discovered) turpentine, thus making it more flexible. Van Eyck's most celebrated work is the *Adoration of the Mystic Lamb*, a stunningly beautiful altarpiece displayed in St-Baafskathedraal in Ghent (see page 94). The painting was revolutionary in its realism, for the first time using elements of the native landscape in depicting biblical themes, and this finely observed realism remains the hallmark of the Flemish Primitives.

The realism also underpins a complex symbolism. Mostly, the symbolism was religious, but sometimes, it was secular, representing a distinct nod to the humanism that was gathering pace in Flanders.

The descriptions on page 52 detail some of the key works held in the Groeninge by four of the principal Flemish Primitives – **Jan van Eyck**, **Hugo van der Goes**, **Gerard David** and **Hieronymus Bosch**. There are also two fine and roughly contemporaneous copies of works by **Rogier van der Weyden** (1399–1464). The first is the tiny *Portrait of Philip the Good*, in which the pallor of the duke's aquiline features, along with the brightness of his hatpin and chain of office, are skilfully balanced by the sombre cloak and hat. The second and much larger painting, *St Luke painting the Portrait of Our Lady*, is a rendering of a popular if highly improbable legend claiming that Luke painted Mary – thereby becoming the patron saint of painters. One of Rogier's pupils was the talented **Hans Memling** (1430–94), who is well represented here by the splendid *Moreel Triptych* and has six works at the St-Janshospitaalmuseum (see page 57).

The Flemish Primitives are the Groeninge's star turn, but the museum also holds a substantial collection of later Belgian art. The collection of late sixteenth- and seventeenth-century paintings isn't especially strong, but there's enough to demonstrate the period's watering down of religious themes in favour of more secular preoccupations. In particular, **Pieter Pourbus** (1523–84) is seen at his best in a series of austere and often surprisingly unflattering portraits of the movers and shakers of his day. There's also his *Last Judgement*, a much larger but atypical work crammed with muscular men and fleshy women. Completed in 1551, its inspiration came from Michelangelo's Sistine Chapel.

The museum also has a significant sample of nineteenth- and early twentieth-century Belgian art, with the obvious highlight being the Expressionists, most memorably the work of the talented **Constant Permeke** (1886–1952). Wounded in World War I, Permeke's grim wartime experiences helped him to develop a distinctive style in which his subjects – usually agricultural workers, fishermen and so forth – were monumental in form but invested with sombre, sometimes threatening emotion. His charcoal drawing *The Angelus* is a typically dark and earthy representation of Belgian peasant life dated to 1934. In a similar vein is the enormous *Last Supper* by **Gustave van de Woestijne** (1881–1947), in which Jesus and the disciples – all elliptical eyes and restrained movement – are trapped within prison-like walls.

Last but not least, the Groeninge has a small but choice selection of **Belgian Surrealists**, including a clutch of works by the inventive **Marcel Broodthaers** (1924–76), notably his tongue-in-cheek *Les Animaux de la ferme*. There's also the spookily stark surrealism of *Serenity* by **Paul Delvaux** (1897–1994). The latter, one of the most interesting of Belgium's modern artists, started as an Expressionist but came to – and stayed with – Surrealism in the 1930s. Two of his pet motifs were train stations, in one guise or another, and nude or semi-nude women set against a classical backdrop, all intended to usher the viewer into the unconscious. At their best, his paintings achieve an almost palpable sense of foreboding. This section also has a couple of minor oil paintings and several etchings and drawings by **James Ensor** (1860–1949), one of Belgium's most innovative painters, and **Magritte**'s (1898–1967) characteristically unnerving *The Assault*.

Most of the individual paintings mentioned should be on display, but the collection is regularly rotated; be sure to pick up a floor plan at reception.

Flemish masterpieces at the Groeninge Museum

The Flemish Primitives at the Groeninge

Jan van Eyck (1385–1441)

Jan van Eyck lived and worked in Bruges from 1430 until his death eleven years later. The Groeninge has two gorgeous examples of his work, beginning with the miniature portrait of his wife, *Margareta van Eyck*, painted in 1439 and bearing his motto, *'als ich can'* ('the best I can do'). The painting is a private picture with no commercial value, marking a step away from the sponsored art and religious preoccupations of previous Flemish artists. The second Van Eyck painting is the remarkable *Madonna and Child with Canon George van der Paele*, a glowing and richly symbolic work with three figures surrounding the Madonna and child: the kneeling canon, St George (his patron saint) and St Donatian, to whom he is being presented. St George doffs his helmet to salute the infant Christ and speaks using the Hebrew word *'Adonaï'* (Lord) inscribed on his chin strap, while Jesus replies through the green parrot he holds. Folklore asserted that this type of parrot was fond of saying *'Ave'*, the Latin for 'welcome' or 'hail'. Audaciously, Van Eyck has broken with religious tradition by painting the canon amongst the saints rather than as a lesser figure.

Hugo van der Goes (d.1482)

Hugo van der Goes is a shadowy figure, though it is known that he became master of the painters' guild in Ghent in 1467. Eight years later, he entered a Ghent priory as a lay brother, perhaps because of the prolonged bouts of acute depression that afflicted him. Few paintings have survived, but his last work, the luminescent *Death of Our Lady*, is here at the Groeninge. Sticking to religious legend, the Apostles have been miraculously transported to Mary's deathbed, where they surround the prostrate woman in a state of agitation. Mary is dressed in blue, but there are no signs of luxury, reflecting Van der Goes' asceticism and his polemic – the artist may well have been appalled by the church's love of glitter and gold.

Gerard David (c.1460–1523)

Born near Gouda, **Gerard David** moved to Bruges in his early twenties. Soon admitted into the local painters' guild, he quickly rose through the ranks, becoming the city's leading artistic light after the death of **Hans Memling** (see page 58). Official commissions rained in on David, primarily for religious paintings, which he approached formally but with a fine eye for detail. The Groeninge holds two delightful examples of his work, starting with the *Baptism of Christ* triptych, in which, in the central panel, a boyish, lightly bearded Christ is depicted as part of the Holy Trinity. One of David's few secular ventures in the Groeninge is the intriguing *Judgement of Cambyses*, painted on two oak panels. Based on a Persian legend related by Herodotus, the first panel's background shows the corrupt judge Sisamnes accepting a bribe, with his subsequent arrest by grim-faced aldermen filling the foreground. The aldermen crowd in on Sisamnes, and tear sweeps over the judge's face as the king sentences him to be flayed alive. In the gruesome second panel, the king's servants carry out the judgement, while behind, in the top-right corner, the fable is completed with the judge's son dispensing justice from his father's old chair, which is now draped with the flayed skin.

Hieronymus Bosch (1450–1516)

The work of **Hieronymus Bosch** excels in its detail. Still, the subject matter was very different from that of his contemporaries, with his *Last Judgement* comprising a trio of oak panels crammed with mysterious beasts, microscopic mutants and scenes of awful cruelty – men boiled in a pit or cut in half by a giant knife. It looks like unbridled fantasy, but the scenes are read as symbols, a veritable strip cartoon of legend, proverb and tradition. Indeed, Bosch's religious orthodoxy is confirmed by the appeal his work had for the most Catholic of Spanish kings, Philip II.

SOUTH OF THE MARKT

Onze-Lieve-Vrouwekerk

MAP P.48, POCKET MAP C7
Mariastraat W museabrugge.be. Free, but charge for the chancel.

The **Onze-Lieve-Vrouwekerk** (Church of Our Lady) is a rambling shambles of a building, a clamour of different dates and styles whose spire is – at 115.5m (378.9ft) – the highest brick tower in Belgium. The **nave** was three hundred years in the making, an architecturally discordant affair, whose thirteenth-century grey-stone central aisle is the oldest part of the church. The central aisle blends in with the south aisle, but the later, fourteenth-century north aisle doesn't mesh at all – even the columns aren't aligned. This resulted from changing fashions, not slapdash work: the high Gothic north aisle was intended to start a complete remodelling of the church, but the money ran out before the project was finished. The church's most acclaimed objet d'art is a delicate marble *Madonna and Child* by Michelangelo in the south aisle. Purchased by a Bruges merchant, this was the only one of Michelangelo's works to leave Italy during the artist's lifetime and it had a significant influence on painters working in Bruges at the time, though its present setting – beneath gloomy stone walls and set within a gaudy Baroque altar – is hardly prepossessing.

The chancel is the most diverting part of the Onze-Lieve-Vrouwekerk, which lies beyond the heavy-duty black-and-white marble rood screen. Here, you'll find the **mausoleums** of Charles the Bold and his daughter Mary of Burgundy (see page 55), two exquisite examples of Renaissance artistry, their side panels decorated with coats of arms connected by the most intricate floral designs. The royal figures are enhanced in the detail, from the helmet and gauntlets placed gracefully by Charles' side to the pair of watchful dogs nestled at Mary's

Onze-Lieve-Vrouwekerk

The earthly remains of Mary of Burgundy and Charles the Bold

The last independent rulers of Flanders were Charles the Bold, the **duke of Burgundy**, and his daughter **Mary of Burgundy**, both of whom died in unfortunate circumstances: Charles during the siege of the French city of Nancy in 1477 and Mary after a riding accident in 1482. Mary's death was a real surprise, but not so her father's – Charles was always fighting someone. Mary was married to **Maximillian**, a Habsburg prince and future Holy Roman Emperor, who inherited her territories on her death. Thus, at a dynastic stroke, Flanders was incorporated into the Habsburg Empire with all the dreadful consequences that would entail.

In the sixteenth century, the Habsburgs relocated to Spain, but they were keen to emphasise their connections with, and historical authority over, Flanders. Nothing did this quite as well as the ceremonial burial – or reburial – of bits of the royal body. Mary was safely ensconced in Bruges's Onze-Lieve-Vrouwekerk, but the body of Charles was in a makeshift grave in Nancy. Emperor Charles V, the great-grandson of Charles the Bold, had his body exhumed and carried to Bruges, where it was reinterred next to Mary. Or at least he thought he had: there were persistent rumours that the French – the traditional enemies of the Habsburgs – had deliberately handed over a dud skeleton. In the 1970s, archaeologists had a bash at solving the mystery by digging beneath Charles and Mary's mausoleums in the Onze-Lieve-Vrouwekerk. Still, among the assorted tombs, they failed to authoritatively identify either the body or even the tomb of Charles. However, things ran more smoothly in Mary's case, with her skeleton confirming the details of her hunting accident. Moreover, buried alongside her was the **urn**, which contained the heart of her son, Philip the Fair, placed here in 1506. More archaeological harrumphing over the remains of poor old Charles is likely at some point or another.

feet. Curiously, the **hole** dug by archaeologists beneath the mausoleums during the 1970s to discover who was buried here was never filled in, so you can see the burial vaults of several unknown medieval dignitaries. However, three have been moved to the Lanchals Chapel (see below). The coats of arms above the choir stalls are those of the knights of the Order of the Golden Fleece (see page 61), who met here in 1468.

In the ambulatory, across from the mausoleums, the **Lanchals Chapel** holds the imposing Baroque gravestone of Pieter Lanchals, a one-time Habsburg official who had his head lopped off by the citizens of Bruges in 1488. Legend asserts that he was beheaded for his opposition to Maximilian's temporary imprisonment in the Craenenburg (see page 30) and that Bruges was later obliged to introduce swans onto its canals to atone for the crime. Both tales are, however, later fabrications: Lanchals had his head lopped off for being corrupt and was soon forgotten by his erstwhile sponsor, while

Coat of arms above the entrance to St-Janshospitaal

the swan story originated with the swan that adorns his gravestone – the bird was the man's emblem, appropriately enough, as his name means 'long neck'. In front of the Lanchals gravestone are the three relocated **medieval burial vaults** moved across from beneath the royal mausoleums. Each is plastered with lime mortar and the inside walls sport brightly coloured **grave frescoes**, a type of art that flourished hereabouts in late medieval times. The iconography is pretty consistent, with the long sides mostly bearing one, sometimes two, angels apiece, and most of the angels are shown swinging thuribles (the vessels in which incense is burnt during religious ceremonies). Typically, the short sides show the Crucifixion and a Virgin and Child. The background decoration is more varied, with crosses, stars and dots all appearing, and two main sorts of flowers – roses and bluebells. The frescoes were painted freehand and executed at

great speed – Flemings were then buried on the day they died – hence the delightful immediacy of the work.

St-Janshospitaal

MAP P.48, POCKET MAP C7
Mariastraat 38 ⓦ museabrugge.be. **Free entry to Apotheek (Apothecary) with museum ticket (see page 57).**

A sprawling complex, **St-Janshospitaal** sheltered the sick of mind and body from medieval times until well into the nineteenth century. The oldest part – at the front on Mariastraat, behind two church-like gable ends – has been turned into the excellent **St-Janshospitaalmuseum** (see page 57), while the nineteenth-century annexe, reached along a narrow passageway on the north side of the museum, has been converted into a rather mundane events and exhibition centre called – somewhat confusingly – **Oud St-Jan**. As you stroll down the passageway, you pass the old **Apotheek**, where one room holds dozens of ex votos, the other an ancient dispensing counter flanked by a brigade of vintage apothecary's jars.

St-Janshospitaalmuseum

MAP P.48, POCKET MAP C7
Mariastraat 38 Ⓦ visitbruges.be. Charge.
At the front of the St-Janshospitaal complex, the **St-Janshospitaalmuseum** occupies three distinct spaces – the old, stone-arched hospital ward, the adjoining chapel and a modern floor inserted above. The hospital ward and the floor above are often used for temporary exhibitions, which means that the museum's collection of artefacts on the hospital itself – including a pair of sedan chairs used to carry the infirm to the hospital in emergencies and a set of photos of nuns in their fanciful habits – can be shunted around or even removed. On the other hand, the chapel and its immediate environs always feature several key works by **Hans Memling** (see page 58), plus several other paintings and objets d'art. Highlights include an exquisite *Deposition of Christ*, a late fifteenth-century version of an original by **Rogier van der Weyden**, and a stylish, intimately observed diptych by **Jan Provoost** with portraits of Christ and the donor (a friar) on the front and a skull on the back – the skull a reminder of the donor's mortality. There's also Jan Beerblock's *The Wards of St Janshospitaal*, a minutely detailed painting of the hospital ward as it was in the late-eighteenth century, the patients tucked away in row upon row of tiny, cupboard like beds. There were 150 beds divided into three sections: one for women, one for men and the third for the dying. The nuns had a fine reputation for the quality of their ministrations, but presumably, being moved to the dying beds was something of a disappointment – though none of the patients have left any records.

View of St-Salvatorskathedraal and the rooftops of Bruges

The Memling Collection

St-Janshospitaalmuseum holds six wonderful works by **Hans Memling** (1433–94). Born near Frankfurt, Memling spent most of his working life in Bruges, where Rogier van der Weyden tutored him. He adopted much of his mentor's style and stuck to the detailed symbolism of his contemporaries, but his painterly manner was distinctly restrained, often pious and grave. Graceful and warmly coloured, his figures also had a velvet-like quality that greatly appealed to the city's burghers, whose enthusiasm made Memling a rich man – in 1480, he was listed among the town's major moneylenders.

The most unusual of the Memling works on display is the **Reliquary of St Ursula**, comprising a miniature wooden Gothic church painted with the story of St Ursula. Memling condensed the legend into six panels, beginning with Ursula and her ten companions landing at Cologne and Basle before reaching Rome at the end of their pilgrimage. Things go badly wrong on the way back: they leave Basle in good order but are then – in the last two panels – massacred by Huns as they pass through Germany. Memling had a religious point to make, but today, it's the mass of incidental detail that makes the reliquary so enchanting, providing an intriguing evocation of the late medieval world. Close by are two **triptychs**, a *Lamentation* and an *Adoration of the Magi*, in which there's a gentle nervousness in the approach of the Magi, here shown as the kings of Spain, Arabia and Ethiopia.

The middle panel of Memling's **St John Altarpiece** displays the exquisite *Marriage of St Catherine* in which the saint, who represents contemplation, is shown receiving a ring from the baby Jesus to seal their spiritual union. Catherine was one of the most popular medieval saints, not least because although she was martyred in the fourth century, her body was reportedly rediscovered on Mount

Sinai several centuries later with a stream of healing oil issuing from her body. Behind Jesus to the left stands St John and behind him, if you look closely, is the giant wooden crane that once dominated the Kraanplein (see page 71). The side panels depict the beheading of St John the Baptist and a visionary St John writing the Book of Revelation on the bare and rocky island of Patmos. Once again, the detail impresses: between the inner and outer rainbows above St John, for instance, the prophets play music on tiny instruments, including a lute, a flute, a harp and a hurdy-gurdy.

In a side-chapel adjoining the main chapel is Memling's **Virgin**

and Martin van Nieuwenhove, a diptych depicting the eponymous merchant in the full flush of youth and with a hint of arrogance: his lips pout, his hair cascades down to his shoulders and he is dressed in the most fashionable of doublets – by the middle of the 1480s, when the portrait was commissioned, no Bruges merchant wanted to appear too pious. Opposite, the Virgin gets the full stereotypical treatment from the oval face and the almond-shaped eyes through to full cheeks, thin nose and bunched lower lip.

Also, in the side chapel, Memling's skill as a portraitist is demonstrated to exquisite effect in his **Portrait of a Young Woman**, where the richly dressed subject stares dreamily into the middle distance, her hands – in a superb optical illusion – seeming to clasp the picture frame. The lighting is subtle and sensuous, with the woman set against a dark background, her gauze veil dappling the side of her face. A high forehead was then considered a sign of great womanly beauty, so her hair was pulled back and probably plucked, as were her eyebrows. There's no knowing who the woman was, but in the seventeenth century, her fancy headgear convinced observers that she was one of the legendary Persian sibyls who predicted Christ's birth; they added the cartouche in the top left-hand corner, describing her as *Sibylla Sambetha* and the painting is often referred to by this name.

St-Salvatorskathedraal

MAP P.48, POCKET MAP B6–B7
Steenstraat ⓦ sintsalvator.be. Free.

Rising high above its surroundings, **St-Salvatorskathedraal** (Holy Saviour Cathedral) is a primarily Gothic edifice that mainly dates from the late thirteenth century. However, the Flamboyant Gothic ambulatory was added some two centuries later. A parish church for most of its history, it was only made a cathedral in 1834 following the destruction of St Donatian's (see page 42) by the French. This change of status prompted ecclesiastical rumblings – nearby Onze-Lieve-Vrouwekerk (see page 54) was bigger and its spire higher – and when part of St Salvator's went up in smoke in 1839, the opportunity was taken to make its tower higher and grander in a romantic rendition of the Romanesque style.

Now, finally emerged from a seemingly interminable restoration, the cathedral's **nave** remains a cheerless, cavernous affair despite lashings of new paint. The star turn is the **set of eight paintings** by Jan van Orley currently displayed in the transepts. Commissioned in the 1730s, the paintings were used to manufacture a matching set of tapestries from a Brussels workshop; remarkably enough, these have survived and are hung sequentially in the choir and nave. Each of the eight scenes features a familiar episode from the life of Christ, complete with a handful of animals, including a remarkably determined Palm Sunday donkey. The tapestries are mirror images of the paintings as the weavers worked with the rear of the tapestries uppermost on their looms; the weavers also had sight of the tapestry paintings, as the originals were too valuable to be kept beside the looms. Also in the choir are the painted escutcheons of the Order of the Golden Fleece members, which met here in 1478 (see page

Interior of St-Salvatorskathedraal

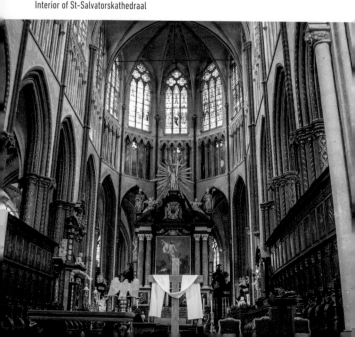

61). Adjoining the nave, on the porch floor behind the old main doors, look out for the recently excavated tombs, whose interior walls are decorated with grave frescoes that follow the same design as those in the Lanchals Chapel (see page 55).

Entered from the cathedral nave, the **Treasury** (Schatkamer; free) occupies the neo-Gothic chapterhouse, whose cloistered rooms are packed with ecclesiastical tackle, from religious paintings and statues to an assortment of reliquaries, vestments and croziers. The labelling is average, so picking up the English-language mini-guide

The Martyrdom of St Hippolytus

Keeping your friends and enemies close: the Order of the Golden Fleece

Philip the Good, the Duke of Burgundy, invented the **Order of the Golden Fleece** in 1430 on his marriage to Isabella of Portugal. Duke since 1419, Philip had spent much of his time curbing the power of the Flemish cities – including Bruges – but he was too economically dependent on them to feel entirely secure. To bolster his position, the duke was always looking for ways to add lustre to his dynasty, hence creating the Order of the Golden Fleece, an exclusive, knightly club that harked back to the (supposed) age of chivalry. The choice of the name was a nod both to the wool weavers of Flanders, who provided him with most of his money, and to the legends of classical Greece. In the Greek story, a winged ram named Chrysomallus – gifted with the power of speech and a golden fleece – saved the life of Phrixus, presented him with his fleece and then flew off to become the constellation of Aries; it was this same fleece that Jason and the Argonauts later sought to recover. The Order's emblem was a golden ram.

Philip stipulated that **membership** of the Order be restricted to 'noblemen in name and proven in valour … born and raised in legitimate wedlock'. He promptly picked the **membership** and appointed himself Grand Master. It was a bit of a con trick, but it went down a treat and the 24 knights who were offered membership duly turned up at the first meeting in Lille in 1431. After that, the Order met regularly, gathering for mutual back-slapping, feasting and exchanging presents. Bruges and Ghent were two favourite venues, and the Order met three times in the former: at St Donatian's Cathedral in 1431, at the Onze-Lieve-Vrouwekerk in 1468, and St-Salvatorskathedraal in 1478. However, the Order was rendered obsolete when the Habsburgs swallowed up Burgundy in the late fifteenth century. The title 'Grand Master' became just one of the family's many dynastic baubles.

Stained glass in St-Salvatorskathedraal

at the entrance is a good idea. The treasury's finest painting is a gruesome, oak-panel triptych, *The Martyrdom of St Hippolytus*, by **Dieric Bouts** (1410–75), who was probably born in Leuven, and **Hugo van der Goes** (d. 1482), from Ghent. The right panel depicts the Roman Emperor Decius, a notorious persecutor of Christians, trying to persuade the priest Hippolytus to abjure his faith. He fails, and in the central

An intricate skill: tapestry making in Bruges

Tapestry manufacture in Bruges began in the middle of the fourteenth century when the city was experiencing something of a boom. This embryonic industry soon came to be based on a dual system of workshop and outworker, the one using paid employees and the other with workers paid on a piecework basis. From the beginning, the town authorities took a keen interest in the business, ensuring consistency through a rigorous quality control system. The other side of this interventionist policy was less palatable: wages were kept down and the workers could hardly ever accumulate enough capital to buy their looms or raw materials, ensuring the burghers remained in tight control.

There were two significant periods of **Bruges tapestry-making**, the first from the early fifteenth until the middle of the sixteenth century and the second from the 1580s to the 1790s. Tapestry production was a cross between **embroidery and ordinary weaving**. It consisted of interlacing a wool weft above and below the strings of a vertical linen 'chain', a process similar to weaving. However, the weaver had to stop to change colour, requiring as many shuttles for the weft as they had colours, as in embroidery. The weft entirely determined the appearance of a tapestry; the design is taken from a painting – or cartoon of a painting – to which the weaver made constant reference. Standard-size tapestries took six months to complete and were produced exclusively for the wealthy. The most famous artists of the day were often involved in the preparatory paintings – among many, Pieter Paul Rubens, Bernard van Orley and David Teniers had tapestry commissions.

There were only two significant **types of tapestry**: decorative, principally verdures, showing scenes of foliage in an almost abstract way, and pictorial (the Bruges speciality) – usually variations on the same basic themes, mainly rural life, knights, hunting parties, classical gods and goddesses and religious scenes. Over the centuries, changes in style were strictly limited. However, the early seventeenth century saw increased use of elaborate woven borders, an appreciation of perspective, and a far brighter, more varied range of colours.

panel, Hippolytus is pulled to pieces by four horses. One other highlight here is the coin-like tokens the churchwardens once gave to the poor. Each is inscribed with an entitlement – 'W.B.', for instance, means bread for a week.

Brouwerij De Halve Maan

MAP P.48, POCKET MAP C7

Walplein 26 Ⓦ halvemaan.be. Charge.
Beside a pleasant square, the long-established **Brouwerij De Halve Maan** (Half Moon Brewery) offers frequent 45-minute-long guided tours of its premises, which include a glass of one of the brewery's most popular beers, either Brugse Zot or Straffe Hendrik. There is a café-bar and a beer shop here too. Interestingly, the brewery recently crowd-funded a 3km (1.9-mile-) long tunnel to take beer from the brewery here on Walplein to its bottling plant – and hey presto, no more brewery delivery vans.

Begijnhof

MAP P.48, POCKET MAP C8

Begijnhof Ⓦ visitbruges.be. Free.
Most tourists visiting Bruges zero in on the **Begijnhof**, just south of the centre, where a rough circle of old and infinitely pretty whitewashed houses surrounds a central green, which looks a treat in spring when a carpet of daffodils pushes up between the wind-bent elms. There were once *begijnhoven* all over Belgium, and this is one of the few to have survived in good nick. They date back to the twelfth century when a Liège priest – a certain Lambert le Bègue – encouraged widows and unmarried women to live in communities, the better to do pious acts, especially caring for the sick. These communities differed from convents in that the **Beguines** (*begijnen*) – did not have to take conventual vows and had the right to return to the secular world if they wished.

Bottling at the Brouwerij De Halve Maan

The entrance to the Begijnhof

Margaret, Countess of Flanders, founded Bruges' Begijnhof in 1245. Although most of the houses now date from the eighteenth century, the medieval layout has survived intact, preserving the impression of the Begijnhof as a self-contained village, with access controlled through two large and particularly handsome gates. The houses are still in private hands, but, with the Beguines long gone, they're now occupied by a mixture of single, older women and Benedictine nuns, whom you'll sometimes see flitting around in their habits, mostly on their way to and from the **Begijnhofkerk**, a surprisingly large church with a set of gaudy altarpieces. Only one house in the Begijnhof is open to the public – the **Begijnenhuisje** (charge), a small-scale celebration of the simple life of the Beguines, comprising a couple of living rooms and a mini-cloister. The prime exhibit is the *schapraai*, a traditional Beguine's cupboard, which was a frugal combination of a dining table, cutlery cabinet and larder.

Minnewater

MAP P.48, POCKET MAP C8

Facing the more southerly of the Begijnhof's two gates is the **Minnewater**, often hyped as the city's 'Lake of Love'. The tag certainly gets the canoodlers going, but the lake – more a large pond – started life as a city harbour. The distinctive stone **lock house** at the head of the Minnewater recalls its earlier function, though it's a fanciful nineteenth-century reconstruction of the medieval original. The **Poertoren**, on the west bank at the far end of the lake, is more authentic, its brown brickwork dating from 1398 and once forming part of the city wall. This is where the city kept its gunpowder – hence the name 'Powder Tower'. Beside the Poertoren, a footbridge spans the southern end of the Minnewater to reach the leafy expanse of **Minnewaterpark**, which trails north back towards Wijngaardstraat, or you can keep on going along the wooded footpath that threads its way along the city's former **ramparts**.

Shops

Brugse Boekhandel

MAP P.48, POCKET MAP D6
Dijver 2 ⓦ brugseboekhandel.be.

Family-owned, the long-established Brugse Boekhandel is an amiable general bookshop that is especially good for books about Bruges, past and present, including tourist guides. It also does a competent side-line in English language novels, has a better-than-average selection of postcards, sells English-language newspapers and stocks an outstanding range of books on local lace.

The Chocolate Line

MAP P.48, POCKET MAP C6
Simon Stevinplein 19
ⓦ thechocolateline.be.

The best chocolate shop in town – and there's some serious competition – with everything handmade using natural ingredients. Truffles and pralines are two specialities and the chocolates come in all sorts of tempting shapes and sizes. Boxes of mixed chocolates are sold in various quantities: a 250g box costs €20.

Classics

MAP P.48, POCKET MAP C6
Oude Burg 32 ⓦ paul-van-hecke-art.be/classics-brugge.

In business since the 1970s, this cosy family-owned art shop is a mixed bag of a place, selling everything from fine art, tapestries, furniture and antiques to more modern objects in traditional styles. It also stocks Indian textiles and is good for handmade jewellery.

Leonidas

MAP P.48, POCKET MAP C7
Katelijnestraat 24 ⓦ leonidas.com.

Leonidas is one of Belgium's biggest chocolate shop chains and has three outlets in Bruges, including one here on Katelijnestraat and another at the train station. This branch offers a wide selection of pralines and candy confectionery, all at very competitive prices (around €16 for 250g). However, their products are more sugary than their exclusive/expensive rivals. As with all chocolate shops along Katelijnestraat, expect queues in the summer.

Neuhaus

MAP P.48, POCKET MAP C6
Steenstraat 66 ⓦ neuhauschocolates.com.

Neuhaus is probably Belgium's best chocolate chain and they sell delicious and beautifully presented chocolates. Check out their specialities, such as the handmade Caprices – pralines stuffed with crispy nougat, fresh cream and soft-centred chocolate – and the delicious Manons – stuffed white chocolates, which come with fresh cream, vanilla and coffee fillings. There are two shops in Bruges; this outlet is the least crowded. Reckon on €25 for a 250g box.

Quicke

MAP P.48, POCKET MAP B6
Zuidzandstraat 23 ⓦ quicke.be.

Neuhaus

The top shoe shop in Bruges, Quicke, showcases the prime European seasonal collections featuring the likes of Prada, Church's and Miu Miu. No surprise, then, that their shoes are expensive. It also sells a wide range of less well-known brands – for instance, Santoni, Hogan and Bambu.

De Striep
MAP P.48, POCKET MAP C7
Katelijnestraat 42 ⓦ stripweb.be.
Comics are a Belgian speciality (remember Tintin), but this is the only comic-strip specialist in Bruges, stocking everything from run-of-the-mill cheapies to collector's items in Flemish, French and English. You'll also find new and second-hand comics, plus a scattering of hang-on-the-wall comic prints.

Cafés

De Bron
MAP P.48, POCKET MAP D8
Katelijnestraat 82 ⓣ 050 33 45 26.

Many of the city's cafés and restaurants offer vegetarian dishes. However, this pleasant little place is the only exclusively vegetarian spot per se, offering fresh, organic food – lentil salad, stewed cabbage, pumpkin, pickled radish and such. There is one main dish of the day, which comes in three sizes – small, medium and large (medium is enough for most appetites). A meal here costs a very reasonable €20–25. Cash only at the time of writing. €

Le Pain Quotidien
MAP P.48, POCKET MAP C6
Simon Stevinplein 15 ⓦ lepainquotidien.be.
This popular café, part of a chain, occupies a grand old building on one of the city's busiest squares and has a large terrace at the back. Much of the chain's success is built upon its bread, whole food and baked every which way. A substantial menu clocks up the likes of salads, light bites and cakes and they also do an excellent home-made soup and bread, which makes a meal in itself, but a full brunch costs €24. €

Le Pain Quotidien on Simon Stevin

Tea-room Laurent

MAP P.48, POCKET MAP C6
Steenstraat 79 ☎ 050 33 94 67.
Located just metres from the
cathedral, this busy café wins no
points for decor or atmosphere, but
its competitive prices attract locals
by the score. The snacks and light
meals are filling if hardly finessed,
but the pancakes are delicious and
begin at a very reasonable €5. €

De Verbeelding

MAP P.48, POCKET MAP C6
Oude Burg 26 Ⓦ de-verbeelding-brugge.be.
This amenable café-restaurant
occupies notably cosy premises in
a handy location. The home-
made food is tasty, filling and
relatively inexpensive, with the
more straightforward dishes (tapas)
perhaps the best – try the meatballs
or the shrimp croquettes. This is a
popular spot.

Restaurants

Boem Patat

MAP P.48, POCKET MAP E6
Minderbroedersstraat 26
Ⓦ boempatatbrugge.be.
This enjoyable restaurant has got
most things dead right – from
the jazzed-up, ersatz medievalism
of the decor (the house is old,
but the wooden beams and
chimneypiece were inserted during
the refurbishment) through to the
simple Flemish cuisine. Fries and
salads are a big deal here, but there
are also veal escalopes and spaghetti
Bolognese. Mains average a very
reasonable €22. €€

Christophe

MAP P.48, POCKET MAP D7
Garenmarkt 34 Ⓦ christophe-brugge.be.
Rural chic furnishings and fittings
make for a relaxing atmosphere at
this pocket-sized bistro, where a
Franco-Flemish menu is especially
strong on meat. One exception is
the excellent bouillabaisse. Daily
specials are a feature and prices are

Boem Patat

competitive, with main courses
averaging around €32. €€€

Goesepitte 43

MAP P.48, POCKET MAP B7
Goezeputstraat 43 Ⓦ goesepitte43.be.
The contemporary decor here is
inventive and creative – there's
even a moss wall made up of real
moss at the entrance – and so is
the menu: try, for example, the red
mullet with garden peas, fava beans
and lemon balm sauce as a starter,
followed by the guinea fowl filet
filled with goose liver as a main.
Many of the dishes are prepared in
a Mibrasa oven. After the kitchen
closes, the place morphs into a
relaxed and rather charming bar.
Starters average €28, €40 for a
main. €€€

Lobster Pot

MAP P.48, POCKET MAP C7
St-Salvatorskerkhof 14
Ⓦ lobsterpotbrugge.be.
Almost in the shadow of the
cathedral, this friendly and well-
maintained family restaurant does a
good line in fish – halibut, sole and
so forth – but really (as the name

Lio's

might suggest) you should come here for the lobster offered up in a variety of ways – there's even a separate lobster menu. €€€

Réliva

MAP P.48, POCKET MAP B7
Goezeputstraat 6 Ⓦ reliva.be.
This chic and relaxed restaurant may not entirely deserve all its rave reviews. Still, there's no denying the inventive, carefully constructed menu and the pride they take in using organic ingredients. A sample dish is a wild duck with celeriac cream with a port jus – indeed, the sauces are genuinely delicious. A three-course set menu will cost you €54 (less at lunchtime). Reservations are absolutely essential. €€€

De Schaar

MAP P.48, POCKET MAP E6
Hooistraat 2 Ⓦ bistrodeschaar.be.
In the cosiest of terrace houses, complete with a stepped gable, this appealing restaurant sits prettily beside the Coupure canal, about ten minutes' walk southeast of

the Burg. The speciality here is grilled meat – for example, a rack of lamb with wok vegetables and mustard sauce – but there are other gastronomic delights, such as duck with a raspberry sauce. All are nicely served and presented. €€€

Tanuki

MAP P.48, POCKET MAP C7
Oude Gentweg 1 Ⓦ tanuki.be.
It's probably the best Japanese restaurant in town and certainly, if you've been in Belgium a long time, a welcome break from the heaviness of Flemish cuisine. The menu features the usual Japanese favourites you'd expect to come across – noodles, sushi and sashimi. Mains average €38. They must be doing something right – Tanuki has been going for nigh-on thirty years. €€€

Bars and clubs

Het Brugs Beertje

MAP P.48, POCKET MAP C6
Kemelstraat 5 Ⓦ brugsbeertje.be.

This small and friendly speciality beer bar – the 'Little Bear' – claims a stock of three hundred brews (plus guest beers on draught), which aficionados reckon is one of the best selections in Belgium. It was opened by an enterprising local woman, Daisy Claeys, in the early 1980s, when she spotted an increasing interest in Belgian beers in general and speciality brews in particular. The bar is now on the tourist trail, attracting an international clientele. Simple food is served here, too, including a cheese board with five types of cheese, paté and toasted sandwiches.

L'Estaminet

MAP P.48, POCKET MAP D6
Park 5 ⓦ estaminet-brugge.be.
Groovy café-bar with a relaxed neighbourhood feel and (for Bruges) a pretty diverse and cosmopolitan clientele. Drink in the dark (almost mysterious) interior or outside on the large sheltered terrace. The beer menu is well chosen, skilfully picking its way through Belgium's vast offering. One of the city's best hangouts, though the name of the place has seedy connotations: according to some local sources, *estaminet* is derived from the Spanish Habsburg garrison's search

for women as in '¿*estan minetas?*' ('Are there girls?').

Lio's

MAP P.48, POCKET MAP C7
Oud St-Jan, off Mariastraat ⓦ liosbrugge.be.
Perhaps the coolest place in town, this popular bar, club and restaurant is kitted out in a very attractive modern style and its canalside outside terrace looks very much like a beach – a visual surprise if ever there was one. Guest DJs play funky, uplifting house and the drinks and cocktails are reasonably priced. The club gets going at about 11pm.

Lokkedize

MAP P.48, POCKET MAP B7
Korte Vuldersstraat 3 ⓦ bistrolokkedize.be.
Attracting a mixed crowd, this inviting and sympathetic bar-cum-bistro is all subdued lighting, fresh flowers and bare brick walls. It does a good job of serving up a nice but limited line in Mediterranean (especially Greek) food, with good value, well-seasoned salads and main courses alongside a selection of cheaper and equally good bar snacks (or finger food as it is called here). There is regular live music, too, everything from jazz and *chanson* to R&B to get those toes tapping.

Het Brugs Beertje

North and East of the Markt

The gentle canals and mazy cobbled streets of northeast Bruges are beautiful. In this uncrowded part of the centre, stretching out from Jan van Eyckplein to the old medieval moat, picturesque brick terraces dating from the town's late medieval golden age blend seamlessly with the grand Classical mansions of later years, all woven round a skein of black-blue canals. Northeast Bruges often surprises the eye with its subtle variety, from discreet shrines and miniature statues to delightful neighbourhood churches, intimate arched doorways, handsome crow-step gables and scores of wonky-looking chimneys. The sheer prettiness of northeast Bruges is its main appeal. Still, there are one or two obvious targets: a pair of Baroque churches – St-Annakerk and St-Walburgakerk – as well as the antique lace of the Kantcentrum (Lace Centre) and the Museum Onze-Lieve-Vrouw ter Potterie (Museum of Our Lady of the Pottery), which has an intriguing chapel and several exemplary Flemish tapestries.

St-Jakobskerk

MAP P.72, POCKET MAP B5
St-Jakobsplein ☏ 050 33 68 41. Free.

Not far from the Markt, the serious exterior of **St-Jakobskerk**

Religious painting in St-Jakobskerk

(St James Church) mainly dates from the fifteenth century. In medieval times, the church was popular with foreign merchants, acting as a prototype community centre. Inside, the church is mainly Baroque, its airy, triple-aisled **nave** interrupted and darkened by a grim marble rood screen with a cumbersome high altar lurking beyond. More appealing is the handsome Renaissance **burial chapel** of Ferry de Gros (d. 1547), to the right of the choir, which sports this well-to-do landowner's elaborate, painted tomb. Unusually, the tomb has two shelves – on the top are the finely carved effigies of Ferry and his first wife, while below, on the lower shelf, is his second. Above the chapel's altar is an enamelled terracotta medallion of the Virgin and Child imported from Florence in the fifteenth century. No one knows quite how it ended up here, but there's no

Monument to Jan van Eyck on Jan van Eyckplein square

doubt that it influenced Flemish artists of the period. The walls of St-Jakobskerk are covered with around eighty **paintings**. They're not an especially distinguished bunch, but look out for the finely executed *Legend of St Lucy* in St Anthony's Chapel – the first chapel on the left-hand side of the nave. A panel triptych by the Master of the St Lucy Legend, the painting illustrates the persecution of this fourth-century saint, who – legend has it – proved extremely difficult to dispose of: the men sent to arrest her found her immovable even with the assistance of a team of oxen (as in the third panel). In the next chapel, look out also for the meditative *Madonna and the Seven Sorrows*, a triptych by **Pieter Pourbus** (1523–84), the leading local artist of his day.

Kraanplein

MAP P.72, POCKET MAP C5

Just off Vlamingstraat lies the **Kraanplein** – Crane Square – whose name recalls the enormous wooden crane that once unloaded heavy goods from the adjoining river. Before it was covered over, the River Reie ran south from Jan van Eyckplein to the Markt, and the Kraanplein dock was one of the busiest parts of this central waterway. Mounted on a revolving post like a windmill, the crane's pulleys were worked using two large treadmills operated by children – a grim existence by any measure. Installed in 1290 – and only dismantled in 1767 – the crane impressed visitors greatly and was a sign of Bruges's economic success. The crane appears in the background of several medieval paintings, notably behind St John in Memling's *St John Altarpiece* (see page 58).

Jan van Eyckplein

MAP P.72, POCKET MAP C4

Jan van Eyckplein is one of the prettiest squares in Bruges, its cobblestones backdropped by the easy sweep of the Spiegelrei canal. The centrepiece of the square is an earnest **statue** of Van Eyck, erected in 1878, while on the north side is the **Tolhuis**, whose fancy Renaissance entrance is decorated

North and east of the Markt

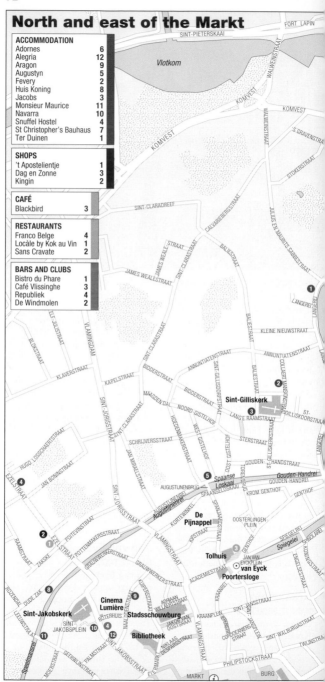

ACCOMMODATION

Adornes	6
Alegria	12
Aragon	9
Augustyn	5
Fevery	2
Huis Koning	8
Jacobs	3
Monsieur Maurice	11
Navarra	10
Snuffel Hostel	4
St Christopher's Bauhaus	7
Ter Duinen	1

SHOPS

't Apostelientje	1
Dag en Zonne	3
Kingin	2

CAFÉ

Blackbird	3

RESTAURANTS

Franco Belge	4
Locàle by Kok au Vin	1
Sans Cravate	2

BARS AND CLUBS

Bistro du Phare	1
Café Vlissinghe	3
Republiek	4
De Windmolen	2

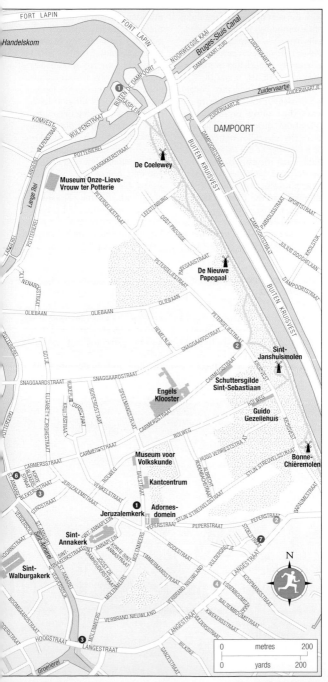

FORT LAPIN

Handelskom

FORT LAPIN

Bruges-Sluis Canal

NOORWEEGSE KAAI

DAMSE VAART-ZUID

Zuidervaartje 2A

ZUIDERVAARTJE.IE

Zuidervaartje

ZUIDERVAARTJE

ZUIDERVAART

KOMVEST

WULPENSTRAAT

BUITEN DE DAMPOORT

DIJKSASPLEIN

DAMPOORT

WILPENSTRAAT

WILPENSTRAAT

POTTERIEREI

HAARAKKERSTRAAT

De Coelewey

BUITEN KRUISVEST

DAMPOORTSTRAAT

SPORTSTRAAT

CAMPGRDSTRAAT

PAPEGUISSTRAAT

KEGLSTDK

Langerei

LANGEREI

Museum Onze-Lieve-
Vrouw ter Potterie

PETERSELIESTRAAT

LEESTENBURG

OOST-PROOSSE

JULIUS DOOGHELAAN

POTTERIEREI

JULI NENABOSTRAAT

PAPEGAAISTRAAT

De Nieuwe
Papegaal

PETERSELIESTRAAT

DAMPOORTSTRAAT

OLIEBAAN

OLIEBAAN

OLIEBAAN

BUITEN KRUISVEST

POTTERIEREI

GOTJE

ELIZABETHZORGHESTRAAT

SNAGGAARDSTRAAT

HEMELRIJK

SNAGGAARDSTRAAT

PETERSELIESTRAAT

Sint-
Janshuismolen

SNAGGAARDSTRAAT

RIJKEPIJN

DERSTRAAT

ROPERDSTRAAT

SPEELMANSSTRAAT

CARMERSSTRAAT

Engels
Klooster

Schuttersgilde
Sint-Sebastiaan

KRUISVEST

CARMERSSTRAAT

KRUISVEST

CARMERSSTRAAT

ROLWEG

HOIWEG

Guido
Gezellehuis

ELIZABETHZORGHESTRAAT

POTTERIEREI

ROLWEG

HUGO VERRIESTSTRAAT

STIJN STREUVELSSTRAAT

Bonne-
Chièremolen

CARMERSSTRAAT

CARMERSSTRAAT

ROLWEG

Museum voor
Volkskunde

BALSTRAAT

ALBRECHT
RODENBACHSTRAAT

RAPAMESTRAAT

VENKELSTRAAT

Kantcentrum

JERUZALEMSTRAAT

KORTE
ELEKES
STRAAT

S-ANNAREI

BLEKERSSTRAAT

SIROSTRAAT

Jeruzalemkerk

Adornes-
domein

PEPERSTRAAT

STIJN STREUVELSSTRAAT

PEPERSTRAAT

STOELSTRAAT

PEPERSTRAAT

VERWERSSTRAAT

HOORNSTRAAT

Sint-Annarei

Sint-
Annakerk

SINT-ANNAPLEIN

MOLENMEERS

RODESTRAAT

KOOPMANSSTRAAT

LANGESTRAAT

Sint-
Walburgakerk

SINT-
ANNAKERKSTRAAT

SINT ANNAREI

OOST DE
MOLENMEERS

JOOST DE
ANNASTRAAT

TIMMERMANSSTRAAT

VERBRAND NIEUWLAND

VLDERSTRAATJE

ESSENBOOMSTR.

BALSEMBOOMSTRAAT

BOOMGAARDSTRAAT

VERVERSSTRAAT

MOLENMEERS

LANGESTRAAT

VLDERSTRAAT

KWEKERSSTRAAT

PEERSTRAAT

HOOGSTRAAT

LANGESTRAAT

Groenerei

VERBRAND NIEUWLAND

GANZESTRAAT

BILKSKE

N

| 0 | metres | 200 |
| 0 | yards | 200 |

with the coat of arms of the dukes of Luxembourg, who long levied tolls here. The Tolhuis dates from the late fifteenth century but was extensively remodelled in medieval style in the 1870s, as was the **Poortersloge** (Merchants' Lodge), whose slender tower pokes up above the rooftops on the west side of the square. Theoretically, every city merchant was entitled to be a member of the Poortersloge, but in fact, membership was restricted to the richest and the most powerful. An informal alternative to the Town Hall, it was here that key political and economic decisions were taken and it was also where local bigwigs could drink and gamble discreetly away from prying eyes.

The Spiegelrei canal and around

MAP P.72, POCKET MAP D4

Running east from Jan van Eyckplein, the **Spiegelrei canal** was once the heart of the foreign merchants' quarter, its frenetic quays overlooked by the trade missions of many of the city's trading partners. The medieval buildings framing the canal were demolished long ago but have been replaced by an exquisite medley of architectural styles from expansive classical mansions to the more modest brick dwellings of lesser merchants, who dug deep into their pockets for the pirouetting crow-step gables that now adorn their former homes. At the far end of Spiegelrei, a left turn brings you onto one of the city's loveliest streets, **Gouden-Handrei**, which, along with adjoining **Spaanse Loskaai**, was once the focus of the Spanish merchants' district. On the far side of the canal stand a string of delightful summer outhouses, privately owned and sometimes surprisingly lavish extensions to the demure houses fronting onto Gouden-Handstraat. The west end of Spaanse Loskaai is marked by the **Augustijnenbrug**, the city's oldest surviving bridge, a sturdy three-arched structure dating from 1391. The bridge was built to help the monks of

The Spiegelrei canal

a nearby (and long-demolished) Augustinian monastery get into the city centre speedily; the benches set into the parapet were cut to allow itinerant tradesmen to display their goods here.

Spanjaardstraat

MAP P.72, POCKET MAP C4

Running south from the Augustijnenbrug (see above) is the narrow **Spanjaardstraat**, also part of the Spanish merchants' enclave – hence the platoon of substantial terrace houses. It was here, at No. 9, in a house formerly known as **De Pijnappel** (The Fir Cone), that the founder of the Jesuits, the Spaniard Ignatius Loyola (1491–1556), spent his holidays while he was a student in Paris in the early 1530s. He befriended Juan Luis Vives (see page 47), who lodged down the street, but unfortunately, his friend's relative liberality – he did, after all, proclaim that 'an unmarried woman should rarely appear in public' – failed to temper Loyola's nascent fanaticism. Spanjaardstraat soon leads back to Jan van Eyckplein (see page 71).

St-Gilliskerk

MAP P.72, POCKET MAP D3–D4

Baliestraat ☏ 050 34 87 05. Free.

The sturdy brick pile of **St-Gilliskerk** dates from the late thirteenth century, though it was considerably enlarged in the 1460s; the church has a broad and appealing three-aisled nave, but its most distinctive feature is its barrel-vaulted roof, which was added in the eighteenth century. Among the **paintings**, the pick is the Hemelsdale polyptych by the prolific **Pieter Pourbus** – on the wall just to the right of the main doors. It's a dainty piece of work with the donors at either end, sandwiching four scenes from the life of Christ: the *Adoration of the Shepherds*, the *Arrival of the Magi*, the *Flight into Egypt* and Jesus' *Circumcision*. The church also

A painting by Jan Maes in St-Gilliskerk

possesses six eighteenth-century paintings illustrating the efforts of the Trinitarian monks to ransom Christian prisoners from the Turks. The paintings are distinctly second-rate, but the two near the organ in the top right-hand corner of the church are interesting in their sinister representation of the East – all glowering clouds and gloomy city walls. The other four paintings, in the bottom left-hand corner of the nave, illustrate the 1198 papal foundation of the Trinitarians, an order devoted to the ransom of Christians held by Muslims, and one that enjoyed the support of St-Gilliskerk.

St-Walburgakerk

MAP P.72, POCKET MAP D5

St-Maartensplein, off Koningstraat ☏ 050 34 87 05. Free.

Southeast of Jan van Eyckplein, **St-Walburgakerk** is a fluent Baroque extravagance built for the Jesuits in the first half of the seventeenth century. Framed by slender pilasters, the sinuous, flowing facade is matched by the stunning opulence of the booming interior, awash with acres of creamy-white paint. The grandiose pulpit, complete with its huffing and puffing cherubs, was the work of Artus II Quellin (1625–1700), an Antwerp woodcarver and sculptor whose family ran a profitable sideline in Baroque pulpits. The pick of the church's scattering of **paintings** is a triptych by **Pieter Claeissens the Younger** (1535–1623) on the right-hand side of the nave. The central panel depicts a popular legend about Philip the Good, a fifteenth-century count of Flanders and the founder of the Order of the Golden Fleece (see page 61). The story goes that as Philip was preparing to fight the French, he encountered the Virgin Mary in a scorched tree; not one to look a gift horse in the mouth, Philip fell to his knees and asked for victory, and his prayers were duly answered.

St-Annakerk

MAP P.72, POCKET MAP E4
St-Annaplein ☎ 050 34 87 05. Free.
Founded in the 1490s, **St-Annakerk** came a cropper in the religious wars of the sixteenth century when the Protestants burnt the place to the ground. Rebuilt in the 1620s, the church is a dinky little structure surmounted by the slenderest of brick towers and set within a pleasant little square. Almost untouched since its reconstruction, the interior is a notably homogeneous example of the Baroque, its barrel-vaulted, single-aisle nave nearly drowning in ornately carved, dark-stained wooden panelling. Pride of artistic place going to the marble and porphyry rood screen of 1628, but you can't miss the massive painting of the *Last Judgement*, hung above the entrance in 1685 and the finest surviving painting by the Flemish artist **Hendrik Herregouts** (1633–1724). Born near Antwerp, Herregouts was an artistic star of the Counter-Reformation, painting religious scenes in a score of churches across Dutch-speaking Belgium. However, he was most popular in Bruges, living in the city from 1680 to 1690.

The Adornesdomein: the Jeruzalemkerk

MAP P.72, POCKET MAP E4
Peperstraat 3 ⓦ adornes.org. Charge.

St-Annakerk

Bruges's medieval gates – and a windmill or two

Medieval Bruges had seven **gates** intercepting the wall and moat that encircled the city. Although the wall has almost entirely disappeared – unlike the moat – four gates have survived in good condition. All four date from the late fourteenth and early fifteenth centuries, though each has been heavily restored. Of the four, the two prettiest are the **Smedenpoort**, on the west side of the city centre at the end of Smedenstraat, and the **Ezelpoort** (Donkey Gate), to the northwest of the centre, both of which exhibit twin, heavily fortified towers, rising above the moat. The **Gentpoort**, on the southeast edge of the centre on Gentpoortstraat, has twin circular brick towers on one side and a church-like facade on the other. The niche statue on the facade is of St Adrian, an early fourth-century figure and member of the Praetorian guard, who was so impressed by the Christians he was torturing that he was converted – and subsequently martyred. Previously, the interior of the Gentpoort held a mildly diverting museum exploring how the city ramparts and gates developed and evolved, but this is currently not open to visitors. Almost identical to the Gentpoort is the fourth and final surviving gate, the **Kruispoort**, at the far end of Langestraat. Belgium's assorted invaders usually chose to enter Bruges via this gate – including the Habsburg Charles V, Napoleon and the German army (twice). Perched on top of the earthen bank near the Kruispoort are a quartet of **windmills** – two visible and another two beyond eyeshot, about 300m (0.18 miles) and 500m (0.3 miles) to the north. You'd have to be a windmill fanatic to want to visit them all. Still, the nearest two are mildly diverting – and the closest, **St-Janshuismolen**, is in working order and the only one that is open (☎ 050 44 87 11; charge).

Beyond the Spiegelrei canal is an old working-class district, whose simple brick cottages surround the **Adornesdomein**, a substantial complex of buildings belonging to the wealthy Adornes family, who migrated here from Genoa in the thirteenth century and then proceeded to make a fortune from alum, a sort of dye fastener made from a hydrated double sulphate. A visit to the *domein* begins towards the rear of the complex, where a set of humble brick almshouses hold a small **museum**, which gives the historical low-down on the family. The most interesting figure was **Anselm Adornes** (1424–1483), whose rollercoaster career included high-power diplomatic missions to Scotland and being punished for corruption – he was fined and paraded through Bruges dressed only in his underwear. Anselm and one of his sons also made the perilous pilgrimage to the Holy Land, where they were much impressed by the Church of the Holy Sepulchre in Jerusalem. On their return, they decided to commission an approximate copy of the church they had visited and the result is the idiosyncratic **Jeruzalemkerk** (Jerusalem Church) that now dominates the *domein*. The church's interior is on two levels: the lower one features a large and ghoulish altarpiece decorated with skulls and ladders, in front of which is the black marble mausoleum of Anselm Adornes and his wife Margaretha – though the only part of Anselm held here is his heart: Anselm was murdered in Scotland, which is where he was buried, but his heart was sent back to Bruges. There's more grisliness at the back of the church, where the small vaulted chapel holds a replica of Christ's tomb – you can glimpse the imitation body down the tunnel behind the iron grating. To either side of the main altar, steps ascend to the choir, right below the eccentric, onion-domed lantern tower.

Kantcentrum

MAP P.72, POCKET MAP E4
Balstraat 16 ⓦ kantcentrum.eu. Charge, including demonstrations.

The ground floor of the **Kantcentrum** (Lace Centre), just metres from the Adornesdomein, traces the history of the lace industry here in Bruges and displays a substantial sample of antique, handmade lace. One of the earliest major pieces is an

The Jeruzalemkerk

exquisite, seventeenth-century Lenten veil with scenes from the life of Ignatius of Loyola, the founder of the Jesuits, and there are also seventeenth- and eighteenth-century collars, ruffs and fans of great delicacy.

Indeed, Belgian lace – or **Flanders lace** as it was formerly known – was renowned for the fineness of its thread and the beauty of its motifs; much desired, it was once worn in all the courts of Europe. It was in the nineteenth century, however, that the Bruges lace industry took a surprising turn. Right across Flanders, lace had always played second commercial fiddle to linen manufacture, but in the 1830s, British clothiers undercut and overwhelmed their Flemish competitors and the results were catastrophic, with thousands of Flemish spinners and weavers left destitute; poor harvests and epidemics of cholera and typhus made things even worse. In these dire circumstances, the Catholic church – or rather its parish priests – and Belgium's liberal bourgeoisie swallowed their mutual hatred to step into the breach, training hundreds of Flemish women in **lace-making** in scores of convents and specialist schools. It might have seemed a foolish initiative, given that **machine-made lace** was very much on the rise, but there was a market for certain sorts of handmade lace – Flemish Valenciennes and Chantilly, for example – and the expansion of the Bruges lace industry did mitigate the worst effects of the economic collapse. There was an ideological point, too: for the clergy, the home-working female lace maker, whom nuns usually trained, was the epitome of domestic virtue, whereas, for Belgium's liberals and socialists, the badly paid and poorly educated Flemish lace maker was a symbol of exploitation – and the difference of opinion fuelled bitter debate.

Lace-making at Kantcentrum

At the start of the twentieth century, there were 47,000 lace-makers in Belgium, of whom over thirty thousand were in Bruges. However, the industry collapsed after World War I when lace, a symbol of an old and discredited order, suddenly had no place in most women's wardrobes. Nowadays, lace-making is a local tradition-cum-hobby and there are **demonstrations** of handmade lace-making upstairs at the Kantcentrum. You can buy pieces here, too – or stroll along the street to the excellent 't Apostelientje (see page 86).

Museum voor Volkskunde

MAP P.72, POCKET MAP E4
Balstraat 43 ⓦ visitbruges.be. Charge.
The unassuming **Museum voor Volkskunde** (Folklore Museum) occupies a long line of low-ceilinged almshouses beside a trim courtyard. The interior is parcelled into small period rooms, with an emphasis on the nineteenth and early twentieth centuries. The labelling is patchy, so it's best to pick up an English guidebook at reception. There's also a small

tavern, *De Zwarte Kat* (*The Black Cat*), done in traditional style, serving ales and average snacks. Room 1 features an old classroom *c.* 1920, but the first high spot is Room 5, which focuses on popular religion and displays an interesting collection of pilgrimage banners and the wax, silver and iron ex votos that still hang in many Flemish churches. With the ex voto, the believer makes a promise to God – say, to behave better – and then asks for a blessing, like the curing of a bad leg. Sometimes, the ex voto is hung up once the promise is made, but mostly, it's done afterward in gratitude for the cure or blessing. Further on in the museum, Room 8 holds a display of pipes and tobacco. There are all sorts of antique smokers' paraphernalia – tobacco cutters, lighters, tinderboxes and so forth – but it's the pipes that catch the eye, especially the long, thin ones made of clay. Clay pipes were notoriously brittle, so smokers invested in pipe cases, of which several are displayed. Room 12 is an old confectioner's shop, where there are demonstrations of traditional

Exhibition at the Museum voor Volkskunde

sweet-making in the summertime on the first and third Sunday of the month, and the next room holds a mildly diverting assortment of biscuit and chocolate moulds as well as cake decorations (*patacons*). Made of clay, these *patacons* were painted by hand in true folksy style, with the three most popular motifs being animals, military scenes and Bible stories.

Guido Gezellehuis

MAP P.72, POCKET MAP F3.
Rolweg 64 ☎ 050 44 87 43. Garden and house free.

The **Guido Gezellehuis** commemorates the poet-priest Guido Gezelle (1830–99), a leading figure in nineteenth-century Bruges. Gezelle was born in this large brick cottage, which now contains a few personal knick-knacks such as Gezelle's old chair and pipes, plus his death mask, though it's primarily devoted to a biographical account of his life. However, the labelling is in Dutch and you need to be a Gezelle enthusiast to get much out of it. Neither is Gezelle to everyone's

taste. His poetry is pretty average and the fact that he translated Longfellow's *Song of Hiawatha* into Dutch is the sort of detail that bores rather than inspires.

More importantly, Gezelle played a key role in the preservation of many of the city's medieval buildings, believing that the survival of the medieval city symbolised the continuity of the Catholic faith, a mindset similar to that of the city's Flemish nationalists, who resisted change and championed medieval – or at least neo-Gothic – architecture to maintain Flemish 'purity'. Gezelle resisted cultural change, too: secular theatre appalled him, prompting him to write that 'We are smothered by displays of adultery and incest … and the foundations of the family and of marriage are [being] undermined'.

Schuttersgilde St-Sebastiaan

MAP P.72, POCKET MAP E3
Carmersstraat 174 ⓦ sebastiaansgilde.be.
By appointment only – booked at least one week ahead of time. Charge.

The guild house of the **Schuttersgilde St-Sebastiaan** – The Marksmen's (or Archers') Guild of St Sebastian – is a large brick pile with a distinctive tower dating from the middle of the sixteenth century. The city's archers had ceased to be of any military importance by the time of its construction, but the guild had redefined itself as an exclusive social club where the bigwigs of the day could spend their time hobnobbing. Nowadays, it's still in use as a social-cum-sports club, with the archers opting either to shoot at the familiar circular targets or to plonk a replica bird on top of a pole and shoot at it from below – the traditional favourite. The house is hardly riveting, but it possesses an attractive old dining hall, where a bust of Charles II surmounts the fireplace, recalling the days when the exiled king was a guild member (see page 83). Visitors can also drop by the shooting gallery, whose medievalist stained-glass windows date from the 1950s, and peek at the modern clubhouse.

Engels Klooster

MAP P.72, POCKET MAP E3
Carmersstraat 85 Ⓦ the-english-convent.be. Free.

During his stay in Bruges, the exiled king Charles II (see page 83) worshipped more or less regularly here at the **Engels Klooster** (English Convent) on Carmersstraat. Founded in 1629, the convent was long a haven for English Catholic exiles, though this didn't deter the very Protestant Queen Victoria from popping in during her visit to Belgium in 1843. Nowadays, the convent's nuns provide an enthusiastic fifteen-minute guided tour of the lavishly decorated Baroque church, whose finest features are the handsome cupola and the altar, an extraordinarily flashy affair made of 23 different types of marble – a gift of the Nithsdales, English

Schuttersgilde St-Sebastiaan

The Engels Klooster

aristocrats whose loyalty to the Catholic faith got them into no end of trouble.

Museum Onze-Lieve-Vrouw ter Potterie

MAP P.72, POCKET MAP D2
Potterierei 79 ⓦ museabrugge.be. Charge.

The **Museum Onze-Lieve-Vrouw ter Potterie** (Museum of Our Lady of the Pottery) was founded as a hospital in the thirteenth century on the site of an earlier pottery – hence the name. The hospital (though 'hospital' is a tad misleading, as the buildings were originally used as much to accommodate visitors as tend the sick) was remodelled on several occasions and the three brick gables that front the building today span three centuries. The middle gable is the oldest, dating from 1359 and was built as part of the first hospital chapel. The left-hand gable belonged to the main medieval hospital ward and the one on the right marks a second chapel, added in the 1620s. Inside, a visit begins in the former **sick room**, where a selection of medieval religious paintings includes several anonymous triptychs and a small but arresting panel painting of *St Michael triumphing over the Devil* by the Master of the St Ursula Legend.

Moving on, the museum's **chapel** is an L-shaped affair distinguished by a sumptuous marble rood screen, whose two side altars recall the museum's location beside what was once one of the city's busiest quays. The altar on the left is dedicated to St Anthony, the patron saint of ships' joiners, and the one on the right to St Brendan, the patron saint of seamen. There's also a finely expressed thirteenth-century stone statue of the Virgin on the main altar, but pride of place goes to the set of old **tapestries** hung in the chapel from Easter to October. These comprise a superbly naturalistic, brightly coloured cartoon strip depicting eighteen miracles attributed to Our Lady of the Pottery, almost all to do with being saved from the sea or a sudden change of fortune in fishing or trade. Each carries an inscription, but you'll need to be good at Dutch to decipher them.

Charles II in Bruges

Charles II of England, who spent three years in exile in Bruges from 1656 to 1659, was an enthusiastic member of the archers' guild. After the Restoration, he sent them a whopping 3,600 florins for their hospitality. Charles's enforced exile had begun in 1651 after his attempt to seize the English crown – following the Civil War and the execution of his father in 1649 – had ended in defeat by the Parliamentarians at the Battle of Worcester. Initially, Charles high-tailed it to France, but Cromwell persuaded the French to expel him and the exiled king sought sanctuary in Spanish territory. He was allowed to settle in **Bruges**, then part of the Spanish Netherlands, though the Habsburgs were stingy when granting Charles and his retinue an allowance. The royalists were, says a courtier's letter of 1657, 'never in greater want ... for Englishmen cannot live on bread alone'. In addition, Cromwell's spies kept an eagle eye on Charles's activities, filing lurid reports about his conduct. A certain Mr Butler informed Cromwell, 'I think I may truly say that greater abominations were never practised among people than at Charles Stuart's court. Fornication, drunkenness and adultery are considered no sins amongst them'. It must have made Cromwell's hair stand on end. Cromwell died of malaria in 1658 and Charles was informed of this while playing tennis in Bruges. The message was to the point – 'The devil is dead' – and Charles was on the English throne two years later. Neither did Charles's hatred of Cromwell end with the Protector's death: Charles had Cromwell disinterred and posthumously executed.

Museum Onze-Lieve-Vrouw ter Potterie

Belgian beer: top brews

These tasting notes should help you through the (very pleasurable) maze that is **Belgian beer** – this is, after all, a country where many bars have **beer menus**.

Brugse Zot (Blond 6%, Brugse Zot Dubbel 7.5%) Brouwerij De Halve Mann, a small brewery in Bruges's centre (see page 63), produces refreshing ales with a dry, crisp aftertaste. Their Blond is a light and tangy pale ale, whereas the Bruin – Brugse Zot Dubbel – is a classic brown ale with a full body.

Bush Beer (7.5% and 12%) A Walloon speciality. At 12%, it's claimed that the original version is the strongest beer in Belgium. It's more like a barley wine, with a lovely golden colour and an earthy aroma. The 7.5% Bush is a tasty pale ale with a hint of coriander.

Chimay (red top 7%, blue top 9%) Made by Trappist monks in southern Belgium, Chimay beers are among the best in the world. Of their several brews, these two are the most readily available: fruity, strong, deep in the body and somewhat spicy with a hint of nutmeg and thyme.

La Chouffe (8%) Produced in the Ardennes, this distinctive beer is instantly recognizable by the red-hooded gnome *chouffe* that adorns its label. It's a refreshing pale ale with a peachy aftertaste.

Gouden Carolus (8%) Named after – and also allegedly the favourite tipple of – the Habsburg emperor Charles V, Gouden Carolus is a full-bodied dark brown ale with a sour and slightly fruity aftertaste. It is brewed in Mechelen.

Hoegaarden (5%) The role model for all Belgian wheat beers, Hoegaarden, from near Leuven, is light and highly refreshing despite its cloudy appearance. The ideal drink for a hot summer's day, it's brewed from equal parts of wheat and malted barley.

Kriek (Cantillon Kriek Lambic 5%, Belle Vue Kriek 5.2%, Mort Subite Kriek 4.3%) A type of beer made from a base Lambic beer to which are added cherries or cherry juice and perhaps even sugar. Other fruit beers are available, such as Framboise. The better versions (including those mentioned above) are not too sweet and taste fantastic.

Orval (6.2%) One of the world's most distinctive malt beers, Orval is made in the Ardennes at the Abbaye d'Orval. Refreshingly bitter, the beer is a lovely amber colour and makes an excellent aperitif.

Rochefort (Rochefort 6 7.5%, Rochefort 8 9.2%, Rochefort 10 11.3%) Produced at a Trappist monastery in the Ardennes, Rochefort beers are typically dark and sweet and come in three main versions: Rochefort 6, Rochefort 8 and the extremely popular Rochefort 10, which has a deep reddish-brown colour and a delicious fruity palate.

Rodenbach (Rodenbach 5% and Rodenbach Grand Cru 6.5%) The Rodenbach brewery produces a reddish-brown ale in several forms, with the best brews aged in oak containers. Their widely available Rodenbach is a tangy brown ale with a hint of sourness. The much fuller – and sourer – Rodenbach Grand Cru is more difficult to get hold of but delicious.

Westmalle (Westmalle Dubbel 7%, Tripel 9%) The Trappist monks of Westmalle, just north of Antwerp, claim their beers not only cure loss of appetite and insomnia but reduce stress. Whatever the truth, the prescription certainly tastes good. Their most famous beer, Westmalle Tripel, is creamy and aromatic, while the Westmalle Dubbel is dark and supremely malty.

Lambic beers

One of the world's oldest styles of beer manufacture, Brussels' **Lambic** beers are tart brews made with at least thirty percent raw wheat with malted barley. **Wild yeast** is used in their production, a spontaneous fermentation process in which the yeasts – specific to the air of Brussels – gravitate down into open wooden casks over two to three years. Draught Lambic is rare, but bottled varieties are more commonplace. **Cantillon Lambic** is perhaps the most authentic, an excellent drink with a lemony zip. It's the best you'll find (5%). **Gueuze** is a blend of old and new Lambics in a bottle, a little sweeter and fuller bodied than straight Lambic, with an almost cider-like aftertaste. Other good brews include Belle Vue Gueuze (5.2%), Timmermans Gueuze (5.5%) and Lindemans Gueuze (5.2%).

PRO DEO

Bistro Pro Deo

Shops

't Apostelientje
MAP P.72, POCKET MAP E4
Balstraat 11 ⓦ apostelientje.be.
This small and infinitely cosy
shop sells a charming variety of
handmade lace pieces of both
modern and traditional designs. It's
easily the best lace shop in Bruges,
with accommodating and well-
informed staff. The smallest pieces
cost about €20.

Dag en Zonne
MAP P.72, POCKET MAP E5
Langestraat 3 ⓣ 050 33 02 93.
This tiny and cramped Aladdin's
cave is jam-packed with
inexpensive trinkets and baubles.
There are clocks and barometers,
vintage prints, antique tiles, shot
glasses, stained-glass pieces, pottery,
a reasonably good selection of
second-hand jewellery, and all sorts
of once-treasured bygones.

Kingin
MAP P.72, POCKET MAP B4
Ezelstraat 27 ⓦ kingin.be.
Handmade, top-quality jewellery is
on sale here at this chic little shop
on the north side of the city centre.
Gold, silver and precious stones are

to the fore – and the designs range
from the more straightforward
to the ambitious and positively
daring. Predictably, it's expensive.

Café

Blackbird
MAP P.72, POCKET MAP C4
Jan van Eyckplein 7 ⓦ blackbird-
bruges.com.
This bright and welcoming café,
with its inventive modern decor,
throws a wide gastronomic net:
breakfasts feature all manner of
healthy options (€15), and there are
sandwiches (from €14), plus superb
lunch-time salads, heaped high
and very fresh (€20). They also do
creative side-lines in Spanish-style
tapas and even cocktails. €

Restaurants

Franco Belge
MAP P.72, POCKET MAP E5
Langestraat 109
ⓦ restaurantfrancobelge.be.
In a straightforward, three-storey
building on one of the city's
main thoroughfares, this smooth
and chic restaurant focuses on
traditional Franco-Belgian cuisine
with a contemporary twist – hake
with leeks, cockles and *paksoi*, veal
tartare with beetroot or guinea
fowl with asparagus. Alfresco
dining at the back. It's pricey at
night and much more affordable at
lunchtime. Reservations are well-
nigh essential. €€€

Locàle by Kok au Vin
MAP P.72, POCKET MAP B4
Ezelstraat 21 ⓦ locale.be.
A slick, informal and inventive
modern restaurant whose well-
considered and ambitious menu
features tapas-style light bites,
anything from Zeeland razor clams
to organic aubergine and *pizette*.
Dishes from around €15 to 30.
Reservations are recommended. €€

Sans Cravate

MAP P.72, POCKET MAP F4

Langestraat 159 ⓦ sanscravate.be.

This pocket-sized, bistro-style, family-owned restaurant is a popular spot, its enterprising menu emphasising traditional Franco-Flemish cuisine: try, for example, the scallops and sauerkraut or the turbot with parsley potatoes and mushrooms. Local, seasonal ingredients take pride of place. A three-course meal costs in the region of €120. €€€

Bars and clubs

Bistro du Phare

MAP P.72, POCKET MAP E1

Sasplein 2 ⓦ duphare.be.

Off the beaten track, this busy, bustling place offers filling food, a good range of beers and a canal setting. There's also a pleasant summer terrace and evening jazz and blues concerts every month or so; come early to get a seat.

Café Vlissinghe

MAP P.72, POCKET MAP D4

Blekersstraat 2 ⓦ cafevlissinghe.be.

With its wood panelling, antique paintings and long wooden tables, this is one of the oldest and most distinctive bars in Bruges, thought to date from 1515. The atmosphere is relaxed and easy-going, with an emphasis on quiet conversation – there are certainly no jukeboxes here – and the bar snacks are traditional Flemish. There's a pleasant garden terrace, too.

Republiek

MAP P.72, POCKET MAP C5

St-Jakobsstraat 36 ⓦ republiekbrugge.be.

One of the most popular café-bars in town, this large and darkly lit café-bar attracts an arty, mostly youthful clientele. Very reasonably priced snacks and light meals, including vegetarian and pasta dishes. There's a terrace at the back for summertime drinking. It also hosts the occasional gig.

De Windmolen

MAP P.72, POCKET MAP F3

Carmersstraat 135 ⓣ 050 33 97 39.

This amiable, neighbourhood café-bar is a pick for its setting – away from the crowds and next to the grassy bank that marks the course of the old city wall. It offers an average line of inexpensive snacks but has a competent beer menu and a pleasant outside terrace.

De Windmolen

Damme

Now a popular day-trippers' destination, the quaint village of Damme, 7km (4.3 miles) northeast of Bruges, was in medieval times the city's main seaport, but those heady days are long gone. Today, Damme has just one main street, Kerkstraat, a few minutes' walk from end to end, and on either side are what remains of the medieval town, principally the Stadhuis (Town Hall) and the Onze-Lieve-Vrouwekerk (Church of Our Lady). A pretty, poplar-lined canal connects Bruges and Damme, starting at Dampoort on the northeast edge of central Bruges and trimming the edge of Damme before proceeding onto Sluis, a tiny village over the border in The Netherlands. This Bruges-Sluis canal slices its way across a delightful parcel of countryside. It is a rural backwater of green fields and whitewashed farmhouses, all shadowed by long lines of slender poplar trees, quivering and rustling in the prevailing westerly winds. It makes perfect cycling country with many possible routes to explore (see page 92).

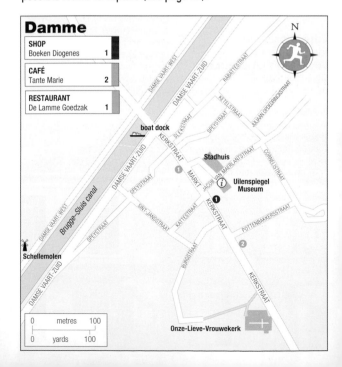

Arrival and information

There are several ways of reaching **Damme from Bruges**, perhaps the most rewarding being the 7km (4.3-mile) cycle ride out along the **Brugge–Sluis canal**, which begins at Dampoort, about 2.5km (1.6km) northeast of the Markt. Cycle rental is available in Bruges (see page 139). If you want to explore the area in depth, you might consider buying a detailed cycling map; the **Fietsnetwerk Brugse Ommeland** (1:50,000), available from any major bookshop in Bruges, is the best choice.

You can also get from Bruges to Damme on a vintage **canal boat**, the *Lamme Goedzak*, with excursions starting about 600m (0.4 miles) east of the Dampoort on the Noorweegse Kaai (April to mid–Nov 4 daily each way; 45min; one-way €11, return €16; tickets can be purchased on board or online; ⓦ lammegoedzakdamme.com). Local **buses Nos 1 and 3** connect Bruges' Markt and the main bus/train station with Sasplein, from where it's a 750m (0.5 mile; 15min) walk to the boat departure point on Noorweegse Kaai, but check at the De Lijn information kiosk, outside the bus/train station, before you set out.

Finally, you can reach Damme on **city bus No. 43** from the bus station, but it is an inferior service that fluctuates with the school terms and holidays – and even if you can get out there, you can't always get back. Again, check at the De Lijn information kiosk. Damme has a **tourist office** across the street from the Stadhuis at Jacob van Maerlantstraat 3 (ⓦ visitdamme.be).

The Stadhuis, Damme

MAP P.88
Markt 1, off Kerkstraat ⓦ visitdamme.be. Free.

Funded by a special tax on barrels of herrings, the fifteenth-century **Stadhuis** is easily the best-looking building in Damme, its elegant, symmetrical facade balanced by the graceful lines of its exterior stairway. In one of the niches, you'll spy Charles the Bold, the last duke of Burgundy, offering a wedding ring to Margaret of York, who stands in the next niche – appropriately enough, as the couple got hitched here in 1468, a prestige event that attracted aristocratic bigwigs from all over western Europe. It was Charles's third marriage – his previous wives had died young – and it greatly irritated the French king: the last thing Louis XI wanted was to cement the alliance between England and his powerful vassal, the duke of

The Stadhuis

The Battle of Sluys

In the summer of 1340, a **French fleet** assembled in the estuary of the **River Zwin** near Damme to prepare for an invasion of England at the start of the Anglo-French **Hundred Years' War**. To combat the threat, however, the English king, Edward III, sailed across the Channel and attacked at dawn. Although they were outnumbered three to one, Edward's fleet won an extraordinary victory, his bowmen causing chaos by showering the French ships with arrows from a safe distance. A foretaste of the Battle of Crécy, there was so little left of the French force that no one dared tell King Philip VI of France until finally, the court jester took matters into his own hands: 'Oh! The English cowards! They had not the courage to jump into the sea as our noble Frenchmen did.' Philip's reply is not recorded.

Burgundy. Indeed, Louis sent a fleet to waylay Margaret on her way to Damme, but it failed to locate her. Margaret arrived at a time when Damme boasted a population of ten thousand and played a key strategic role in guarding the banks of the River Zwin, which gave Bruges direct access to the sea. The subsequent silting up of the river – and the decline of Damme – has been the subject of much historical debate: some have argued that the silting of the river led to Bruges's decline, others that it was the city's inability to pay for the continued dredging of the river that reflected the downturn.

Uilenspiegel Museum

MAP P.88
Jacob van Maerlantstraat 3
Ⓦ visitdamme.be. Charge.

The **Uilenspiegel Museum**, in the same building as tourist information (see page 145), is devoted to the eponymous folkloric figure, who started as an obnoxious fool-cum-prankster in Germany in the early fourteenth century. There has been much speculation as to the meaning of his name. Still, it's usually translated from the original High German as 'owl mirror' – a somewhat confused version of 'arse wiper', as in Uilenspiegel's addiction to all things scatological. Whatever the truth, Uilenspiegel stories spread into Flanders. As they did so, he became more of a scoundrel than a joker until a Belgian author, **Charles de Coster** (1827–79), subverted the legend in his 1867 novel *The Legend of the Glorious Adventures of Tyl Ulenspiegel in the Land of Flanders & Elsewhere*. Coster's Ulenspiegel (alternate spelling) is a seventeenth-century Protestant hero, embodying the Belgian hankering for religious and political freedom. He made

Tijl Ulenspiegel Museum

Damme his home and added
Nele, Ulenspiegel's fiancée, and
Lamme Goedzak, a loyal, lazy and
good-natured friend, as well as
a mother, Soetkin, and a father,
Claes. Ulenspiegel becomes the
sworn enemy of King Philip II of
Spain after the Spanish take Claes
prisoner and burn him at the stake.

Onze-Lieve-Vrouwekerk

MAP P.88

Kerkstraat ☏ 050 28 86 10. Free.

A sturdy brick structure in classic
Gothic style, the **Onze-Lieve-
Vrouwekerk** (Church of Our
Lady) is attached to a ruined
segment of the original nave (open
access) that speaks volumes about
Damme's decline: the church was
built in the thirteenth century,
but when the population shrank
it was just too big and so the
inhabitants abandoned part of
the nave. The remnants are now
stuck between the present church
and its clumpy tower. Climb the

Onze-Lieve-Vrouwekerk

tower for panoramic views over
the surrounding polders. Beside
the tower, the large and enigmatic,
three-headed modern statue, the

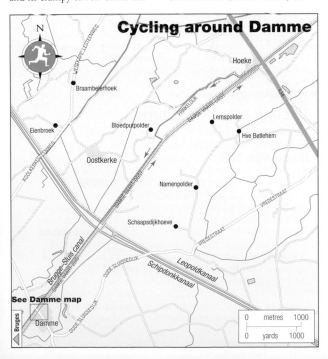

View from the top of Onze-Lieve-Vrouwekerk

Blik van Licht (Look of Light), is the work of the Belgian painter and sculptor **Charles Delporte** (1928–2012), who had strong connections with Damme. A prolific artist, Delporte had his work displayed worldwide – and nigh-on three hundred are exhibited in various locations.

Just beyond the church, on the right-hand side of Kerkstraat, a **footpath** branches off along a narrow canal to loop round the west side of Damme, an enjoyable ten-minute stroll through the poplars which brings you out just west of the village beside the Brugge-Damme-Sluis canal.

Cycling around Damme

Beginning in Bruges at the Dampoort, about 2.5km (1.6 miles) northeast of the Markt, the country lanes on either side of the **Brugge-Sluis canal** cut a handsome, poplar-lined route across the Flemish countryside. After about 7km (4.3 miles), these parallel lanes slip past the northern end of **DAMME**'s main street, Kerkstraat. After that, one especially rewarding cycle route is a 15km (9.3-mile-) long round-trip that begins by pressing on from Damme along the same Brugge–Sluis canal. The route then crosses over the wide and murky-green **Leopoldkanaal** before continuing to the tiny and inordinately pretty hamlet of **HOEKE**. Just over the bridge, turn hard left for the narrow causeway – the **Krinkeldijk** – which meanders back toward Damme, running just north of the Brugge-Sluis canal. Just over 3km (1.9 miles) long, this causeway drifts across a beguiling landscape of bright, whitewashed farmhouses and deep-green grassy fields before reaching an intersection where you turn left to regain the main waterway.

Shop

Boeken Diogenes

MAP P.88
Kerkstraat 22A ☎ 0477 28 25 92.
Damme has a handful of tourist-orientated shops, including several art galleries, and, to justify its claim to be a 'book town', it possesses half a dozen bookshops dotted along the main street and its immediate surroundings. There is also a book market every second Sunday of the month on the main square, Damme Plaats, in the summer and inside the Stadhuis during winter. Amongst the bookshops, *Diogenes* is one of the more diverting, a pocket-sized antiquarian bookshop focusing on literature and art with many English titles.

Café

Tante Marie

MAP P.88
Kerkstraat 38 Ⓦ tantemarie.be.
This pleasant and modern café-bistro and patisserie does an incredibly delicious line in breakfasts and lunches. The latter features salads and pasta, not to mention one of their specialities, shrimp croquettes. There's also a tasty range of vegetarian options and superb pastries – the lemon curd tarts go down a storm. For a full lunch, reckon on around €25. €

Restaurant

De Lamme Goedzak

MAP P.88
Kerkstraat 13 Ⓦ delammegoedzak.be.
In attractively refurbished old premises, this is perhaps the best restaurant in Damme – and certainly one of the most popular. The menu covers most of the traditional Flemish dishes – for example, the roasted slices of lamb with vegetables – and some more inventive dishes, like the lobster ravioli with crab sauce. Most main courses hover around €30, but the lobster will cost you no less than €60. It also sells house ales. There is a garden terrace at the back and a pavement terrace at the front. €€

DAMME

Book market on Damme Plaats

Central Ghent

Ghent may be less immediately picturesque than Bruges, its great and ancient rival. However, it still musters a string of superb Gothic buildings and a bevy of delightful, intimate streetscapes, where antique brick houses are woven around a lattice of narrow canals. The city's star turn is undoubtedly St-Baafskathedraal, home to Jan van Eyck's remarkable *Adoration of the Mystic Lamb*. Still, it's ably supported by other attractions, including exquisite medieval guild houses, enjoyable museums and a brigade of lively bars and first-class restaurants. But perhaps most importantly, Ghent remains a quintessentially Flemish city with a tourist industry – rather than the other way round – and, if you find the tweeness of Bruges overpowering, this is the place to decamp, just twenty minutes away by train.

St-Baafskathedraal

MAP P.96, POCKET MAP D13
St-Baafsplein Ⓦ sintbaafskathedraal.be.
Free, Mystic Lamb charge; timed tickets,
bookable online.

The best place to start an exploration of the city is the mainly Gothic St-Baafskathedraal

(St Bavo's Cathedral), squeezed into the eastern corner of St-Baafsplein and named after a local seventh-century landowner turned Christian missionary. The third church on this site, and 250 years in the making, the cathedral is a tad lop-sided, but there's no

The vaulted roof at St-Baafskathedraal

denying the imposing beauty of the west tower, with its long, elegant windows and perky corner turrets. Some 82m high, the tower was the last major part of the church to be completed, topped off in 1554 – just before the outbreak of the religious wars that were to wrack the country for the next hundred years.

Inside, the mighty fifteenth-century nave is supported by tall, slender columns and these give the whole interior a cheerful sense of lightness, though the Baroque marble screen spoils the effect by darkening the choir. The nave's principal item of interest is the rococo pulpit, a whopping oak and marble affair, where the main timber represents the Tree of Life with an allegorical representation of Time and Truth at its base. There's more easy-to-unravel symbolism above the high altar, where St Baaf (aka St Bavo) is shown ascending to heaven on an untidy heap of clouds.

Nearby, in the north transept, is the entrance to the Adoration of the Mystic Lamb (see page 110), where you start your visit in the dank and capacious crypt, a survivor from the earlier Romanesque church. Here in the crypt, you can don the appropriate gear for a virtual reality show on the altarpiece and/or have a look at the clothed version of the painting's nude Adam and Eve, which an offended Emperor Joseph II had installed in the 1780s. Here also is The Crucifixion of Christ, a superb triptych by Justus van Gent (1410–80), who trained in Flanders but went on to live in Italy. This

The ornate pulpit at St-Baafskathedraal

depicts the crucified Christ flanked, on the left, by Moses purifying the waters of Mara with wood, and to the right by Moses and the bronze serpent, which cured poisoned Israelites on sight. As the Bible has it: "So Moses made a bronze serpent [as the Lord had commanded] and set it on a pole; and if a serpent bit any man, he would look at the bronze serpent and live".

On the floor above the crypt, the Adoration of the Mystic Lamb is displayed in a side-chapel at the back of the cathedral ambulatory.

Stadhuis

MAP P.96, POCKET MAP C13
Botermarkt. Guided tours only, check with the tourist office (see page 145). Charge.

CityCard Ghent

A bargain if you're set on seeing most of the sights, a **CityCard Gent** (🔾 visit.gent.be) covers all of the key attractions, provides free and unlimited use of the city's buses and trams and includes a boat trip and a day's bike rental; it costs €38 for 48hr, €44 for 72hr. It's on sale at any of the participants and from the tourist information office (see page 145).

Central Ghent

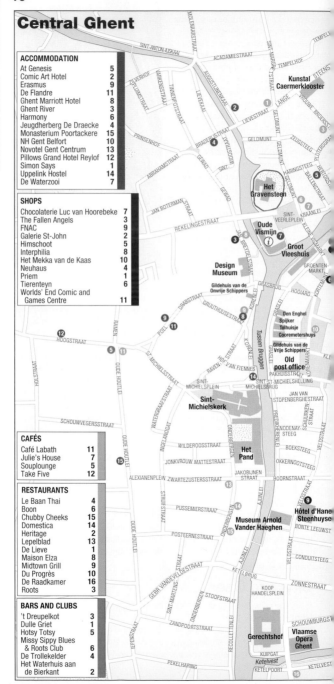

ACCOMMODATION

At Genesis	5
Comic Art Hotel	2
Erasmus	9
De Flandre	11
Ghent Marriott Hotel	8
Ghent River	3
Harmony	6
Jeugdherberg De Draecke	4
Monasterium Poortackere	15
NH Gent Belfort	10
Novotel Gent Centrum	13
Pillows Grand Hotel Reylof	12
Simon Says	1
Uppelink Hostel	14
De Waterzooi	7

SHOPS

Chocolaterie Luc van Hoorebeke	7
The Fallen Angels	3
FNAC	9
Galerie St-John	2
Himschoot	5
Interphilia	8
Het Mekka van de Kaas	10
Neuhaus	4
Priem	1
Tierenteyn	6
Worlds' End Comic and Games Centre	11

CAFÉS

Café Labath	11
Julie's House	7
Souplounge	5
Take Five	12

RESTAURANTS

Le Baan Thai	4
Boon	6
Chubby Cheeks	15
Domestica	14
Heritage	2
Lepelblad	13
De Lieve	1
Maison Elza	8
Midtown Grill	9
Du Progrès	10
De Raadkamer	16
Roots	3

BARS AND CLUBS

't Dreupelkot	3
Dulle Griet	1
Hotsy Totsy	5
Missy Sippy Blues & Roots Club	6
De Trollekelder	4
Het Waterhuis aan de Bierkant	2

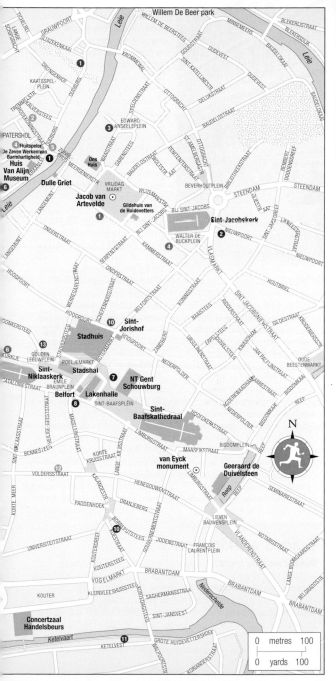

Willem De Beer park

Leie

GRAUWPOORT
SLUIZEKENKAAI
SLEEPSTRAAT
DUDDIGE
DROGENHOF
KAATSSPEL-PLEIN
KROMMEWAL
WILLEM DE BEERSTEEG
MINNEMEERS
BLEKERIJSTRAAT
BLEKERSDIJK
GOUDSTRAAT
OUDEVEST
OUDEVEST
BAUDELOKAAI

Leie

BAUDELOKAAI

TICHELREI
LANGE SCHIPGRACHT
TROMMELSTR
KALVERSTEEG
NIEUWBROEKSTEEG
PATERSHOL
SPELDESTRAAT
EDWARD ANSEELEPLEIN
OTTOGRACHT
GELUKSTRAAT
SINT-KATELIJNESTR
BAUDELOSTRAAT
OTTOGRACHT
PENITENTENSTRAAT
ST-AMELBERGASTR

BAUDELOSTRAAT
MOLENAAT
HEMBERT DODDENSDREEF
STEENDAM
STEENDAM

1
2
Fluitspeler
3
De Zeven Werken van Barmhartigheid 1
Huis Van Alijn Museum 6
Ons Huis
Dulle Griet
ZWIJNAARDE
KRAANLEI
GROOT
MEERSENIERSTR
VRIJDAG MARKT
GARENSTEEG
WIJZEMANSTRAAT
BEVERHOUTPLEIN
BIBLIOTHEEKSTRAAT
QUEISTE-AAI
LIKNOESTRAAT

Leie
LANGEMUNT
LANGEMUNT
LANGEMUNT

Jacob van Artevelde ⊙
1
Gildehuis van de Huidevetters
BIJ SINT-JACOBS
Sint-Jacobskerk 2
NIEUWPOORT
SINT-JACOBSSTR
NIEUWPOORT
NIEUWPOORT

ONDERSTRAAT
HOOGPOORT
SERPENTSTRAAT
ONDERSTRAAT
BIJ SINT-JACOBS
WALTER DE BUCKPLEIN
KAMMERSTRAAT
VLASMARKT
KONINGSTRAAT
HOUTBRIEL
4

HOOGPOORT
WEBEREGHEMSTRAAT
SCHEPENHUISSTRAAT
BELFORTSTRAAT
BAANSTEEG
SINT-JACOBSNIEUWSTRAAT
GILDESTRAAT
VLAENDERENSTR
DONKERSTEEG
HOOGPOORT
STADHUISSTEEG
BOTERMARKT
Sint-Jorishof 10
Stadhuis
ZANDBERG
RIDDERSTRAAT
EPPELSTEEG
BIJDONKELSTEEG
URSULINENSTRAAT
KWAATHAM
JAN PALFIJNSTRAAT
KWAATHAM
BARRESTRAAT
OUDE BEESTENMARKT

8
TURKIJE
GOUDEN LEEUWPLEIN 13
CATALONIËSTRAAT
Sint-Niklaaskerk
POELJEMARKT
EMILE BRAUNPLEIN
Stadshal
Belfort 8
Lakenhalle
SINT-BAAFSPLEIN
NT Gent Schouwburg 7
NEDERPOLDER
NEDERPOLDER
NEDERWAADHAM
BISDOMKAAI
BISDOMKAAI
REEP
REEP

SINT-NIKLAASSTRAAT
HEILIGE GEESTSTRAAT
Sint-Baafskathedraal
HOOFDKERKSTRAAT
MAGELEINSTRAAT
BENNESTEEG
KORTE KRUISSTRAAT
LANGE KRUISSTRAAT
LIMBURGSTRAAT
BISDOMPLEIN
REEP

N

VOLDERSSTRAAT 12
KALANDESTR
van Eyck monument ⊙
Geeraard de Duivelsteen
REEP
SEMINARIESTRAAT

KORTE MEER
PADDENHOEK
ORANJEBERG
HENEGOUWENSTRAAT
LIMBURGSTRAAT
LIEVEN BAUWENSPLEIN

UNIVERSITEITSTRAAT
KOUTERDREEF
NEDERSTRAAT
BORLUUTSTEEG
GOUVERNEMENTSTRAAT
JODENSTRAAT
FRANÇOIS LAURENTPLEIN
VLAENDERENSTRAAT
NOTARISSTRAAT
10

KOUTERSTEEG
BRABANTDAM
LANGE BOOMGAARDSTRAAT
BELGRADOSTR
BRABANTDAM
BRABANTDAM

KOUTER
VOGELMARKT
KLEINVLEESHUISSTEEG
KORTE DAGSTEEG
SAGHERMANSSTRAAT
SINT-JANSVEST
Nederschelde

Concertzaal Handelsbeurs
Ketelvaart
KETELVEST
11
GROTE HUIDEVETTERSHOEK
WALPOORTSTR
KORIANDERSTRAAT

0	metres	100
0	yards	100

Stadhuis

Stretching along the Botermarkt is the striking **Stadhuis** (City Hall), whose discordant facade comprises two distinct sections. The later section, framing the central stairway, dates from the 1580s and offers a fine example of Italian Renaissance architecture, its crisp symmetries faced by many black-painted pilasters. In stark contrast are the wild, curling patterns of the section to the immediate north, carved in Flamboyant Gothic style at the beginning of the sixteenth century to a design by the celebrated architect **Rombout Keldermans** (1460–1531). The whole of the Stadhuis was to have been built by Keldermans, but the money ran out and the city couldn't afford to finish it off until much later – hence today's mixture of styles. Look carefully at Keldermans' work and you'll spot all sorts of charming details, especially in the elaborate tracery, decorated with oak leaves and acorns as well as vines laden with grapes, though the statuettes in the niches, representing important historical personages in characteristic poses, were only added in the nineteenth century.

Guided tours of the Stadhuis amble round a series of halls and chambers, the most interesting being the old Court of Justice or **Pacificatiezaal** (Pacification Hall), where the Pacification of Ghent was signed in 1576. A plaque commemorates this treaty, which momentarily bound the rebel armies of the Low Countries (today's Belgium and The Netherlands) together against their rulers, the Spanish Habsburgs. The carrot offered by the dominant Protestants was the promise of religious freedom, but they failed to deliver and much of the south (present-day Belgium) soon returned to the Spanish fold. The hall's charcoal-and-cream **tiled floor** is designed as a maze. No one's quite sure why, but it's thought that more privileged felons (or sinners) had to struggle round the maze on their knees as a substitute punishment for a

Guided walking tours

Guided walking tours are popular in Ghent. The standard walking tour is a two-hour jaunt around the city centre, including a visit to the Stadhuis or the cathedral. You can hire a guide yourself, though this is expensive, or join a group, in which case you can expect to pay €15 per person. Tickets are on sale at the tourist information office (see page 145) and booking – at least a few hours ahead – is strongly recommended. Among several, the best operator of these walking tours is GhentCityGuide (ⓦ ghentcityguide.be).

pilgrimage to Jerusalem – a good deal if ever there was one.

Lakenhalle

MAP P.96, POCKET MAP C13

Botermarkt. No public access except to the attached Belfort (see page 99).

The conspicuous **Lakenhalle** is a hunk of a building with an unhappy history. Work began on the hall in the early fifteenth century, but the cloth trade collapsed before it was finished and was only grudgingly completed in 1903. Since then, no one has ever quite worked out what to do with it and today, the building is little more than an empty shell. However, the basement once held the municipal prison, whose entrance was on the west side of the building through the **Mammelokker** (The Suckling), a grandiose Louis XIV-style portal of 1741. Part gateway and part warder's lodging, the Mammelokker displays a sculpture illustrating the classical legend of Cimon, whom the Romans condemned to death by starvation; his daughter, Pero, saved the day by suckling him – hence the name.

Belfort

MAP P.96, POCKET MAP C13

St-Baafsplein ☎ 09 266 70 70. Charge.

The first-floor entrance on the south side of the Lakenhalle is the only way to reach the **Belfort** (Belfry), a much-amended medieval edifice whose soaring spire is topped by a corpulent gilded copper dragon. Once a watchtower and storehouse, the interior is now largely empty except for a few old bells and incidental statues alongside the rusting remains of a brace of antique dragons, which formerly perched on top of the spire. The belfry is equipped with a **glass-sided lift** that climbs up to the roof, where consolation is provided in the form of excellent views over the city centre.

St-Niklaaskerk

MAP P.96, POCKET MAP C13

Cataloniestraat ☎ 09 234 28 69. Free.

An architectural hybrid dating from the thirteenth century, **St-Niklaaskerk** is a handsome affair, its arching buttresses and pencil-thin turrets elegantly attenuating the lines of the nave, in a classic example of the early Scheldt Gothic. Many of the Baroque

The Belfort at the Lakenhalle

Boat trips

Boat trips explore Ghent's inner waterways, departing from the Korenlei quay, just near the Korenmarkt, and from the Vleeshuisbrug, beside the Kraanlei (April–Oct daily 10am–6pm). Trips last about forty minutes and leave every fifteen minutes or so. Queues are common at the height of the season, especially on the weekend. There is also a useful **Hop-on/Hop-off boat** running between the Gravensteen, the Korenlei, STAM and St-Pietersabdij and the cathedral (April–Oct 5 daily; Whoponhopoff.be/en).

furnishings and fittings have been removed and the windows un-bricked, thus returning the church to its early – and lighter – appearance. The highlight is the giant-sized Baroque **high altar** with its mammoth God the Father glowering down its back, blowing the hot wind of the Last Judgement from his mouth and surrounded by a flock of cherubs.

Korenmarkt

MAP P.96, POCKET MAP C13

St-Niklaaskerk marks the southern end of the **Korenmarkt** (Corn Market), the traditional focus of the city, comprising a long and wide cobbled area where the

St-Niklaaskerk

grain that once kept the city fed was traded after it was unloaded from the boats that anchored on the Graslei dock nearby (see page 102). The one noteworthy building is the former **post office**, now a shopping mall, whose combination of Gothic Revival and neo-Renaissance styles illustrates the eclecticism popular in Belgium at the beginning of the twentieth century – the building was completed in 1909. The carved heads encircling the building represent the great and the good of the time, including – curiously enough – Florence Nightingale.

St-Michielsbrug

MAP P.96, POCKET MAP B13

Behind the old post office, **St-Michielsbrug** (St Michael's Bridge) offers fine views of the towers and turrets that pierce the Ghent skyline. This is no accident: the bridge was built in 1913 to provide visitors to the Great Exhibition with a vantage point from which to admire the city centre. The bridge also overlooks the city's oldest harbour, the **Tussen Bruggen** (Between the Bridges), from whose quays boats leave for trips around the canals (see box, page 100).

St-Michielskerk

MAP P.96, POCKET MAP B13

St-Michielsplein ⓦ visit.gent.be. Free. Beside St-Michielsbrug rises the bulky mass of **St-Michielskerk**, a heavy-duty Gothic structure begun in the 1440s. The city's

St-Michielsbrug

Protestants seem to have taken a particularly strong disliking to the place, ransacking it twice – once in 1566 and again in 1579 – and the repairs were never quite finished, as witnessed by the clumsily truncated tower. The interior is a handsome affair, the broad sweep of the five-aisled nave punctuated by tall and slender columns that shoot up to the arching vaults of the roof. Most of the furnishings and fittings are Gothic Revival. Still, they are enlivened by a scattering of sixteenth- and seventeenth-century paintings, the pick of which is an impassioned *Crucifixion* by **Anthony van Dyck** (1599–1641) displayed in the north transept. Trained in Antwerp, where he worked in Rubens' workshop, van Dyck made extended visits to England and Italy in the 1620s before returning to Antwerp in 1628. He stayed there for four years – during which time he painted this *Crucifixion* – before migrating to England to become a portrait painter for Charles I and his court, dying in London just before the outbreak of the English Civil War.

Markets

Ghent does a good line in open-air **markets**. There's a large and popular flea market (**prondelmarkt**) on Bij St Jacobs and adjoining Beverhoutplein (Fri, Sat & Sun 8am–1pm), where you can pick up any and everything from a pair of old cords to a well-worn statuette of a saint; an extensive Saturday and Sunday morning flower market on the Kouter, on the south side of the centre, just off Veldstraat (7am–4pm); organic foodstuffs on the Groentenmarkt (Fri 7.30am–1pm); a weekly second-hand book market on the Ajuinlei (Sun 8am–1pm); a weekend craft and bygones market on the Groentenmarkt (Sat & Sun 7.30am–1pm); and a bird and small pets market (not perhaps for the squeamish) on the Oude Beestenmarkt on Sundays (7am–1pm).

The doorway to one of the guild houses of the Graslei

Graslei

MAP P.96, POCKET MAP B13

Ghent's boatmen and grain weighers were crucial to the functioning of the medieval city, and they built a row of splendid **guild houses** along the **Graslei**, each gable decorated with an appropriate sign or symbol. Working your way north from St-Michielsbrug, the first building of distinction is the **Gildehuis van de Vrije Schippers** (Guild House of the Free Boatmen), at No. 14, where the badly weathered sandstone is decorated with scenes of boatmen weighing anchor, plus a delicate carving of a caravel – the type of Mediterranean sailing ship used by Columbus – located above the door. Medieval Ghent had **two boatmen guilds** – the Free, who could discharge their cargoes within the city, and the Unfree, who were obliged to unload their goods into the vessels of the **Free Boatmen** at the edge of the city in an arrangement typical of the complex regulations governing the guilds.

Next door, at Nos 12–13, the seventeenth-century **Cooremetershuys** (Corn Measurers' House) was where city officials weighed and graded corn behind a facade graced by cartouches and garlands of fruit. Next to this, at No. 11, stands the quaint **Tolhuisje**, another delightful example of Flemish Renaissance architecture, built to house the customs officers in 1698, while the adjacent limestone **Spijker** (Staple House), at No. 10, boasts a surly Romanesque facade dating from around 1200. Here, the city stored its grain supply for over five hundred years until a fire gutted the interior. Finally, two doors down at No. 8, the splendid **Den Enghel** is named after the banner-bearing angel that decorates the facade; the building was originally the stonemasons' guild house, as evidenced by the effigies of the four Roman martyrs who were the guild's patron saints, though they are depicted in medieval attire rather than togas and sandals.

Groentenmarkt

MAP P.96, POCKET MAP C12

Just north of Graslei is the **Groentenmarkt** (Vegetable

Market), where a jangle of old buildings includes one especially distinctive shop, Tierenteyn, the mustard specialist (see page 113). The west side of the square is flanked by a long line of stone gables which once enclosed the **Groot Vleeshuis** (Great Butchers' Hall), a covered market where meat was sold under the careful control of the city council – the private sale of meat was forbidden in medieval Ghent. The gables date from the fifteenth century and could do with a brush-up and the interior, with its intricate wooden roof, now holds a delicatessen.

Korenlei
MAP P.96, POCKET MAP B13

Across the Grasbrug (Grass Bridge) from the Graslei lies the **Korenlei**, which trips along the western side of the old city harbour. Unlike the Graslei opposite, none of the medieval buildings have survived here and instead, there's a series of expansive, high-gabled Neoclassical merchants' houses, mostly dating from the eighteenth century. It's the general ensemble that appeals rather than any particular building. Still, the **Gildehuis van de Onvrije Schippers** (Guild House of the Unfree Boatmen), at No. 7, does boast a fetching eighteenth-century facade decorated with whimsical dolphins and bewigged lions, all bulging eyes and rows of teeth.

Design Museum
MAP P.96, POCKET MAP B12
Jan Breydelstraat 5 ⓦ designmuseumgent. be. Closed for refurbishment until 2026.
Currently closed for a significant overhaul, the **Design Museum** has long focused on Belgian decorative and applied arts, with its wide-ranging collection traditionally divided into two distinct sections. At the front, squeezed into what was once an eighteenth-century patrician's mansion, there has always been an attractive sequence of **period rooms**, mostly

illustrating the Baroque and the Rococo. The original dining room is lovely, from its fancy painted ceiling, ornate chandelier and Chinese porcelain to its intricately carved elm panelling. The second section, at the back of the mansion, formerly comprised a **modern display** area used for temporary exhibitions and to showcase the museum's collection of applied arts, dating from 1880 onwards. This area will be expanded and refreshed during the refurbishment – and undoubtedly, due prominence will be given to the museum's outstanding collection of Art Nouveau material, especially the finely crafted furnishings of **Henry van der Velde** (1863–1957).

St-Veerleplein
MAP P.96, POCKET MAP B12
Public punishments ordered by the counts and countesses of Flanders were carried out in front of the castle on **St-Veerleplein**, now an attractive cobbled square with an ersatz punishment post plonked here in 1913; it is topped off by a lion carrying the banner

Merchants' houses on the Korenlei

of Flanders. In case the citizenry became indifferent to beheading, it was here also that currency counterfeiters were thrown into boiling oil or water.

Oude Vismijn

MAP P.96, POCKET MAP B12
St-Veerleplein.

Standing proud at the back of St-Veerleplein, beside the junction of the city's two main canals, is the Baroque facade of the **Oude Vismijn** (Old Fish Market), which features Neptune on a chariot drawn by sea horses. To either side are allegorical figures representing the River Leie (Venus) and the River Scheldt (Hercules), the two rivers that spawned the city. After years of neglect, the Oude Vismijn has been redeveloped and is now home to the tourist office (see page 145).

Het Gravensteen

MAP P.96, POCKET MAP B12
St-Veerleplein ℹ 09 225 93 06. Charge.

The cold, forbidding walls and unyielding turrets of **Het Gravensteen**, the castle of the counts of Flanders, look sinister

enough to have been lifted from a Bosch painting. They were first raised in 1180 as much to intimidate the town's unruly citizens as to protect them, and, considering the castle has been used for all sorts of purposes since then (even a cotton mill), it has survived in remarkably good nick. The imposing **gateway** comprises a deep-arched, heavily fortified tunnel leading to a large **courtyard** framed by protective battlements with ancient arrow slits and apertures for boiling oil and water. Overlooking the courtyard are the castle's two main buildings: the **count's residence** on the left and the **keep** on the right, the latter riddled with narrow, interconnected staircases set within the thickness of the walls. A **self-guided tour** takes you through this labyrinth, the first highlight being a room full of medieval military hardware, from suits of armour, pikes, swords, daggers and early pistols to a pair of exquisitely crafted sixteenth-century crossbows. Beyond is a gruesome collection of instruments of torture, a particularly dank underground dungeon (or oubliette), and the

Het Gravensteen

counts' vaulted session room (or council chamber). It's also possible to walk along most of the castle's encircling wall, from where there are pleasing views over the city centre.

Kraanlei

MAP P.96, POCKET MAP C12

The **Kraanlei** cuts an attractive course along the canalised River Leie, passing the Huis van Alijn Museum (see page 106) before encountering two magnificent facades. First up, at No. 79, is **De Zeven Werken van Barmhartigheid** (The Seven Works of Mercy), which takes its name from the miniature panels that decorate its front. The panels on the top level, from left to right, illustrate the mercies of visiting the sick, ministering to prisoners and burying the dead, while those below (again from left to right) show feeding the hungry, providing water for the thirsty and clothing the naked. The seventh good work – giving shelter to the stranger – was provided inside the building, which was once an inn, so, perhaps rather too subtly, there's no decorative panel. The adjacent **Fluitspeler** (The Flautist), the corner house at No. 81, dates from 1669. The six rather weathered bas-relief terracotta panels on this facade sport allegorical representations of the five senses plus a flying deer; above, on the cornice, are the figures of Faith, Hope and Charity.

Patershol

MAP P.96, POCKET MAP C12

Behind Kraanlei are the lanes and alleys of the **Patershol**, a tight web of brick-terraced houses dating from the seventeenth century. Once the heart of the Flemish working-class city, the Patershol hit the skids in the 1890s when the industry moved to the outskirts of town, leaving a district known for its drinking dens and down-at-heel lodgings. By the 1970s,

The Fluitspeler on the Kraanlei

the Patershol had become a slum threatened with demolition, but after much debate, the area was saved from the developers and a restoration process began, resulting in today's modernised terrace houses and apartments. The process is still underway and the Patershol fringes remain a ragbag of decay and restoration. However, it's still one of Ghent's most diverting districts with one specific sight: the Kunsthal Caermersklooster.

Kunsthal Caermersklooster

MAP P.96, POCKET MAP C11

Lange Steenstraat 14 ⓦ kunsthal.gent. Entrance fee varies with the exhibition, but it is often free.

The capacious former Carmelite Monastery on the edge of the Patershol has been turned into the **Kunsthal Caermersklooster**, which offers an ambitious programme of temporary exhibitions. There is space for two or three shows at any one time. They mix things up with contemporary art, photography, design and fashion displayed alongside more socially engaged exhibitions – with one recent

Exhibition at Huis van Alijn Museum

exhibitions – with one recent highlight being an immaculately researched feature on 'Poverty in Belgium'.

Huis van Alijn Museum

MAP P.96, POCKET MAP C12
Kraanlei 65 W huisvanalijn.be. **Charge.**
The Huis van Alijn folklore museum occupies a series of pretty little almshouses set around a central courtyard. Dating from the fourteenth century, the almshouses were built following a major scandal reminiscent of Romeo and Juliet. In 1354, two members of the Rijms family murdered three of the rival Alijns when they were at Mass in St-Baafskathedraal. The immediate cause of the affray was jealousy – one man from each clan was after the same woman – but the dispute went deeper, reflecting the commercial animosity of two guilds, the weavers and the fullers. The murderers fled for their lives and were condemned to death in absentia, but were eventually – eight years later – pardoned on condition that they paid for the construction of a set of almshouses, which was to be named after the

victims. The result was the Huis van Alijn, which became a hospice for elderly women and then a workers' tenement until the city council snapped it up in the 1940s.

The museum consists of two sets of rooms, either side of the courtyard, depicting local life and work in the nineteenth and twentieth centuries. One set is devoted to temporary exhibitions, some of which are very good indeed, the other houses the permanent collection, where the most interesting rooms are thematic, illustrating particular aspects of traditional Flemish society – marriage, school, mourning, birth, growing up, misfortune and so forth. Each display features a scattering of artefacts, a short illustrative film gleaned from the archives and an explicatory text. Clearly, a lot of thought has gone into these displays and they really are fascinating. On this side also, one of the rooms has a bank of miniature TV screens showing short, locally-made amateur films in a continuous cycle. Some of these date back to the 1920s, but most are post-war including a snippet featuring a local 1970s soccer team in terrifyingly tight shorts.

Overlooking the central courtyard is the chapel, a pleasantly gaudy affair built in the 1540s and now decorated with folksy shrines and votive offerings. When they aren't out on loan, the chapel is also home to a pair of "goliaths", large and fancily dressed wooden figures that are a common feature of Belgian street processions and festivals.

Dulle Griet

MAP P.96, POCKET MAP C12

From the Kraanlei, an antiquated little bridge leads over to **Dulle Griet** (Mad Meg), a lugubrious fifteenth-century **cannon** whose failure to fire provoked a bitter row between Ghent and the nearby Flemish town of Oudenaarde, where it was cast. In the 1570s, fearful of a Habsburg attack, Ghent purchased the **cannon** from Oudenaarde. It seemed a good buy as it was the region's most powerful siege gun, able to propel a 340kg (749.6lb) cannonball several hundred metres. Still, when Ghent's gunners tried it out, the barrel cracked on first firing and,

much to the chagrin of Ghent's city council, Oudenaarde refused to offer a refund. The useless lump was then rolled to the edge of the Vrijdagmarkt, where it has stayed ever since.

Vrijdagmarkt

MAP P.96, POCKET MAP C12

A wide and open square, the **Vrijdagmarkt** was long the political centre of Ghent, the site of both public meetings and executions – sometimes at the same time. In the middle of the square stands a nineteenth-century statue of the guild leader **Jacob van Artevelde** (see page 108), portrayed addressing the people in a heroic style. Of the buildings flanking the Vrijdagmarkt, the most appealing is the former **Gildehuis van de Huidevetters** (Tanners' Guild House), at No. 37, a tall, Gothic structure whose stepped gables culminate in a dainty and distinctive corner turret – the Toreken.

Also worth a second glance is the old headquarters of the trade unions, the **Ons Huis** (Our House), a sterling edifice built in eclectic style at the turn of the twentieth century.

Dulle Griet

Jacob van Artevelde comes to a sticky end

One of the most powerful of Ghent's medieval leaders, **Jacob van Artevelde** (1290–1345), was elected captain of all the guilds in 1337. Initially, he steered a delicate course during the interminable wars between France and England, keeping the city neutral – and the textile industry going – despite the machinations of both warring countries. Ultimately, he was forced to take sides, plumping for England. This proved his undoing: in a burst of Anglomania, Artevelde rashly suggested that a son of Edward III of England become the new count of Flanders. This unpopular notion prompted a mob to storm his house and hack him to death.

Bij St-Jacobs

MAP P.96, POCKET MAP D12
St-Jacobskerk Bij St-Jacobs
Ⓦ visit.gent.be. Free.

Adjoining the Vrijdagmarkt is **Bij St-Jacobs**, a sprawling and irregularly shaped square whose centrepiece is the whopping **St-Jacobskerk**. This glum-looking edifice partly dates from the twelfth century, its proudest features being its twin west towers and central spire. Inside, the heavily vaulted nave is awash with Baroque decorations from the gaudy pulpit to the kitsch high altar. The square hosts the city's biggest and best **flea market** (*prondelmarkt*; Fri–Sun 8am–1pm).

St-Jorishof

MAP P.96, POCKET MAP C13
Corner Botermarkt and Hoogpoort.

Facing the Stadhuis, **St-Jorishof** is one of the city's oldest buildings, its heavy-duty stonework dating from the fifteenth century. This was once the home of the Crossbowmen's Guild, and although the crossbow was a dead military duck by the time it was built, the guild was still a powerful political force – and long remained so. It was here, in 1477, that Mary of Burgundy (see page 55) was pressured into signing the Great Privilege confirming the city's commercial freedoms. Beyond St Jorishof, lining up along **Hoogpoort**, are some of the oldest facades in Ghent, sturdy if sometimes sooty Gothic structures also dating from the fifteenth century.

Geeraard de Duivelsteen

MAP P.96, POCKET MAP D14
Reep. No admission.

The forbidding **Geeraard de Duivelsteen** is a fortified palace of splendid Romanesque design built of grey limestone in the thirteenth century. The stronghold takes its name from Geeraard Vilain, who earned the soubriquet 'Duivel' (Devil) for his acts of cruelty. Medieval Ghent was dotted with fortified houses (*stenen*) like this one, reflecting the fear the privileged few had of the rebellious guildsmen. The last noble moved out of the Duivelsteen in about 1350 and since then, the building has been put to a bewildering range of uses, but today it stands empty.

Lieven Bauwensplein

MAP P.96, POCKET MAP D14

Across from the Duivelsteen is **Lieven Bauwensplein**, a square that takes its name from – and has a statue of – the local entrepreneur who founded the city's machine-manufactured textile industry. Born in 1769, Bauwens was an intrepid soul who posed as an ordinary textile worker in England to learn how its (more technologically advanced) machinery worked. In the 1790s, he smuggled a spinning jenny to the continent and soon opened cotton mills in Ghent. It didn't, do him much good: his factories went bust and he died in poverty.

Van Eyck monument

MAP P.96, POCKET MAP D14
Limburgstraat.

In the shadow of the Cathedral, the **Van Eyck monument** celebrates the Eyck brothers, Hubert and Jan, the painter(s) of the *Adoration of the Mystic Lamb* (see page 110). The monument is a stodgy affair, knocked up for the Great Exhibition of 1913 but it's an interesting piece of art propaganda, proclaiming Hubert as co-painter of the altarpiece.

Veldstraat

MAP P.96, POCKET MAP C13–B14
Museum Arnold Vander Haeghen,
Veldstraat 82 ☎ 09 269 84 60. Charge.
Hôtel d'Hane-Steenhuyse, Veldstraat 55
☎ 09 266 85 00. Charge.

The city's main shopping street, Veldstraat, leads south from the Korenmarkt, running parallel to the River Leie. It's a fairly ordinary strip, but the eighteenth-century mansion at no.82 holds the mildly diverting Museum Arnold Vander Haeghen, where pride of place goes to the Chinese salon, whose original silk wallpaper has survived intact. The Duke of Wellington stayed here in 1815 after the Battle of Waterloo, popping across the street to the Hôtel d'Hane-Steenhuyse, at no.55, to bolster the morale of the refugee King of France, Louis XVIII, who had hot-footed it to Ghent soon after Napoleon landed in France following his escape from Elba. While others did his fighting for him, Louis waited around gorging himself. Thanks to Wellington's ministrations, Louis was persuaded to return to France and his entourage left for Paris on June 26, 1815, one week after Waterloo. The grand facade of Louis's hideaway, dating to 1768, has survived in good condition Nearby rise a pair of Neoclassical buildings. On the right is the Gerechtshof (Law Courts). Opposite stands Opera Ghent – home to De Vlaamse Opera.

Geeraard de Duivelsteen

The Adoration of the Mystic Lamb

Ghent cathedral's greatest treasure is a winged altarpiece known as **The Adoration of the Mystic Lamb** (De Aanbidding van het Lam Gods), a seminal work of the early 1430s, though of dubious provenance. Since the discovery of a Latin verse on its frame in the nineteenth century, academics have been arguing about who actually painted it. The inscription reads that Hubert van Eyck "than whom none was greater" began, and Jan van Eyck, "second in art", completed the work, but as nothing else is known of Hubert, some art historians doubt his existence. They argue that Jan, who lived and worked in several cities, including Ghent, was responsible for the painting and that only later, after Jan had firmly rooted himself in the rival city of Bruges, did the citizens of Ghent invent "Hubert" to counter his fame. No one knows for sure, but what is certain is that the artist was able to capture a needle-sharp, luminous realism that must have stunned his contemporaries and remains a marvel today. What's more, the altarpiece is looking better than it has for centuries after a long restoration. This has returned the altarpiece to its former splendour and revealed one surprise: the Lamb of God at the centre of the painting was shown to have a humanoid face – the more sheep-like version was an over-paint.

The cover screens

At the back of the altarpiece, the **cover screens** hold a beautiful Annunciation scene with the archangel Gabriel's wings reaching up to the timbered ceiling of a Flemish house. The shadows of the angel dapple the room, emphasising the reality of the apparition – a technique repeated on the opposite cover panel around the figure of Mary. Below, the donor, Joos Vydt – one-time city mayor – and his wife, Isabella Borlout, kneel piously alongside statues of the saints.

The upper level

By design, the restrained exterior was but a foretaste of what lay within – a striking, visionary work of art whose brilliant colours and precise draughtsmanship still takes the breath away. On the **upper level** sit God the Father (some say Christ Triumphant), the Virgin

and John the Baptist in gleaming clarity; to the right are musician-angels and a nude, pregnant Eve; and on the left is Adam plus a group of singing angels, who strain to read their music.

The lower central panel

In the **lower central panel**, the Lamb, the symbol of Christ's sacrifice, is depicted in a heavenly paradise. The Lamb stands on an altar whose rim is minutely inscribed with a quotation from the Gospel of St John, 'Behold the Lamb of God, which taketh away the sins of the world' – hence the wound in the lamb from which blood issues into a gold cup. Four groups of religious figures converge on the Lamb from the corners of the central panel.

The side panels

On the **side panels**, approaching the Lamb across symbolically rough and stony ground, are more saintly figures. On the right are two groups: St Anthony with his hermits and St Christopher, shown here as a giant with a band of pilgrims. On the left side panel come the horsemen, the inner group symbolising the Warriors of Christ

including St George bearing a shield with a red cross – and the outer the **Just Judges**, a replica panel.

Scares and alarms

The **Just Judges panel** was added during the 1950s to replace the original, which was stolen in 1934. The lost panel features in Albert Camus's novel *The Fall*, whose protagonist keeps it in a cupboard, declining to return it. There has been endless speculation as to who stole it and why. Some argue that it was the Nazis, but suspicion ultimately rested on Arsène Goedertier, a local stockbroker and conservative politician, who made a deathbed confession.

The theft was just one of many dramatic events to befall the painting – indeed, it's remarkable that it survived. The Calvinists tried to destroy it; Philip II of Spain tried to acquire it; the Emperor Joseph II disapproved of it so violently that he replaced the nude Adam and Eve with a clothed version of 1784 (now in the crypt); and, near the end of World War II, the Germans hid it in an Austrian salt mine, where it remained until American soldiers rescued it in 1945.

Galerie St-John

Shops

Chocolaterie Luc van Hoorebeke

MAP P.96, POCKET MAP C13
St–Baafsplein 15
Ⓦ chocolatesvanhoorebeke.be.

Right in the city's centre, in a handsome twentieth-century building across from the Lakenhalle, is the *Chocolaterie Luc van Hoorebeke*. This excellent, family-owned chocolate shop was established in 1982. It offers prime chocolates varying in size and shape, not to mention chocolate spread and chocolate/orange slices – and everything is delectably tasty. A 250g box will cost you €18.

The Fallen Angels

MAP P.96, POCKET MAP B12
Jan Breydelstraat 29–31 Ⓦ the-fallen-angels.com.

Mother and daughter run these two adjacent shops, selling all manner of antique bric-a-brac, from postcards, posters and religious images to teddy bears and toys. Intriguing at best, twee at worst, but a distinctive source of unusual gifts nonetheless.

FNAC

MAP P.96, POCKET MAP C14
Veldstraat 47 Ⓦ fnac.be.

This is a mixed bag of a chain store whose several floors sell electrical appliances, cameras, TVs and all sorts of gadgets. It also has a modest selection of English-language books, mostly fiction, and a wide range of road, cycling and hiking maps with good coverage of Belgium. It sells tickets for many mainstream cultural events, too.

Galerie St-John

MAP P.96, POCKET MAP D12
Nieuwpoort 2 Ⓦ st-john.be.

Arguably the best antique shop in Ghent – and there is competition – this well-regarded place specialises in nineteenth- and twentieth-century fine and applied art, everything from silverware and furniture to chandeliers, ceramics, glass, crystal and oil paintings.

Himschoot

MAP P.96, POCKET MAP C12
Groentenmarkt 1 ⓦ bakkerijhimschoot.be.
Traditional bakery, where the bread is baked in the basement before being packed tight into the shop shelves above. Over sixty different sorts of bread, plus tasty tarts, cakes and scones – all at bargain prices. No wonder there are queues at peak times.

Interphilia

MAP P.96, POCKET MAP C13
St-Baafsplein 4 ⓦ interphila.be.
Temptingly old-fashioned stamp and coin shop, with every nook and cranny stuffed to the gills. It also sells antique postcards, vintage badges, posters and insignia.

Het Mekka van de Kaas

MAP P.96, POCKET MAP C14
Koestraat 9 ⓦ hetmekkavandekaas.be.
Literally the 'Cheese Mecca', this small specialist cheese shop offers a remarkable range of traditional and exotic cheeses – try some of the delicious Ghent goats' cheese (*geitenkaas*). It sells a good range of wine, too.

Neuhaus

MAP P.96, POCKET MAP C12
Groentenmarkt 16
ⓦ neuhauschocolates.com.
Probably Belgium's best chocolate chain, with mouthwatering chocolates at €20 for 250g – you can go cheaper, but not better. Try their Manons – stuffed white chocolates with fresh cream, vanilla and coffee fillings – or the Caprices – pralines stuffed with crispy nougat, fresh cream and soft-centred chocolate. Of the two stores in Ghent, this is the more central.

Priem

MAP P.96, POCKET MAP C12
Zuivelbrugstraat 1 ⓣ 09 223 25 37.
One of the oddest shops in Ghent, *Priem* has an extraordinary range of vintage wallpaper dating from the 1950s. Zuivelbrugstraat is the location of the main shop, but there are three other neighbouring premises on the Kraanlei.

Tierenteyn

MAP P.96, POCKET MAP C12
Groentenmarkt 3 ⓦ tierenteyn-verlent.be.
This traditional shop, one of the city's most delightful, makes its mustards – wonderful, tongue-tickling stuff displayed on shelves of ceramic and glass jars. A small jar will set you back about €7.

Worlds' End Comic and Games Centre

MAP P.96, POCKET MAP C15
Ketelvest 51 ⓦ worldsendcomics.com.
Comics are a Belgian speciality and national obsession. This substantial shop delves deep into every part of its subject – from manga to Marvel, horror to sci-fi, the *Adventures of Luther Arkwright*, for one. Collectables and games, too. Down a narrow alley on the south side of the city centre.

Tierenteyn

Cafés

Café Labath

MAP P.96, POCKET MAP A13
Oude Houtlei 1 Ⓦ cafelabath.be.
Specialist coffee house in neat,
modern premises that makes much
of the quality of its beans – with
good reason. Try the Java or the
Ethiopian. Sells snacks, soups and
teas, too. Attracts a boho, avant-
garde crew.

Julie's House

MAP P.96, POCKET MAP C12
Kraanlei 13 Ⓦ julieshouse.be.
Squeezed into an ancient and
somewhat rickety terrace house
in one of the prettiest parts of the
city, *Julie's* serves goodies 'baked
with love, served with joy'. The
boast may be a little OTT, but the
home-made cakes and patisseries
are genuinely delicious. They also
serve breakfasts (till 2pm) and
pancakes.

Souplounge

MAP P.96, POCKET MAP C12
Zuivelbrugstraat 4, just off Vrijdagmarkt
Ⓦ souplounge.be.

Café Labath

Bright and cheerful self-service
café, where the big bowls of
freshly made soup are the main
event – from just €5.50. They
serve filling sandwiches and
salads, too.

Take Five

MAP P.96, POCKET MAP C14
Voldersstraat 10 Ⓦ take-five-
espressobar.be.
Bright, brisk coffee bar with a cool
soundtrack, jazz meets house and
pleasing modern decor. Offers
a great range of specialist-bean
coffees, plus a selection of teas and
delicious cakes and pastries.

Restaurants

Boon

MAP P.96, POCKET MAP C12
Geldmunt 6. Ⓦ boon.gent.
Across the street from the castle,
this neat and trim vegetarian
restaurant offers a wide range
of well-prepared dishes that are
perfect for lunch. The salads
are particularly good – try, for
example, the salad with kale, ricotta
and carrot. €

Le Baan Thai

MAP P.96, POCKET MAP C12
Corduwaniersstraat 57
Ⓦ lebaanthai.be/nl.
Down a narrow, cobbled street, in
a distinguished old house in the
Patershol, this is generally reckoned
to be the best Thai restaurant in
the city. Its menu covers all the
classics and then some: try, for
instance, the *Nua phad* fried beef
with chilli and basil for €26. It
has a charming, leafy terrace out
the back, too. Reservations are
recommended. €€

Chubby Cheeks

MAP P.96, POCKET MAP B14
Onderbergen 33 Ⓦ chubbycheeks.be.
This fabulous restaurant is food as
an adventure with an ingenious
menu featuring tapas-style dishes

Dish at Heritage

like Swiss chard and beetroot or the dark meat of Cecina de León. There's an open kitchen, so you can sit on a bar stool and watch the chefs at work, or choose one of a handful of tables – the place is small and cosy. €€€

Domestica

MAP P.96, POCKET MAP B14
Onderbergen 27 Ⓦ domestica.be.
Smart and chic restaurant, whose principal chef and owner serves up an excellent range of Belgian dishes – both French and Flemish – in nouvelle cuisine style. Has a garden terrace for good-weather eating. Try, for example, the filet of lamb with peas, carrots and beans (€33). €€€

Heritage

MAP P.96, POCKET MAP C12
Rodekoningstraat 12 Ⓦ heritage.gent.
Cosy, somehow rather rustic decor sets the scene for this enterprising restaurant, where there's no meat, just fish and vegetarian dishes with a strong Latin American influence. Try, for starters, the fennel, seitan and vegan cheese. A set three-

course menu at lunchtime will set you back a very reasonable €40. €€€

Lepelblad

MAP P.96, POCKET MAP B14
Onderbergen 40 Ⓦ lepelblad.be.
Popular restaurant with a heaving pavement terrace if you can get a seat on it, where the ever-changing menu is inventive and creative with pasta dishes, salads and traditional Flemish cuisine to the fore; mains average €30. The arty decor is good fun, too. €€

De Lieve

MAP P.96, POCKET MAP B11
St-Margrietstraat 1 Ⓦ eetkaffee-delieve.be.
On the edge of the Patershol, this informal, bistro-style restaurant features traditional Flemish dishes that taste wonderful – don't miss the risotto with wild mushrooms or the rabbit with prunes. The main courses are very reasonable at around €25. A popular spot with so-called BVs (*Bekende Vlamingen*, 'Famous Flemings'). €€€

Het Waterhuis aan de Bierkant

Maison Elza

MAP P.96, POCKET MAP B12
Jan Breydelstraat 36 W maisonelza.be.
Idiosyncratic, split-level café-
restaurant liberally sprinkled with
Edwardian bric-a-brac – you'll
even spot some vintage models'
dummies. They serve a tasty
breakfast and afternoon tea here
(several days a week). In the
evening, the dinner menu offers a
limited but well-chosen selection
of freshly prepared meat and
fish dishes (mains average €30).
However, seafood, in general,
and shellfish, in particular, are
the house speciality. The window
tables overlook a canal and if the
weather holds, you can eat out on
the pontoon at the back. €€

Midtown Grill

MAP P.96, POCKET MAP B13
Korenlei 10 W midtowngrillgent.com.
It's surprisingly difficult to find a
good-quality restaurant open on
Sunday in Ghent – so this smart,
medium-sized place can fill the
gap. Attached to the *Marriott
Hotel* (see page 134), meat
dominates the menu – especially
steak from around €35. There

is a bit of tomfoolery with the
specialist steak knives – but
nothing too unbearable. €€€

Du Progrès

MAP P.96, POCKET MAP C13
Korenmarkt 10 W duprogres.be.
This long-established, family-
owned restaurant is popular with
tourists and locals alike – and with
good reason. The house speciality
is steak (from €26) – and very
tasty they are too. Rapid-fire
service and a central location. €€

De Raadkamer

MAP P.96, POCKET MAP B15
Nederkouter 3 W de-raadkamer.be.
A family-run restaurant in neat,
modern premises offering a short
but well-conceived menu of
Belgian favourites, such as the
turbot risotto with asparagus and
lobster sauce. Mains average €28.
Impeccable service. €€

Roots

MAP P.96, POCKET MAP C12
Vrouwebroersstraat 5 W rootsgent.be.
This cool and collected Patershol
haunt, hidden behind its
ancient brickwork, may have
the simplest boho decor. Still,
the menu is subtle and complex,
always featuring local, seasonal
ingredients. Pumpkin and
parmesan with red gurnard gives
the flavour. Fixed menus are the
order of the day here – €45 at
lunchtime, €75 at night. €€€

Bars and clubs

't Dreupelkot

MAP P.96, POCKET MAP C12
Groentenmarkt 12 W dreupelkot.be.
Cosy bar specializing in *jenever*
(Dutch gin), which stocks more
than two hundred brands, all kept
at icy temperatures – the vanilla
flavour is particularly delicious. It's
down a little alley leading off the
Groentenmarkt – and next door to
Het Waterhuis (see page 117).

Dulle Griet

MAP P.96, POCKET MAP C12
Vrijdagmarkt 50 ⓌW dullegriet.be.
Long, dark, atmospheric bar with
all manner of incidental bygones –
with barrels and puppets hanging
from the ceiling and vintage vehicle
number plates on the walls. But
the magnet is the beer of course –
over five hundred brews on tap or
bottled.

Hotsy Totsy

MAP P.96, POCKET MAP A13
Hoogstraat 1 ⓘ 09 224 20 12.
Long the gathering place of the
city's intelligentsia – though less
so today – this ornately decorated
bar, with its Art Nouveau
flourishes, has ranks of drinkers
lining up along its long wooden
bar. Regular live jazz and blues
sessions, too.

Missy Sippy Blues & Roots Club

MAP P.96, POCKET MAP C13
Klein Turkije 16 ⓌW missy-sippy.be.
Ghent has always had more than its
fair share of quirky pubs and bars
– and this cramped and crowded
place is a real humdinger. Dark and
atmospheric, some of the decor
is positively eccentric and retro,
but their commitment to keeping
blues, jazz, roots music and swing
alive means there are lots of great
live acts – both domestic and
foreign. Right in the centre, just off
the Korenmarkt.

De Trollekelder

MAP P.96, POCKET MAP D12
Bij St-Jacobs 17 ⓌW trollekelder.be.
This dark and atmospheric bar
offers a wonderful selection of beers
in an ancient merchant's house –
don't be deterred by the trolls in the
window.

Het Waterhuis aan de Bierkant

MAP P.96, POCKET MAP C12
Groentenmarkt 9 ⓘ 09 225 06 80.
More than a hundred types of beer
are available in this engaging canal-
side bar, which is popular with
tourists and older locals. Be sure
to try *Stropken* (literally 'noose'),
a delicious local brew named after
the time Charles V compelled the
rebellious city burghers to parade
outside the town gate with ropes
around their necks in 1540.

Dulle Griet

Southern and eastern Ghent

Although most of Ghent's leading attractions are within easy strolling distance of the Korenmarkt, three of the city's principal museums are some 2km (1.2 miles) south of the centre. The nearest is STAM, an ingenious and well-conceived museum that tracks through the city's history from its premises on the sprawling campus of what was once the old Cistercian Bijlokeabdij (Bijloke Abbey). A little further afield are both MSK (Museum voor Schone Kunsten), with Ghent's most comprehensive fine art collection, and the adjacent Museum of Contemporary Art, known as S.M.A.K. Many visitors hop on a tram at the Korenmarkt for the quick trip down to the three, but with a little more time, the twenty-minute walk there makes for a reasonably pleasant and very easy stroll. Elsewhere, east of St-Baafskathedraal, Ghent's eighteenth- and nineteenth-century suburbs stretch toward the Dampoort train station. Few tourists venture this way, which is a pity as this is a particularly interesting part of Ghent. However, there is only one specific sight as such, the enchanting ruins of St-Baafsabdij (St Bavo's Abbey).

STAM

STAM

MAP P.120, POCKET MAP A16–B16
Bijlokesite, Godshuizenlaan
Ⓦ stamgent.be. Charge.

Once wealthy and powerful, the former Cistercian **Bijlokeabdij** (Bijloke Abbey), just to the west of the River Leie, dates from the thirteenth century. Much of the medieval complex has survived and, with subsequent additions, now occupies a sprawling multiuse site. At its core is **STAM**, an ambitious museum that explores the city's history via paintings and a battery of original artefacts. Visits begin in a bright, modern cube-like structure and continue in the former abbey church and cloisters, with one of the early highlights being the two delightful medieval wall paintings in the former refectory. Look out also for the room full of medieval illuminated books and incidental sculpture; a selection of vintage military hardware; a good section on the city's guilds; and, the pick of the lot, a detailed section on the mysterious theft of **The Just Judges panel** of the *Adoration of the Mystic Lamb* (see page 110), which may or may not have involved neo-fascists, crooks and/ or eccentrics.

Citadelpark

MAP P.120, POCKET MAP B18
Koning Léopold II-laan. Free.

A large chunk of greenery, **Citadelpark** takes its name from the fortress that stood here until the 1870s, when the land was cleared and prettified with the addition of grottoes and ponds, statues and fountains, a waterfall and a bandstand. These nineteenth-century niceties survive today and, as a bonus, a network of footpaths crisscross the park. Even better, if you have spent much time in Ghent, which is almost universally flat, Citadelpark seems refreshingly hilly. In the 1940s, a large brick complex was built on the east

A statue in Citadelpark

side of the park and after various incarnations, it now divides into two – a Conference Centre and the **S.M.A.K. art gallery**.

S.M.A.K. (Stedelijk Museum voor Actuele Kunst)

MAP P.120, POCKET MAP C18
Jan Hoetplein 1 Ⓦ smak.be. Charge.

S.M.A.K. (Municipal Museum of Contemporary Art) is one of Belgium's most adventurous and experimental contemporary art galleries. Nowadays, it's primarily devoted to temporary displays of international standing. These exhibitions are supplemented by a regularly rotated selection of sculptures, paintings and installations often drawn from the museum's wide-ranging permanent collection. S.M.A.K. possesses examples of all the major artistic movements since World War II – everything from surrealism, the CoBrA group and pop art through to minimalism and conceptual art, as well as their forerunners, most notably René Magritte and Paul Delvaux. Perennial favourites

SOUTHERN AND EASTERN GHENT

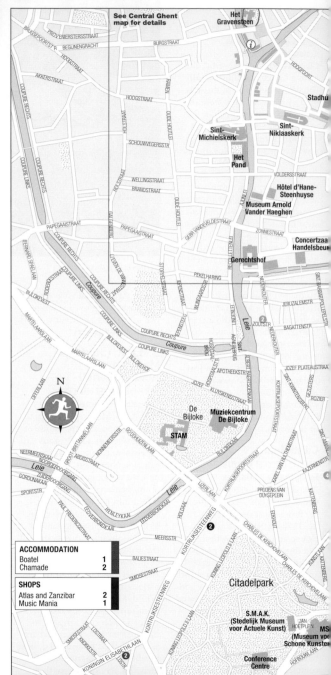

See Central Ghent map for details

Het Gravensteen

Burgstraat

Stadhu

Sint-Michielskerk

Sint-Niklaaskerk

Het Pand

Hôtel d'Hane-Steenhuyse

Museum Arnold Vander Haeghen

Concertzaa Handelsbeu

Gerechtshof

De Bijloke

Muziekcentrum De Bijloke

STAM

Citadelpark

S.M.A.K. (Stedelijk Museum voor Actuele Kunst)

MS (Museum voo Schone Kunster)

Conference Centre

ACCOMMODATION
Boatel 1
Chamade 2

SHOPS
Atlas and Zanzibar 2
Music Mania 1

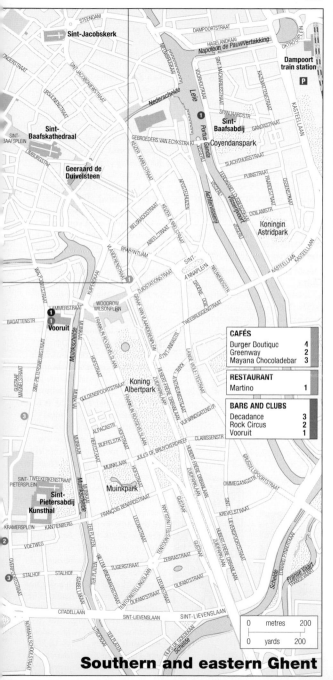

CAFÉS

Durger Doutique	4
Greenway	2
Mayana Chocoladebar	3

RESTAURANT

Martino	1

BARS AND CLUBS

Decadance	3
Rock Circus	2
Vooruit	1

0	metres	200
0	yards	200

Southern and eastern Ghent

SOUTHERN AND EASTERN GHENT

include the installations of the influential German **Joseph Beuys** (1921–86), who played a leading role in the European avant-garde art movement of the 1970s; the Belgian **Panamarenko**'s (1940–2019) eccentric polyester zeppelin entitled *Aeromodeller*, and a characteristically unnerving painting by Dublin-born **Francis Bacon** (1909–92) entitled *A Figure Sitting*. Look out also for the strange and varied works of the Dutch conceptual artist Pieter Engels (1938–2019), who featured in one of the gallery's temporary exhibitions in 2023.

MSK (Museum voor Schone Kunsten)

MAP P.120, POCKET MAP C18
Fernand Scribedreef 1 Ⓦ mskgent.be.
Charge.

One of the city's prime attractions, **MSK** (Fine Art Museum), just opposite S.M.A.K., holds the city's principal art collection and runs an ambitious programme of temporary exhibitions. It occupies an imposing Neoclassical edifice and the paintings are well displayed, but the interior can be a

MSK

tad confusing – be sure to pick up a floor plan at reception.

One highlight of the museum's small but eclectic collection of early Flemish paintings is **Rogier van der Weyden**'s (1399–1464) *Madonna with Carnation*. In this charming work, the proffered flower, in all its exquisite detail, symbolises Christ's passion. Nearby also are two superb works by **Hieronymus Bosch** (1450–1516); his *Bearing of the Cross* shows Christ mocked by some of the most grotesque and deformed characters he ever painted. Among the grotesques, you'll spy a singularly wan penitent thief confessing to a monstrously ugly monk and St Veronica, whose cloak carries the imprint of Christ's face. This struggle between good and evil is also the subject of Bosch's *St Jerome at Prayer*, in the foreground of which the saint prays, surrounded by a brooding, menacing landscape.

From the seventeenth century, there's a powerful *St Francis* by **Rubens** (1577–1640), in which a very sick-looking saint bears the marks of the stigmata, while **Jacob Jordaens** (1593–1678), whom Rubens greatly influenced, is well represented by the whimsical romanticism of his *Allegory of Fertility*. Jordaens was, however, capable of much greater subtlety and his *Studies of the Head of Abraham Grapheus* is an example of the high-quality preparatory paintings he completed, most of which were later recycled within larger compositions. In the same section, **Anthony van Dyck**'s (1599–1641) *Jupiter and Antiope* wins the bad taste award for portraying the lecherous god with his tongue hanging out in anticipation of sex with a sleeping Antiope. Elsewhere, there's a fine collection of seventeenth-century Dutch genre paintings, plus several works by Kortrijk's talented **Roelandt Savery** (1576–1639), who trained in Amsterdam and worked for the Habsburgs in Prague

Vooruit performing arts centre

and Vienna before returning to the Low Countries. To suit the tastes of his German patrons, he infused many of his landscapes with the romantic classicism that they preferred – Orpheus and the Garden of Eden were two favourite subjects – but the finely observed detail of his paintings was always in the true Flemish tradition as in his striking *Plundering of a Village*, where there's a palpable sense of outrage.

The museum's eighteenth- and nineteenth-century collection includes a handful of romantic historical canvases, plus – and this is a real surprise – a superbly executed portrait of a certain *Alexander Edgar* by the Scot **Henry Raeburn** (1756–1823). Also displayed are several key paintings by Ostend's **James Ensor** (1860–1949), notably the ghoulish *Skeleton looking at Chinoiserie and Pierrot and Skeleton in Yellow Robe*. However, you must take potluck with the museum's most famous Ensor, his much-lauded *Self-Portrait with Flower Hat*, as this is often out on loan. Other high points include a

batch of Expressionist paintings by the likes of **Constant Permeke** (1886–1952) and **Gustave de Smet** (1887–1943), as well as several characteristically unsettling works by both **Paul Delvaux** (1897–1994) and **René Magritte** (1898–1967). Two cases in point are Delvaux's *The Staircase* and Magritte's *Perspective II, Manet's Balcony*, in which wooden coffins have replaced the figures from Manet's painting.

Vooruit

MAP P.120, POCKET MAP D15
St-Pietersnieuwstraat 23
Ⓦ viernulvier.gent/en.

The **Vooruit** performing arts centre (see page 147), now largely rebranded as Viernulvier, has a valid claim to be the cultural centre of the city (at least for the under-40s), offering a wide-ranging programme of rock and pop through to theatre and dance. It also occupies a splendid building, a twin-towered and turreted former festival hall built for Ghent's socialists in an eclectic rendition of Art Nouveau in 1914.

St-Pietersabdij

Overpoortstraat

MAP P.120, POCKET MAP C17–C18

Running south from Vooruit,
St-Pietersnieuwstraat and then
Overpoortstraat cut through the
heart of the city's student quarter,
a gritty and grimy but vivacious
district, jam-packed with late-
night bars and cafés. En route is
one of Ghent's biggest churches,
St-Pietersabdij (St Peter's Abbey;
see below).

St-Pietersabdij

MAP P.120, POCKET MAP D17

St-Pietersplein ☎ 09 266 85 00. Church,
gardens & most of the complex: free;
Kunsthal: usually free, but admission is
sometimes charged.

The sprawling mass of **St-
Pietersabdij** (St Peter's Abbey)
flanks St-Pietersplein, a very wide
and long cobbled square. The abbey
dates back to the city's earliest days
and was probably founded by St
Amand in about 640. The Vikings
razed the original buildings three
centuries later, but it was rebuilt
on a grand scale and became rich
and powerful in equal measure. In
1578, the Protestants destroyed
the abbey as a symbol of much
of what they hated. The present
complex – a Baroque whopper
incorporating a church and two
courtyard complexes – was erected
in the seventeenth and eighteenth
centuries. The last monks were
ejected during the French
occupation of the 1790s and
since then – as with many other
ecclesiastical complexes in Belgium
– it's been hard to figure out any
suitable use. Today, much of the
complex serves as municipal offices.
Still, several sections are open to
the public, beginning with the
domed **St-Pieterskerk**, modelled
on St Peter's in Rome, though the
interior is no more than a plodding
Baroque. Elsewhere, there is a
small art exhibition centre, the
Kunsthal St Pietersabdij, where
they feature temporary displays of
modern art and local history, and
you can wander the **gardens** with
their incidental ruins, herb garden,
orchard and mini-vineyard.

St-Baafsabdij

MAP P.120, POCKET MAP F13

Spanjaardstraat ⊕ historischehuizen.stad.
gent/en/st-bavos-abbey. Free.

The extensive ruins of **St-
Baafsabdij** (St Bavo's Abbey)
ramble over a narrow parcel of

The life and times of St Bavo

The patron saint of Ghent, **St Bavo** – or St Baaf – was an early seventh-century Frankish nobleman who – in the way of such things – started out bad and then turned good. Fond of the drink and even fonder of his sword, Bavo led a wild and violent life until he was converted to Christianity by the French missionary St Amand. After that, he gave his possessions to the poor and became a hermit monk living in a hollow tree on the edge of Ghent. His remains were allegedly buried at St-Baafsabdij.

land beside the River Leie in what was once a strategically important location. It was here, in 630, that the French missionary St Amand (584–675) founded an abbey, though the locals could not have been overly impressed as they ended up drowning him in the river. Nonetheless, St Amand's abbey flourished as a place of pilgrimage because of its guardianship of the remains of St Bavo (622–659). In the ninth century, the abbey suffered a major disaster when the Vikings decided this was the ideal spot to camp while they raided the surrounding region. Still, the order was eventually restored, another colony of monks moved in and the abbey was rebuilt in 950. The Emperor Charles V had most of this second abbey knocked down in the 1540s and the monks decamped to St Baafskathedraal, but somehow the ruins managed to survive. Tucked away behind a stone retaining wall, the abbey's extensive **ruins** include the remnants of an ivy-covered Gothic cloister, whose long, vaulted corridors are attached to a distinctive, octagonal tower comprising a toilet on the bottom floor and the storage room – the *sanctuarium* – for the St Bavo relic up above. Attached to the cloister is a substantial two-storey building, whose lower level holds all sorts of architectural bits and pieces retrieved from the city during renovations and demolitions. There are gargoyles, finely carved Gothic heads, terracotta panels,

broken-off chunks of columns and capitals, and several delightful mini-tableaux. There's precious little labelling, but the skill of the carving impresses. If you've already explored the city, one or two pieces are identifiable: the original lion from the old punishment post on St-Veerleplein (see page 103).

Close by, a flight of steps leads up to the Romanesque **refectory**, a splendid chamber whose magnificent, hooped timber roof dates from the twelfth century. The abbey's grounds are small but delightful, a partly wild flurry of shrubs and flowers – and perfect for a picnic.

St-Baafsabdij

SOUTHERN AND EASTERN GHENT

Shops

Atlas and Zanzibar

MAP P.120; POCKET MAP B17
Kortrijksesteenweg 19 Ⓦ atlaszanzibar.be.
Outstanding travel bookshop with
a comprehensive range of English-
language travel guides and road
and hiking maps. They also sell
globes, extreme sports guides and
educational toys. Well-informed
staff will help you on your way.
About 2km (1.2 miles) south of the
city centre.

Music Mania

MAP P.120, POCKET MAP D15
St-Pietersnieuwstraat 19
Ⓦ musicmaniarecords.be.
Opened way back in the late
1960s, this excellent record shop
sells vinyl in just about every
musical genre you can think
of – from jazz, blues and folk to
disco and Afro-funk. It's primarily
second-hand stuff, but there are
reissues and new vinyl. You may
spy some big-name DJs if you
are familiar with Ghent's live
music scene.

Cafés

Burger Boutique

MAP P.120, POCKET MAP C17
St-Amandstraat 48 Ⓦ burgerboutique.be.
In brisk modern premises, this
burger bar serves up what some
locals claim to be the best – and
most pleasingly presented – beef
burgers in town. They also do
chicken and fish burgers and finger
food – croquettes with Iberico
ham, for instance. Burgers begin at
just €7. €

Greenway

MAP P.120, POCKET MAP C15
Nederkouter 42 Ⓦ greenway.be.
Straightforward café-cum-takeaway
decorated in sharp modern style,
selling a wide range of eco-friendly
foods, from bio-burgers to pasta,
noodles and baguettes, all for just a
few euros. €

Mayana Chocoladebar

MAP P.120, POCKET MAP D16
St-Pietersnieuwstraat 208 Ⓦ mayabna.be.
Chocolate aficionados will get their
fix in this bright and modern café

Mayana Chocoladebar

Concert at Vooruit.

devoted to the cocoa bean. Treats on offer range from the humble chocolate chip cookie to a chocolate fondue for two, as well as a plethora of chocolate-flavoured drinks – and coffee. Takeaway available.

Restaurant

Martino

MAP P.120, POCKET MAP E15
Vlaanderenstraat 125 ☎ 09 225 01 04.
Something of a local institution, this unpretentious, family-owned place is a diner-like affair with a workers' menu – steaks, burgers, sandwiches and a local favourite, the 'Martino', comprising raw beef with mustard, Tabasco, tomato and anchovy. A tasty spaghetti Bolognese costs just €15, crevettes €25. €

Bars and clubs

Decadance

MAP P.120, POCKET MAP C18
Overpoortstraat 76 ⓦ facebook.com/
decadance.ghent.
Long a standard-bearer for the city's nightlife, this club, which is near the university (hence the

abundance of students), offers one of the city's best nights out, with either live music – most of Belgium's bands have played here at one time or another – or DJs. Three rooms with three styles of music: reggae, hip-hop, drum 'n' bass and garage-techno vibes, etc.

Rock Circus

MAP P.120, POCKET MAP C17
Overpoortstraat 22
ⓦ facebook.com/rockcircusgent.
At the heart of the student quarter, this busy, sometimes raucous bar prides itself on its range of beers – 58 or so on draft and a further regiment of bottled beers.

Vooruit

MAP P.120, POCKET MAP D15
St-Pietersnieuwstraat 23
ⓦ viernulvier.gent/en.
The Vooruit performing arts centre (see page 147) – Viernulvier – offers a wide range of rock, pop and jazz concerts, dance, theatre and DJ nights. The main area, the ground-floor café-bar, is short of creature comforts – it's a sizeable barn-like affair – but it attracts an avant-garde crew and gets jam-packed on the weekend.

ACCOMMODATION

De Orangerie, Bruges

Accommodation

The great thing about staying in Bruges or Ghent is that most of the more enjoyable hotels and B&Bs are in or near the centre, precisely where you want to be. The main difference is that you're spoilt for choice in Bruges as the city has scores of places, whereas Ghent has a more limited – albeit just as select – range. A bonus is that you'll be offered breakfast almost everywhere at no extra (or minimal) charge, ranging from a roll and coffee at the less expensive places to full-scale banquets at the top end of the range. In Bruges, less so in Ghent, you'll also find that most hotels are small – twenty rooms, often fewer – and chains are few and far between. In both cities, standards are generally high among the hotels and B&Bs but a tad more inconsistent when you come to the hostels. One word of caution, however, is that many hotels offer rooms of widely divergent size and comfort – be pushy if you have to be – and some hoteliers are wont to deck out their foyers rather grandly, in contrast to the spartan rooms beyond.

Bruges

Bruges has over a hundred hotels, scores of B&Bs and several youth hostels. However, it still can't accommodate all its visitors at busy times, especially in the high season (roughly late June to early Sept) and at Christmas – so you'd be well advised to **book ahead**. Most of the city's hotels are small – twenty rooms, often fewer – and very few are chains. Standards are generally high among the hotels and B&Bs, whereas the city's hostels are more inconsistent. We've reviewed a batch of the best places below and there are comprehensive listings on the city's official tourist website (Ⓦ visitbruges.be).

Hotels in Bruges

ADORNES MAP P.72, POCKET MAP D4. St Annarei 26 Ⓦ adornes.be. Medium-sized three-star hotel in two tastefully converted old Flemish townhouses with a plain, high-gabled facade. Both the public areas and the comfortable bedrooms are decorated in bright whites and creams, emphasising the place's antique charm. It's in an excellent location, too, at the junction of two canals near the east end of Spiegelrei. It's very child-friendly, with high chairs in the dining room so children can enjoy a delicious breakfast too. €€

ALEGRIA MAP P.72, POCKET MAP C5. St-Jakobsstraat 34 Ⓦ alegria-hotel.com. Formerly a B&B, this appealing, family-run, three-star hotel has a dozen or so large and attractive rooms in a central location near the Markt. The rooms at the back, overlooking the garden, are quieter than those at the front. The owner is a mine of information about where and what to eat. €€

ARAGON MAP P.72, POCKET MAP C5. Naaldenstraat 22 Ⓦ aragon.be/en. Behind this attractive, elongated facade, this four-star hotel has a wide range of rooms – from budget to executive – in both

Hotel stars and accommodation price codes

All licensed **Belgian hotels** carry a blue permit shield indicating the number of **stars** allocated (up to a maximum of five). This classification system is, by necessity, measured against easily identifiable criteria – toilets, room service, lifts and so on – rather than aesthetics or specific location, and consequently can only provide a general guide as to quality and prices.

All the **hotels** detailed in this guide have been graded according to the three price categories listed below. These represent how much you can expect to pay in each establishment for the **least expensive double or twin room with breakfast in high season**, barring special deals and discounts, though prices do fluctuate wildly depending on demand; for a single room, where available, expect to pay around 80 percent of the cost of a double. Our categories are simply a guide to prices and do not indicate the facilities you might expect; as such, they differ from the star system the tourist authorities apply. At **hostels**, there is much less price fluctuation and we have provided the cost of a dormitory bed and/or a double room.

€	€40-120
€€	€120–200
€€€	€200+

the main building and the neighbouring annexe. The decor is crisp and modern; the hotel is friendly and well-run. The location is convenient too – beside a narrow but attractive side street, a five-minute walk from the Markt. €€

AUGUSTYN MAP P.72, POCKET MAP C4. Augustijnenrei 18 ⓦ hotelaugustyn. com. In a great location, in one of the prettiest parts of the city, this smart, modern hotel occupies a late-nineteenth-century town house overlooking a canal about five minutes' walk north of the Burg. Competitively priced with a variety of room categories – including an apartment. €€€

FEVERY MAP P.72, POCKET MAP D3. Collaert Mansionstraat 3 ⓦ hotelfevery. be. With good eco credentials – saving water, waste and energy – this unassuming, three-star hotel occupies a substantial, albeit standard-issue, three-storey brick building on a pleasant side street about fifteen minutes' walk north of the Burg. The rooms are neat, trim, modern and competitively priced: the smallest doubles cost €75. €

DE GOEZEPUT MAP P.48, POCKET MAP B7. Goezeputstraat 29 ⓦ hotelgoezeput.be. This enjoyable two-star hotel occupies a thoroughly refurbished eighteenth-century convent in a charming location near the cathedral. The guest rooms, which vary considerably in size, have been done in contemporary style in shades of brown and cream, though the entrance, with its handsome wooden beams and staircase, has been left untouched. €€

JACOBS MAP P.72, POCKET MAP C4. Baliestraat 1 ⓦ hoteljacobs.be. Pleasant three-star hotel set in a creatively modernised old-brick building complete with a precipitous crow-step gable. The twenty-odd rooms are decorated in a brisk modern style, though some are a little on the small side. It's in a quiet location though in an attractive part of the city centre, a ten-minute walk northeast of the Markt. €€

JAN BRITO MAP P.38, POCKET MAP C6. Freren Fonteinstraat 1 ⓦ janbrito.com. Something of a mixed bag of a place, the best (and most expensive) guest rooms

Top picks

Luxury:
Bruges: De Orangerie (see page 132); Ghent: Pillows Grand Boutique Hotel Reylof (see page 135).

Charming:
Bruges: Ter Duinen (see page 133); Ghent: Erasmus (see page 134).

Family:
Bruges: Adornes (see page 130); Ghent: Harmony (see page 134).

Location:
Bruges: Die Swaene (see page 132); Ghent: Boatel (see page 134).

Budget:
Bruges: Jacobs (see page 131); Ghent: Monasterium Poortackere (see page 131).

at this large and rambling hotel are in the restored patrician mansion at the front. However, most rooms are in the more modest brick annexe at the back – they are okay if nothing special; the same applies to the breakfasts. Handily located, a short walk from the Burg. €€

MONSIEUR ERNEST MAP P.48, POCKET MAP B6. Wulfhagestraat 43 ⓦ monsieurhotels.com. Sister to the Monsieur Maurice (see below), this agreeable, smallish hotel with its unassuming brick facade occupies tastefully modernised premises with neat and trim modern rooms and a splendid staircase as a reminder of grander times. It's located beside a canal on an appealing side street west of the Markt, although this is only visible from a few rooms. Minimum two-night stay. €€

MONTANUS MAP P.48, POCKET MAP D7. Nieuwe Gentweg 76 ⓦ denheerd.be. This four-star hotel occupies a big old house that has been sympathetically modernised with simple yet luxurious decor. The twelve rooms are large, comfortable and modern – and there are twelve more at the back, in chalet-like accommodation at the far end of the large garden. The garden also accommodates an up-market restaurant tha. €€

NAVARRA MAP P.72, POCKET MAP B5. St-Jakobsstraat 41 ⓦ hotelnavarra.

com. This immaculate four-star hotel occupies one of the city's finest buildings, a handsome mansion built in the French style in the early eighteenth century. The grand facade, with its balanced symmetries, has an elegant open courtyard at the front and a garden terrace at the back. There are nigh-on a hundred guest rooms here and although they don't quite match the setting – most are modern – they are still extremely comfortable. On a busy street just north of the Markt. €€€

DE ORANGERIE MAP P.38, POCKET MAP C6. Kartuizerinnenstraat 10 ⓦ hotelorangerie.be. In a former convent and one-time bakery, this classy, family-owned, four-star hotel has twenty guest rooms, the pick of which are kitted out in an exuberant version of the country-house style. The wood-panelled lounge oozes a relaxed and demure charm – as does the breakfast room – and a tunnel leads down to a canal-side terrace. It's in a great central location, too. €€€

RED ROSE MAP P.38, POCKET MAP C5. Cordoeaniersstraat 18 ⓦ hotelrosered.be. This medium-sized, family-run, two-star hotel is handily located in a narrow side street a few minutes' walk north of the Burg. Mosquitoes can be a problem here, but the 22 rooms are neat, trim and modern. €€

DIE SWAENE MAP P.38, POCKET MAP D6. Steenhouwersdijk 2 ⓦ dieswaene.

com. In a perfect location, beside a pretty and peaceful section of the canal close to the Burg, this long-established, four-star hotel has thirty guest rooms decorated in individual, rather sumptuous antique style. There's also a heated pool and sauna, and the extremely generous breakfast will set you up nicely for the best part of the day. €€€

TER DUINEN MAP P.72, POCKET MAP D3. Langerei 52 Ⓦ hotelterduinen.eu. This charming three-star hotel is located in a lovely part of the city, beside the Langerei canal, and just a fifteen-minute walk from the Markt. It is housed in a beautifully maintained eighteenth-century villa with period public areas and appealing modern rooms. Superb breakfasts start the day off on the right footing, too. €€

B&Bs in Bruges

BARABAS MAP P.38, POCKET MAP D5. Hertsbergestraat 8–10 Ⓦ barabas.be. Deluxe affair in a pair of handsome – and handsomely restored – eighteenth-century houses, with four large guest rooms/suites kitted out in grand period style down to the huge, flowing drapes. It is in a central location, with a garden that backs onto a canal. €€€

HET WIT BEERTJE MAP P.48, POCKET MAP A7. Witte Beerstraat 4 Ⓦ hetwitbeertje.be. This modest little guesthouse-cum-B&B, with just three en-suite rooms, is a particularly good deal. It's located a bit further out, about a twenty-minute walk west of the Markt, beyond the Smedenpoort. €€

HUIS KONING MAP P.72, POCKET MAP B5. Oude Zak 25 Ⓦ huiskoning.be. A plush renovated B&B in a seventeenth-century, step-gable terrace house with a pleasant canal-side garden. The four en-suite guest rooms are decorated in a fresh, modern style and two have rather romantic canal views – ask for one of these when booking. €€

NUMBER 11 MAP P.38, POCKET MAP B5. Peerdenstraat 11 Ⓦ number11.be. In the heart of old Bruges, on a traffic-free side street, this first-rate B&B, set in an ancient terrace house, has just four lavish guest rooms – all wooden floors, beamed ceilings and expensive wallpaper. Every comfort is laid on, and the breakfasts are smashing. €€

SINT-NIKLAAS B&B MAP P.48, POCKET MAP C6. St-Niklaasstraat 18 Ⓦ sintnik. be. This well-kept B&B has three modern, en-suite guest rooms in a good-looking, three-storey, eighteenth-century townhouse near the Markt. One has a lovely view of the Belfort. €€

Hostels in Bruges

BRUGES EUROPA Map p.48, Pocket map D9. Baron Ruzettelaan 143 Ⓦ jeugdherbergen.be. Located 2km (1.2 miles) south of the centre in the suburb of Assebroek, this good-value HI hostel is set in a large, institution-like building and has its own grounds. There are more than two hundred beds in a mix of rooms from doubles through to six-bed dorms, most en suite. Breakfast is included in the price and there are security lockers, wi-fi, free parking, a bar and a lounge. City bus No. 4 or No. 6 from outside Bruges train station passes within 300m (0.19 miles) of the Bruges Europa – ask the driver to let you off at the Wantestraat bus stop. Dorms €, doubles €

SNUFFEL HOSTEL MAP P.72, POCKET MAP B4. Ezelstraat 42 Ⓦ snuffel.be. With its bright and cheery modernist facade, this is the best-looking hostel in Bruges by a country mile. It has around 120 beds and good facilities, including a fully equipped guest kitchen, showers, bicycle store, laundry and a patio/terrace. €

ST CHRISTOPHER'S BAUHAUS MAP P.72, POCKET MAP F4. Langestraat 133–137 Ⓦ bauhaus.be. This lively, laid-back hostel, located just a fifteen-minute walk east of the Burg, has a boho air and offers a mishmash of rooms with between two and six bunks each, some with pod beds. Bike rentals, lockers, a bar and a café are also available on the premises. Dorms €, doubles €

Ghent

Ghent has around seventy hotels, ranging from the delightful to the mundanely modern, with several of the most stylish and enjoyable – but not necessarily the most expensive – located right in the centre. There's also a small army of B&Bs, though these are more widely dispersed, and a couple of bright and cheerful hostels. The tourist information website has comprehensive listings (ⓦ visit.gent.be).

Hotels in Ghent

BOATEL MAP P.120, POCKET MAP E13. Voorhuitkaai 44 ⓦ theboatel.com. Arguably the most distinctive of the city's hotels, the one-star Boatel is, as its name implies, a converted boat – an imaginatively and attractively refurbished canal barge, to be precise. It's moored in one of the city's outer canals, a ten- to fifteen-minute walk east from the centre. The seven-odd bedrooms are decked out in crisp modern style, and breakfasts, taken on the poop deck, are very good. €€

CHAMADE MAP P.120, POCKET MAP A19. Koningin Elisabethlaan 3 ⓦ chamade.be. Standard, three-star accommodation in bright, modern bedrooms at this family-run hotel, which occupies a distinctive, six-storey modern block, a five-minute walk north of the train station. €€

COMIC ART HOTEL MAP P.96, POCKET MAP B11. Augustijnenkaai 2 ⓦ comicarthotel. be. In a large and good-looking building that was formerly a school, this relatively new hotel has a smart modern interior distinguished by the specially commissioned (comic) artwork in many of its rooms. It's all good fun – and the location, beside one of the city's prettiest and quietest stretches of canal, is first-rate. €€

ERASMUS MAP P.96, POCKET MAP B13. Poel 25 ⓦ erasmushotel.be. Friendly, family-run, two-star in a commodious old townhouse a few metres away from the Korenlei. Each room is thoughtfully decorated and furnished in traditional style with many antiques. The breakfast is excellent. Reservations are strongly advised in summer. €€

DE FLANDRE MAP P.96, POCKET MAP B13. Poel 1 ⓦ hoteldeflandre.be. Medium-sized, four-star hotel in a thoroughly refashioned, nineteenth-century mansion with a modern annexe at the back. The rooms vary considerably in size, style and comfort, and those towards the rear are much quieter than those on the road. Competitively priced. €€

GHENT MARRIOTT HOTEL MAP P.96, POCKET MAP B13. Korenlei 10 ⓦ marriott. com. This smart and slick hotel may be part of an international chain, but full marks to the architects – for the discrete pedestrian entry from the historic Korenlei and the capacious, arching glass ceiling enclosing reception, lounge and coffee bar. The rooms are banked up to the sides of the glass ceiling, but each is modern and comfortable. The hotel's Midtown Grill (see page 116) is one of the few restaurants in Ghent open on Sunday. Wide fluctuations in price. €€€

GHENT RIVER MAP P.96, POCKET MAP C12. Waaistraat 5 ⓦ ghent-river-hotel. be. A four-star hotel whose austere modern facade doesn't do it any favours, but persevere: the interior is much more appealing and most of the guest rooms occupy the part of the building that was once a cotton mill – hence the bare-brick walls and industrial trappings. €€

HARMONY MAP P.96, POCKET MAP C12. Kraanlei 37 ⓦ hotel-harmony.be. In an immaculately renovated old mansion, this deluxe four-star hotel has just twenty-odd guest rooms decorated in an attractive modern style – all wooden floors and shades of brown and cream. The best rooms are on the top floor and come complete with a mini-terrace, affording grand views over the city. €€

MONASTERIUM POORTACKERE MAP P.96, POCKET MAP B13. Oude Houtlei 56 ⓦ monasterium.be. This unusual three-star hotel-cum-guesthouse occupies a rambling and somewhat spartan former nunnery and orphanage, whose ageing brickwork dates from the nineteenth century. There's a choice of en-suite double rooms, with some of the cheapest being in the former doctor's house; others are in the old orphanage. There are also single rooms with shared facilities (€75) in what was formerly nuns' cells – the nearest thing you'll get to the authentic monastic experience. Breakfast is usually taken in the former chapterhouse. A five-minute walk west of Veldstraat. €€

NH GENT BELFORT MAP P.96, POCKET MAP C13. Hoogpoort 63 Ⓦ nh-hotels.com. Under previous owners, this four-star chain hotel was one of the smartest in Ghent. Some of the gloss may have worn off, but it still has a great location – just across from the Stadhuis – and the 174 rooms are comfortable enough in a chain sort of way. There are several categories of rooms to choose from – standard, superior and family – plus a gym with a sauna. €€

NOVOTEL GENT CENTRUM MAP P.96, POCKET MAP C13. Goudenleeuwplein 5 Ⓦ all.accor.com. The guest rooms at this brisk, three-star chain hotel are pretty routine, but the location near the cathedral is hard to beat. The price is very competitive and there's an outdoor swimming pool – a rarity in central Ghent – which is great if the sun is out. €€

PILLOWS GRAND BOUTIQUE HOTEL REYLOF MAP P.96, POCKET MAP A13. Hoogstraat 36 Ⓦ pillowshotels.com. This superb chain hotel occupies a spacious nineteenth-century mansion whose elegant, high-ceilinged foyer sets a perfect tone. Beyond the 158 rooms vary in size and facilities, but most are immaculate, spacious and decorated in an appealing rendition of country-house style. The former coach house is now a spa and there is a patio terrace too. The least expensive deals exclude breakfast. €€€

B&Bs in Ghent
AT GENESIS MAP P.96, POCKET MAP C12. Hertogstraat 15 Ⓦ bedandbreakfast.eu/nl/a/350303/at-genesis. In the heart of the Patershol, in a sympathetically modernised old terrace house, this lovely B&B offers two second-floor guest rooms – one for two

guests, the other catering for six – located above an artist's studio. Both come with a kitchenette with many nice decorative touches and traditional beamed ceilings. €

SIMON SAYS MAP P.96, POCKET MAP C11. Sluizeken 8 Ⓦ simon-says.be. On the edge of the Patershol, in a good-looking building with an Art Nouveau facade, this combined coffee bar and B&B has just two guest rooms, both fairly small and straightforwardly modern, en-suite affairs. The breakfasts are splendid and reasonably priced – try the croissants. €€

DE WATERZOOI MAP P.96, POCKET MAP B12. St-Veerleplein 2 Ⓦ dewaterzooi.be. This superbly renovated eighteenth-century mansion offers a handful of handsome rooms that manage to make the most of their antique setting but are extraordinarily comfortable at the same time – the split-level attic room is the most ambitious. There are wonderful views of the castle; if the weather is good, have breakfast on the garden patio. Minimum two- or sometimes three-night stay at peak periods. €€€

Hostels in Ghent
JEUGDHERBERG DE DRAECKE MAP P.96, POCKET MAP B12. St-Widostraat 11 Ⓦ jeugdherbergen.be. Well-equipped, HI-affiliated hostel that's just a five-minute walk north of the Korenmarkt. It has around 120 beds in two- to six-bunk, en-suite rooms, a library, bar and lounge. Reservations are advised, especially in summer. Breakfast included. Dorms €, doubles €

UPPELINK HOSTEL MAP P.96, POCKET MAP B13. St-Michielsplein 21 Ⓦ hostel uppelink.com. A family-owned hostel in a prime location, occupying a rambling late-nineteenth-century building beside St-Michielsbrug (bridge). Some rooms have great views over the city centre and the public areas are a fetching mix of antique fittings and boho-distressed furnishings. Laundry facilities, free luggage storage and – more unusually – kayak rental (single kayak €29 for 3 hours, twin kayak €39 for 3 hours per person). Dorms have between six and fourteen bunk beds. Minimum two-night stay during the summer. Dorms €, doubles €

ESSENTIALS

Cycling in Bruges

Arrival

Bruges and Ghent are easy to reach by road and rail. The **E40 motorway**, linking Brussels with Ostend, runs just south of both cities and there are fast and frequent **trains** to Ghent and Bruges from Brussels and a batch of other Belgian cities. Long-distance **international buses** also run directly to Bruges and Ghent from several capital cities, including London with FlixBus (⊕ flixbus.co.uk), and there are **car ferries** from Hull to Zeebrugge near Bruges. The nearest airport to both cities is Brussels. There are three trains an hour between Bruges and Ghent; the journey time between the two is about twenty minutes.

The train and bus station are next to one another in Bruges, about 2km (1.2 miles) southwest of the city centre. If the flat and easy twenty-minute walk into the centre doesn't appeal, local buses depart for the main square, the Markt, from outside the train station every few minutes; other services stop on the side streets adjoining the Markt. All local buses have destination signs at the front, but if in doubt, check with the driver. A taxi from the train station to the centre should cost about €15.

Ghent has three train stations, but you're almost sure to arrive at Ghent St-Pieters, which adjoins the main bus station some 2km (1.2 miles) south of the city centre. From outside the train station. Tram No. 1 (destination Evergem, NOT Flanders Expo) runs up to the Korenmarkt at the heart of the city every few minutes. All trams have destination signs and numbers at the front, but if in doubt, check with the driver. The taxi fare from the train station to the Korenmarkt is about €20.

By air

The nearest airport to Bruges and Ghent is **Brussels international airport**. From the airport, there are three or four trains every hour to Brussels' three main stations: **Bruxelles-Nord, Bruxelles-Centrale** and **Bruxelles-Midi**. The journey to Bruxelles-Nord is about twenty minutes, a few minutes more to the others. You can change at any of these stations for the twice-hourly train from Brussels to Bruges and Ghent, though changing at Bruxelles-Nord is a tad more convenient since it isn't usually as crowded as the other two. The journey from Brussels takes an hour to Bruges and 35 minutes to Ghent. There are also direct trains from the airport to Ghent (1–2 hourly), from where there are onward connections to Bruges (3 hourly; 20min), but this isn't much quicker. The one-way fare from Brussels Airport to Bruges is currently €30.20, including an airport supplement of €6.40 (twice that for a return); the fare to Ghent is slightly less. Note that some flights to Brussels (including Ryanair) land at **Brussels South Charleroi Airport**, well to the south of the capital and an hour or so away from Brussels by airport bus.

By train

Bruges and Ghent are exceptionally well served by train (⊕ belgiantrain. be/en), with fast and frequent services from several Belgian towns and cities, including Brussels and Ostend. Trains from Brussels to Bruges and Ghent depart from all three of the capital's mainline stations, including Bruxelles-Midi, the terminus of Eurostar trains from London. **Eurostar** trains (⊕ eurostar.com) take two hours to get from London St Pancras to Bruxelles-Midi station, from where it's another hour or so by domestic train to get to Bruges, forty minutes to Ghent; there's through-ticketing with Eurostar too. Bruxelles-Midi station is also served by **Thalys** (⊕ thalys.com) international express trains from the likes of Amsterdam, Cologne, Aachen and Paris.

By car
To reach Belgium by car or motorbike from the UK, you can either take the Hull-Zeebrugge car ferry (see below) or use **Le Shuttle train** (Ⓦ eurotunnel. com; formerly Eurotunnel) through the Channel Tunnel from near Folkestone (exit the M20 at junction 11a). Le Shuttle only carries cars (including occupants) and motorbikes, not cyclists and foot passengers. From the exit in Calais, it's just 120km (74.6 miles) to Bruges and 200km (124.3 miles) to Brussels.

Bruges is signed from the E40 motorway, and its oval-shaped centre is encircled by the R30 ring road, which follows the course of the old city walls. **Parking** in the centre can be a real tribulation, with on-street parking almost impossible to find and the city centre's handful of car parks often filled to the gunnels. Easily the best option is to use the massive 24/7 car park by the train station, particularly as the price – €6.10 per day – includes the cost of the bus ride to and from the centre.

Ghent is also well-signed from the E40 motorway and encircled by a ring road. There are free P+R **car parks** on the edge of town and a dozen or so large and metered car parks within the city centre – reckon on €26 for a 24-hour stay, around €14 for six hours. The 24-hour car park beneath the Vrijdagmarkt is one of the best located.

By ferry
At the time of writing, no car ferries are operating between the UK and Belgium – the Hull to Zeebrugge service has been halted, probably for good. The nearest you'll get by car ferry from the UK is on the Hull to Rotterdam service with **P&O Ferries** (Ⓦ poferries.com); the sailing time is around eleven hours; Rotterdam port is 190km (118 miles) from Ghent. Tariffs vary enormously, depending on when you leave, how long you stay, what size your vehicle is and how many passengers are in it; there's also the cost of a cabin to consider.

Getting around

By bus and tram
Local buses in Bruges and buses and trams in Ghent are all operated by **De Lijn** (Ⓦ delijn.be) with a standard one-way fare costing €2.50. Tickets are valid for an hour and can be purchased at automatic ticket machines. A 24-hour city transport pass, the **Dagpas**, costs €7.50. In both cities, there's a **De Lijn information kiosk** outside the train station and they issue free maps of the transport system – as does the tourist information office (see page 145). Note also that a **Ghent city pass** (see page 139) includes public transport.

By bike
Flat as a pair of pancakes, Bruges and Ghent are great places to cycle, especially as there are cycle lanes on many roads and cycle racks dotted across both city centres. Bruges has about a dozen bike rental places – tourist information has the complete list. The largest is **Fietspunt Brugge**, beside the train station (ⓟ 050 39 68 26), where a standard-issue bike costs €15 per day (€6 one hour), plus a small refundable deposit. In Ghent, bike rental is available at St-Pieters train station with the **Blue-bike scheme** (Ⓦ blue-bike.be; registration €12 & €3.5 per day), at the basement of the Stadshal (town pavilion), the distinctive modern building in the city centre beside the Lakenhalle; and from **Biker** (Ⓦ bikerfietsen.be), on the northeast side of the city centre at Steendam 16; for a standard bike, Biker charges €9 per day.

By canal boat

Throughout the season, canal trips explore **Ghent**'s inner waterways, departing from the Korenlei quay, just near the Korenmarkt, as well as from the Vleeshuisbrug, beside the Kraanlei (April–Oct daily 10am–6pm; €9.50). Trips last forty minutes and leave every fifteen minutes or so, though the wait can be longer as boats often delay their departure until they are reasonably full. Similarly, Bruges has canal trips along the city's central canals with boats departing from several jetties south of the Burg (March–Nov daily 10am–6pm; €12). Boats leave every few minutes, but long queues can still build up; in winter (Dec–Feb), there's only a spasmodic service at weekends. There are boat excursions out from Bruges to the town of **Damme** (see page 88).

By horse-drawn carriage

In Bruges, horse-drawn carriages line up on the Markt (daily 10am–10pm; €60 per carriage) to offer a thirty-minute trot around the town centre; expect to queue at the weekend.

By guided cycling tour

In Bruges, **Quasimundo** (ⓦquasimundo.com) runs several cycling tours from outside their bike shop, a short walk east of the Burg at Predtkherenstraat 28. Their 'Bruges by Bike' excursion (March–Oct 1 daily; 2.5hr; €33) zips round the main sights and then explores less-visited parts of the city, while their 'Border by Bike' tour (March–Oct 1 daily; 4hr; €38) is a 25km (15.5 miles) ride out along the poplar-lined canals to the northeast of Bruges, visiting Damme and Oostkerke along the way. The price includes mountain bike and rain-jacket hire; reservations are required.

By guided tour

In Ghent, there are several different types of guided walking tours to choose from. Still, the standard tour, operated by GhentCityGuide (ⓦghentcityguide. be), is a two-hour jaunt around the city centre (May–Sept 1–3 daily; €15); some of these tours include a visit to either the Stadhuis (Mon–Fri) or the cathedral (Sat & Sun). Tickets are on sale at tourist information (see page 145) and booking is recommended. Bruges has a bewildering range of guided tours – beer, scooter, minibus and so forth – and tourist information (see page 145) has the complete list. One of the better options is the '**Bruges from the Heart**' guided walking tour organised by the city's Guides' Association (April–Sept at least 3 weekly; 2hr; €12.50); booking is strongly recommended via ⓦvisitbruges.be.

By taxi

Bruges has several taxi ranks, including one on the Markt and another outside the train station. Fares are metered – and the most common journey, from the train station to the centre, costs about €15; Bruges to Damme costs about €25. Similarly, Ghent has several taxi ranks, including one outside the train station; a taxi from Ghent train station to the centre should cost about €20.

Mosquitoes

These pesky blighters thrive in the canals of Bruges and Ghent and can be a real handful (or mouthful). An antihistamine cream such as Phenergan is the best antidote, although this can be difficult to find – in which case preventative sticks like Autan or citronella are the best bet.

Directory A–Z

Accessible travel

The most obvious difficulty facing people with **mobility problems** is negotiating the cobbled streets and narrow, often broken pavements of the older districts, where the key sights are mainly located. Similarly, provision for people with disabilities on the **public transport system** is only average, although improving – many new buses, for instance, are now wheelchair accessible. And yet, while it can be challenging to get around, practically all **public buildings**, including museums, theatres, cinemas, concert halls and hotels, provide access. Hotels and hostels certified wheelchair-accessible carry the **International Accessibility Symbol (ISA)**. However, remember that many older, narrower hotels are not allowed to install lifts for conservation reasons, so check first.

Addresses

In Flemish-speaking Belgium, the first line of the address gives the name of the street, which is followed by (and joined to) its category – hence Krakeelplein is Krakeel 'square', Krakeelstraat is Krakeel 'street'; the number comes next. The second line gives the area or zip code followed by the town or area. Consequently, Flemish abbreviations occur at the end of words: thus, *Hofstr* for Hofstraat. An exception is *Grote Markt* (Main Square), which is not abbreviated.

Children

Belgian society is generally sympathetic to its children and the tourist industry follows suit. Extra beds in hotel rooms are usually easy to arrange; many restaurants (but not the smartest) have children's menus; concessions for children are the rule, from public transport to museums; and baby-changing stations are commonplace. Pharmacists carry all the kiddy stuff you would expect – nappies, baby food and so forth – and a few hotels offer a babysitting service.

Cinema

Films are usually shown in the original language, with Dutch subtitles as required. In **Bruges**, the Cinema Lumière St-Jacobstraat 36 (Ⓦlumiere-brugge.be) is the premier venue for alternative, cult, foreign and art-house movies, with three screens. In **Ghent**, the Sphinx (Sint-Michielshelling 3 Ⓦ sphinx-cinema.be) focuses on foreign-language and art-house films (with original soundtrack); Studio Skoop (St-Annaplein 63 Ⓦ studioskoop. be) is the cosiest of the city's cinemas, but still with five screens.

Crime and personal safety

Ghent and Bruges are relatively crime-free, though guarding against petty theft is always advisable. If you are robbed, you'll need to go to the police to report it, not least because your insurance company will require a police report; remember to note the report number – or, better still, ask for a copy of the statement itself. As for personal safety, it's generally possible to walk around without fear of harassment or assault, but certain parts of Ghent require a little caution.

Discount passes

In **Bruges**, the **Museum Card**, valid for three days, covers entry to all the main museums and costs €33 (18–25-year-olds €25; 13–17-year-olds €17; Ⓦ museabrugge.be/en/). Depending on exactly which museums you visit, the pass can offer a significant saving compared to buying individual tickets.

Emergency number
For police, fire & emergency medical assistance, call ☎ 112.

Sites not covered by the pass include St-Salvatorskathedraal and gimmicky new attractions like the **Historium** on the Markt, where you can don virtual reality goggles to 'visit' medieval Bruges. Museum passes can be bought at any of the thirteen participants and from the tourist office (see page 145); note that most museums close one day a week, often on Mondays.

In **Ghent**, the money-saving **CityCard Gent** (ⓦ visit.gent.be) covers all the key attractions, provides free and unlimited use of the city's buses and trams and includes a boat trip and a day's bike rental; it costs €38 for 48 hours, €44 for 72 hours. It's on sale at any participant and from tourist information (see page 145).

Electricity
The current is 220 volts AC, with standard European-style two-pin plugs. British equipment needs only a plug adaptor; American apparatus requires a transformer and an adaptor.

Embassies & consulates
For further information, consult ⓦ diplomatie.belgium.be/en
Australia ⓦ australia.diplomatie.belgium.be/en
Canada ⓦ canada.diplomatie.belgium.be/en
Ireland ⓦ ireland.diplomatie.belgium.be/en
Luxembourg ⓦ luxembourg.diplomatie.belgium.be
New Zealand No embassy – see Australia – but there is consular representation in Wellington.
South Africa ⓦ southafrica.diplomatie.belgium.be/en
UK ⓦ unitedkingdom.diplomatie.belgium.be/en

US ⓦ unitedstates.diplomatie.belgium.be/en

Entry requirements
Citizens of the EU (European Union), EEA (European Economic Area), and citizens of the UK, Australia, New Zealand, Canada and the US do not need a visa to enter Belgium if staying for ninety days or less. Still, they need a current passport (or EU national identity card) whose validity exceeds the length of their stay by at least three months. Travellers from South Africa, on the other hand, need a passport and a tourist visa for visits of less than ninety days; visas must be obtained before departure and are available from the appropriate embassy (see below). For stays of longer than ninety days, EU/EEA residents will have few problems, but everyone else needs a mix of visas and permits. In all cases, consult the appropriate embassy at home before departure (see page 146).

Football
Both Ghent and Bruges have top-flight football (soccer) teams. They are Club Brugge (ⓦ clubbrugge.be), who often win the league, and KAA Gent (ⓦ kaagent.be), who rarely win anything. The former plays at the Jan Breydel Stadion, about 5km (3.1 miles) southwest of Bruges city centre; the latter play at the multi-use Ghelamco Arena, about 6km (3.7 miles) south of Ghent city centre. There are buses to the stadiums from both city train stations.

Health and insurance
Under reciprocal health care arrangements, all citizens of the **EU** and **EEA** are entitled to free, or at least subsidised, **medical treatment** within

Belgium's public health care system. With the exception of certain countries, for example, **Australia**, whose governments have reciprocal health agreements with Belgium, **non-EU/EEA** nationals are not entitled to free treatment and should, therefore, take out medical insurance. However, EU/EEA citizens may also want to consider private health insurance to cover the cost of items not within the EU/EEA scheme, such as dental treatment and repatriation on medical grounds and to enable them to seek treatment within the private sector. Note also that the more worthwhile insurance policies promise to sort matters out before you pay (rather than after) in the case of significant expenses; if you have to pay upfront, get and keep the receipts. No inoculations are currently required for Belgium.

If you're seeking treatment under EU/EEA reciprocal health arrangements, it may be necessary to double-check that the medic you see is working within (and seeing you as) a patient of the public system. That being the case, you'll receive subsidised treatment like the locals. Technically, you should have your passport and **European Health Insurance Card (EHIC)** to hand to prove that you are eligible for EU/EEA health care, but often, no one bothers to check. English-speaking medical staff are commonplace. Your hotel will usually be able to arrange – or help to arrange – an appointment with a doctor/dentist, but note that they will almost certainly see you as a private patient.

Finally, minor ailments can often be remedied at a **pharmacy** (*apotheek*): pharmacists are highly trained, willing to give advice and can dispense many drugs that would only be available on prescription in many other countries. Pharmacies are ubiquitous and late-night duty rotas are usually displayed in every pharmacist's window.

LGBTQ+

The LGBTQ+ scene in Ghent, especially Bruges, is distinctly low-key. The legal framework, however, is notably progressive, with, for example, same-sex marriages legalised in Belgium in 2003. The age of consent for men and women is 16.

Money

In Belgium, the currency is the **euro** (€). Each euro is made up of 100 cents. There are seven notes – in denominations of €500, €200, €100, €50, €20, €10 and €5 – and eight different **coins**, specifically €2 and €1, then 50, 20, 10, 5, 2 and 1 cents. Euro notes and coins feature a common EU design on one face but different country-specific designs on the other. Many retailers will not touch the €500 and €200 notes with a bargepole – you must break them down into smaller denominations at the bank. The EU is also considering abolishing the 2 and 1 cent coins. At the time of writing, the **exchange rate** for €1 is £0.86;

Eating out price codes

All the restaurants detailed in this guide have been graded according to the three price categories listed below. These represent how much you can expect to pay in each establishment for a two-course meal for one, excluding a drink.

€	€20–25
€€	€25–40
€€€	€40-plus

US$1.10; CA$1.47; AU$1.67; NZ$1.80; ZAR20.28. For the most up-to-date rates, check the currency converter website ⓦ oanda.com.

All major **credit/debit cards** are widely accepted in both cities. In addition, **ATMs** are liberally distributed across both Bruges and Ghent – and they take a host of debit cards without charging a transaction fee. Credit cards can also be used in ATMs, but in this case, transactions are treated as loans, with interest accruing daily from the withdrawal date. Typically, ATMs give instructions in a variety of languages.

You can change **foreign currency** into euros at most banks, which are ubiquitous; **banking hours** are usually Monday to Friday from 9am to 3.30/4pm, with a few banks also open on Saturday mornings.

Opening hours

Business hours (office hours) generally run from Monday to Friday 9.30/10am to 4.30/5pm. Regular **shopping hours** are Monday through Saturday 10am to 5.30/6pm, though many smaller shops open late on Monday morning and/or close a tad earlier on Saturdays. At the other extreme, larger establishments – primarily supermarkets and department stores – are likely to have extended hours, often on Fridays when many remain open till 9pm and/or on Sundays, usually 10am–5pm. Bruges and Ghent also have a smattering of convenience stores (*avondwinkels*) that stay open all night or until 1/2am daily. Belgium has ten national **public holidays** annually and two regional/provincial holidays (see page 146). For the most part, these holidays are keenly observed, with most businesses and many attractions closed and public transport reduced to a Sunday service.

Phones

All but the remotest parts of Belgium are on the **mobile phone (cell phone)** network at GSM900/1800, the band common to the rest of Europe, Australia and New Zealand. Mobile/cell phones bought in North America will need to be able to adjust to this GSM band. If you intend to use your mobile/cell phone in Belgium, check call rates with your supplier before departing. You may find buying a local SIM card cheaper, though this can get complicated: some mobiles/cells will not permit you to swap SIM cards and the connection instructions for the replacement SIM card may not be in English. If you overcome these problems, you can buy local SIM cards at high-street phone companies, which offer myriad deals beginning at about €5 per SIM card.

There are **no area codes**, but Belgian numbers mostly begin with a zero, a relic of former area codes, which have now been incorporated into the numbers. Telephone numbers starting ☎ 0900 or ☎ 070 are premium-rated, while ☎ 0800 are toll-free. There's no distinction between local and long-distance calls – in other words, calling Ostend from Bruges costs the same as calling a number in Brussels.

ATMs in Bruges and Ghent

Bruges: There is a central ATM at Europabank, Vlamingstraat 13. There are also ATMs at the train station.
Ghent: ING has ATMs at most of its branches, including Belfortstraat 18, and Europabank has an ATM at their branch on the Groentenmarkt.

International calls

To make an international phone call from Belgium, dial the appropriate international access code below, then the number you require, omitting the initial zero where there is one.

Australia ☎0061
Canada ☎001
Republic of Ireland ☎00353
New Zealand ☎0064
South Africa ☎0027
UK ☎0044
US ☎001

Phoning Belgium from abroad

To call Belgium from abroad, dial your international access code, then ☎32 (the country code for Belgium), followed by the subscriber number minus its initial zero where there is one.

Post

Belgium has an efficient postal system with its **post boxes** painted red. Mail to the US takes seven days or so; within Europe, it takes two to three days. **Post offices** are now thin on the ground, but stamps are sold at various outlets, including many shops and hotels. The main post office in Bruges is well to the west of the city centre at Smedenstraat 57 (Mon–Fri 9am–6pm, Sat 9am–3pm); in Ghent, the main post office is at Lange Kruisstraat 55 (Mon–Fri 9.30am–6pm, Sat 9.30am–3pm).

Time

Belgium is on **Central European Time (CET)**, one hour ahead of Greenwich Mean Time (UK), six hours ahead of US Eastern Standard Time, nine hours ahead of US Pacific Standard Time, nine hours behind Australian Eastern Standard Time, and eleven hours behind New Zealand. There are, however, minor variations during the changeover periods involved in **daylight saving**.

Tipping

There's no need to tip when there's a **service charge** – as there often is – but restaurant waitpersons will anticipate a 10 to 15 percent gratuity when there isn't. In **taxis**, passengers should round up the fare.

Toilets

Public toilets are comparatively rare, but some cafés and bars run what amounts to an ablutionary sideline, with an attendant keeping the toilets scrupulously clean and making a minimal charge. Where it still applies, you'll spot the plate for the money as you enter.

Tourist information

In **Bruges**, there are three **tourist information offices**: a small one at the train station (daily 10am–5pm); the main one in the Concertgebouw (Concert Hall) complex, on the west side of the city centre on 't Zand (Mon–Sat 10am–5pm, Sun 10am–2pm); and a third on the Markt (daily 10am–5pm), in the same building as the Historium. They have a common website (ⓦ visitbruges.be).

Ghent's tourist office is located in the Oude Vismijn, opposite the castle on St-Veerleplein (daily: mid-March–mid-Oct 10am–6pm; mid-Oct–mid-March 9.30am–4.30pm; ⓦ visit.gent.be).

Festivals and events

Bruges and Ghent are big on festivals and special events – everything from religious processions to cinema, fairs and contemporary musical binges – and we have listed a selection below. Information on upcoming festivals and events is easy to come by from tourist information and their websites (see page 145).

Late April to mid-May

Meifoor (Bruges) Late April to mid-May; ⓦvisitbruges.be. Bruges's main annual funfair, held on 't Zand and in the adjoining Koning Albertpark.

May

Festival van Vlaanderen (Flanders Festival) (Bruges & Ghent) May–Oct across Flanders; ⓦfestival.be. For over forty years, the Flanders Festival has provided classical music in churches, castles and other impressive venues in over sixty Flemish towns and cities. The festival now comprises more than 120 concerts and features international orchestras. Each big Dutch-speaking city – including Ghent and Bruges – gets a fair crack of the cultural whip, with the festival celebrated for about two weeks in each city before it moves on to the next.

Heilig Bloedprocessie (Procession of the Holy Blood) (Bruges) Ascension Day (forty days after Easter); ⓦvisitbruges.be. One of medieval Christendom's holiest relics, the phial of the Holy Blood, is carried through the centre of Bruges once annually. Nowadays, the procession is as much a tourist attraction as a religious ceremony, but it remains an important event for many citizens of Bruges.

July

Cactusfestival (Bruges) Three days over the second weekend of July; ⓦcactusfestival.be. Going strong for over twenty years, the Cactusfestival is something of a classic. Known for its amiable atmosphere, it proudly pushes against the musical mainstream with rock, reggae, rap, roots and R&B all rolling along together. The festival features both domestic and foreign artists. It's held in Bruges's city centre, in the park beside the Minnewater.

Gentse Feesten (Ghent Festival) Mid- to late July, but always including 21 July; ⓦgentsefeesten.stad.gent. Ghent gets stuck into partying round the clock for ten days every July.

Public holidays in Flanders

New Year's Day (1 Jan)
Easter Monday
Labour Day (1 May)
Ascension Day (forty days after Easter)
Whit Monday
Flemish Day (Flemish-speaking Belgium only; 11 July)
Belgium National Day (21 July)
Assumption (mid-Aug)
All Saints' Day (1 Nov)
Armistice Day (11 Nov)
Christmas Day (25 Dec)
(Note that if any of the above falls on a Sunday, the next day becomes a holiday).

Local bands perform free open-air gigs throughout the city and street performers turn up all over the place.

There's also an outdoor market selling everything from *jenever* (gin) to handmade crafts.

Major venues

Bruges

CONCERTGEBOUW
MAP P.48, POCKET MAP B7
't Zand 34 Ⓦ concertgebouw.be.
Outstanding concert hall, built in 2002, hosting all the performing arts, from opera and classical music to big-name bands. It offers enjoyable fifty-minute guided tours, too.

STADSSCHOUWBURG
MAP P.72, POCKET MAP C5
Vlamingstraat 29 Ⓦ ccbrugge.be.
Occupying a big neo-Renaissance building from 1869, with a wide-ranging programme, including theatre, dance, musicals, concerts and opera.

Ghent

CONCERTZAAL HANDELSBEURS
MAP P.96, POCKET MAP C14
Kouter 29 Ⓦ haconcerts.be/en.
The city's primary concert hall has two auditoria and hosts a diverse programme.

MUZIEKCENTRUM DE BIJLOKE
MAP P.120., POCKET MAP D16
Godhuizenlaan 2 Ⓦ bijloke.be.
The old Bijloke abbey complex now holds the STAM historical museum (see page 119) and a Muziekcentrum, which includes a smart new Concert Hall.

NT GENT SCHOUWBURG
MAP P.96, POCKET MAP C13
ST-BAAFSPLEIN 17 Ⓦ NTGENT.BE.
Municipal theatre accommodating the Nederlands Toneel Gent, the regional repertory company. Most of their performances are in Flemish, though they host touring English-language theatre companies.

VLAAMSE OPERA GENT
MAP P.96, POCKET MAP C14
Schouwburgstraat 3 Ⓦ operaballet.be.
Handsomely restored nineteenth-century opera house, where the city's opera company performs when not on tour.

VOORUIT – VIERNULVIER
MAP P.120, POCKET MAP D15
St-Pietersnieuwstraat 23 Ⓦ viernulvier.gent/en.
The leading venue for rock, pop, dance, theatre and jazz (see page 123).

Moods (Bruges) Two weeks, usually from the last weekend of July; ⓦmoodsbrugge.be. Bruges's biggest annual knees-up and the chance for city folk to let their hair down. There are big-time concerts on the Markt and the Burg, the city's two main squares, more intimate performances in various bars and cafés, plus all sorts of other entertainments. It's Bruges at its best and most events are free.

Musica Antiqua (Bruges) Four days in early August; ⓦmafestival.be. Part of the Festival van Vlaanderen (see page 146), this well-established and well-regarded festival of medieval music offers an extensive programme of live performances at a variety of venues in Bruges. The evening concerts are built around themes, while the lunchtime concerts are more episodic. Tickets go on sale in February and are snapped up fast.

August

Praalstoet van de Gouden Boom (Pageant of the Golden Tree) (Bruges) Held over two days on the last weekend of August, this pageant features all sorts of mock-medieval heartiness, and thousands congregate in central Bruges to join in the fun. First staged in 1958, it was traditionally held every five years – but now it seems to have been moved to every two; the next one is due in 2024.

October

Ghent Film Festival (Ghent) Eleven days in October; ⓦfilmfestival.be. This is one of Europe's foremost cinematic events in which the city's cinemas (see page 141) combine to present around two hundred feature films and a hundred shorts from all over the world. Many movies are screened long before they hit the international circuit. There's also a particular focus on music in film.

December

The Arrival of St Nicholas (aka Santa Klaus) (Bruges and Ghent) 6 Dec. The arrival of St Nicholas from his long sojourn abroad is celebrated by processions and the giving of sweets to children across Belgium.

Kerstmarkt (Christmas Market) (Bruges) December daily 11am–10pm. Bruges' Christmas Market occupies the Markt with brightly lit stalls selling food, drink, souvenirs and everything Christmassy. Part of the Markt is also turned into an ice rink – and you can rent skates.

Chronology

630 The French missionary St Amand establishes an abbey on the site of present-day Ghent, at the confluence of the rivers Leie and Scheldt.

865 The splendidly named Baldwin Iron Arm, the first count of Flanders, founds Bruges as a coastal stronghold against the Vikings.

Tenth century The wool industry takes root in Flanders. The leading Flemish cloth towns are Bruges and Ghent.

Twelfth to late-fourteenth century The Flemish cloth industry becomes dependent on English wool. Flanders enjoys an unprecedented economic boom and its merchants become immensely rich. However, there is increasing tension – and bouts of warfare – between the merchants and weavers of Flanders, for whom friendship with England is vital, and their feudal overlords, the counts of Flanders, who are vassals of England's traditional enemy, the kings of France. Ghent becomes the seat of the counts of Flanders and the largest town in Western Europe.

1302 The citizens of Bruges massacre the French garrison that had been billeted upon them during the Bruges Matins (May) – anyone who fails to correctly pronounce the Flemish shibboleth *schild en vriend* (meaning 'shield and friend') is put to the sword. At the Battle of the Golden Spurs (July), the Flemish militia defeat the French army, slaughtering hundreds of heavily armoured knights

1384 The dukes of Burgundy inherit Flanders.

1419 Philip the Good, duke of Burgundy, makes Bruges his capital. The Burgundian court becomes known across Europe for its cultured opulence and its male courtiers' elongated, pointy shoes.

1467 Philip the Good dies.

1482 The Habsburg Empire absorbs Flanders when Mary, the last of the Burgundians, dies and her husband, Maximilian, a Habsburg prince, inherits her territories.

1480s onwards The Flemish cloth industry enters a decline.

1530s Bruges's international trade collapses and the town slips into a long decline. Ghent merchants switch from industry to trade to keep the city going – if not exactly flourishing.

Mid-sixteenth to seventeenth century The Protestants of the Low Countries (modern-day Belgium and The Netherlands) rebel against their Catholic Habsburg rulers. A long and cruel series of wars ensues. Eventually, The Netherlands wins its independence – as the United

Provinces – but the south, including Flanders, fails to escape the Habsburgs and is reconstituted as the Spanish Netherlands.

1700 The last of the Spanish Habsburgs, Charles II, dies; the War of the Spanish Succession follows.

1713 The Treaty of Utrecht cedes what is now Belgium, including Flanders, to the Austrians – as the Austrian Netherlands.

1794 Napoleon occupies the Austrian Netherlands and annexes it to France the following year.

1815 Napoleon is defeated at Waterloo, near Brussels, and the Austrian Netherlands becomes half of the new 'Kingdom of The Netherlands'.

1830 A rebellion led to the new kingdom's collapse and the creation of an independent Belgium, including Flanders.

Mid- to late nineteenth century Much of Belgium industrialises, including Ghent but not Bruges, whose antique charms attract a first wave of tourists.

1913 Ghent stages the Great Exhibition, showing the best contemporary design and goods.

1914–1945 The Germans occupy Bruges and Ghent in both world wars. The cities remain largely unscathed, but many citizens are not so lucky. Post-war retribution for Belgian collaborators: 56,000 alleged collaborators are prosecuted, 250 are executed.

Late 1940s to 1950s Historical tensions between Belgium's French- and Dutch-speaking regions augment and ferment.

1962 Entrenching animosities: creation of the Belgian 'Language Frontier' distinguishing French- from Flemish-speaking Belgium.

1980 More communal entrenchment: Belgium adopts a federal form of government with three regions – the Flemish north, the Walloon (French-speaking) south and bilingual Brussels. Dutch-speaking Flanders includes the two provinces of East and West Flanders (Ghent is in East Flanders, Bruges in the West).

1990 A right royal pantomime when Catholic King Baudouin abdicates for the day while the law legalising abortion is ratified.

2002 Out with the Belgian franc and in with the euro.

2003 Belgium becomes the second country in the world to legalise same-sex marriage.

2010–14 Political failure: after Belgium's federal elections in 2010, it takes more than a year to create a ruling coalition amidst much Walloon/Flemish disputation. There is a repeat performance four years later – but this time, the interregnum lasts for five months. The Flemish Parliament carries on pretty much regardless.

2013 Philippe/Filip becomes king of the Belgians to a mixed reception.

2014 In regional elections, the conservative, nationalistic New Flemish Alliance (N-VA; *Nieuw-Vlaamse Alliantie*) cements its position as the largest party in Flanders.

2016 Savage jihadist attack on Brussels' airport leaves 35 dead.

2018 Embarrassments galore: the Belgian army is much mocked for its plans to allow homesick recruits to sleep at home rather than in barracks; Prince Laurent, the younger brother of King Philippe, has his federal allowance reduced after a series of mistakes, which have earnt him the nickname the *écolo-gaffeur* (eco-blunderer).

2019 In federal elections, many voters switch from the political centre to the right and left. Nearly half of the Flemish voters support one of the right-wing separatist parties, principally the New Flemish Alliance (N-VA; *Nieuw-Vlaamse Alliantie*).

2020 Alexander De Croo becomes prime minister at the head of an unwieldy coalition.

2022 King Phillippe visits the Congo and regrets his country's colonial record there – but doesn't offer reparations.

Language

Throughout the northern part of Belgium, including West and East Flanders – which covers Bruges and Ghent – the principal language is Dutch, which is spoken in a variety of distinctive dialects commonly described as 'Flemish'. Dutch-speaking Belgians commonly refer to themselves as Flemish speakers and most of them, particularly in the tourist industry, also speak English to varying degrees of excellence. Indeed, Flemish speakers have a seemingly natural talent for languages, and your attempts at speaking theirs may be met with bewilderment – though this can have as much to do with your pronunciation (Dutch/Flemish is tough to get right) as surprise that you're making an effort.

Consequently, the following words and phrases should be the most you'll need to get by. We've also included a basic **food and drink** glossary, though menus are nearly always multilingual; where they aren't, ask, and one will almost invariably appear.

Pronunciation

Dutch is **pronounced** much the same as English, though a few Dutch sounds don't exist in English and these can be difficult to get right without practice.

Consonants

j is an English **y**, as in **y**ellow

ch and **g** indicate a throaty sound, as at the end of the Scottish word loch. The Dutch word for canal – *gracht* – is especially tricky since it has two of these sounds – it comes out sounding something like *khrakht*. A common word for hello is *Dag!* – pronounced like *daakh*

ng as in bring

nj as in onion

y is not a consonant, but another way of writing ij

Double-consonant combinations generally keep their separate sounds in Flemish: **kn**, for example, is never like the English 'knight'.

Vowels and diphthongs

A good rule of thumb is doubling the letter lengthens the vowel sound.

a is like the English **a**pple

aa like c**a**rt

e like l**e**t

ee like l**a**te

o as in p**o**p

oo in p**o**pe

u is like the French t**u** if preceded by a consonant; it's like w**oo**d if followed by a consonant

uu is like the French t**u**

au and **ou** like h**ow**

ei and **ij** as in fine, though this varies from region to region; sometimes, it can sound more like l**a**ne

oe as in s**oo**n

eu is like the diphthong in the French l**eu**r

ui is the hardest Dutch diphthong of all, pronounced like h**ow** but much further forward in the mouth, with lips pursed (as if to say 'oo').

Words and phrases

Basic expressions

ja yes
nee no
alstublieft please
dank u or bedankt thank you
hallo or dag hello
goedemorgen good morning
goedemiddag good afternoon
goedenavond good evening
tot ziens goodbye
tot straks see you later
Spreekt u Engels? Do you speak English?
Ik begrijp het niet I don't understand
vrouwen/mannen women/men
kinderen children
heren/dames men's/women's toilets
Ik wil ... I want ...
Ik wil niet... I don't want to ... **(+verb)**
Ik wil geen ... I don't want any ... **(+noun)**
Wat kost ...? How much is ...?
sorry sorry
hier/daar here/there
goed/slecht good/bad
groot/klein big/small
open/gesloten open/closed
duwen/trekken push/pull
nieuw/oud new/old
goedkoop/duur cheap/expensive
heet or warm/koud hot/cold
met/zonder with/without
Hoe kom ik in ...? How do I get to ...?
Waar is ...? Where is ...?
Hoe ver is het How far is it to ...?
Wanneer? When?
ver/dichtbij far/near
links/rechts left/right
rechtdoor straight ahead
alle richtingen all directions (road sign)
postkantoor post office
postzegel(s) stamp(s)
geldwisselkantoor money exchange
kassa cash desk

spoor or **perron** railway platform
loket ticket office

Useful cycling terms

fiets bicycle
fietspad bicycle path
band tyre
lek puncture
rem brake
ketting chain
wiel wheel
trapper pedal
pomp pump
stuur handlebars
kapot broken

Numbers

nul 0
een 1
twee 2
drie 3
vier 4
vijf 5
zes 6
zeven 7
acht 8
negen 9
tien 10
elf 11
twaalf 12
dertien 13
veertien 14
vijftien 15
zestien 16
zeventien 17
achttien 18
negentien 19
twintig 20
een en twintig 21
twee en twintig 22
dertig 30
veertig 40
vijftig 50
zestig 60
zeventig 70
tachtig 80
negentig 90
honderd 100
honderd een 101
twee honderd 200

twee honderd een 201
vijf honderd 500
vijf honderd vijf en twintig 525
duizend 1000

Days

maandag Monday
dinsdag Tuesday
woensdag Wednesday
donderdag Thursday
vrijdag Friday
zaterdag Saturday
zondag Sunday
gisteren yesterday
vandaag today
morgen tomorrow
morgenochtend tomorrow morning
jaar year
maand month
week week
dag day

Months

januari January
februari February
maart March
april April
mei May
juni June
juli July
augustus August
september September
oktober October
november November
december December

Time

uur hour
minuut minute
Hoe laat is het? What time is it?
Het is ... It's ...
drie uur 3.00
vijf over drie 3.05
tien over drie 3.10
kwart over drie 3.15
tien voor half vier 3.20
vijf voor half vier 3.25
half vier 3.30
vijf over half vier 3.35
tien over half vier 3.40

kwart voor vier 3.45
tien voor vier 3.50
vijf voor vier 3.55
acht uur 's ochtends 8am
een uur 's middags 1pm
acht uur 's avonds 8pm
een uur 's nachts 1am

Food and drink terms

Basic terms and ingredients

belegd filled or topped, as in belegde
broodjes (bread rolls topped with cheese, etc)
boter butter
boterham/broodje sandwich/roll
brood bread
dranken drinks
eieren eggs
gerst barley
groenten vegetables
Hollandse saus hollandaise sauce
honing honey
hoofdgerechten main courses
kaas cheese
koud cold
nagerechten desserts
peper pepper
pindakaas peanut butter
sla/salade salad
smeerkaas cheese spread
stokbrood french bread
suiker sugar
vis fish
vlees meat
voorgerechten starters/hors d'oeuvres
vruchten fruit
warm hot
zout salt

Cooking methods

doorbakken well-done
half doorbakken medium well-done
gebakken fried or baked
gebraden roast
gegrild grilled
gekookt boiled
geraspt grated
gerookt smoked
gestoofd stewed
rood rare

Starters and snacks

erwtensoep/snert thick pea soup with bacon
or sausage
huzarensalade potato salad with pickles
koffietafel light midday meal of cold meats,
cheese, bread, and perhaps soup
patat/friet chips/french fries
soep soup
uitsmijter ham or cheese with eggs on bread

Meat and poultry

biefstuk (hollandse) steak
biefstuk (duitse) hamburger
eend duck
fricandeau roast pork
fricandel frankfurter-like sausage
gehakt minced meat
ham ham
kalfsvlees veal
kalkoen turkey
karbonadea chop
kip chicken
kroket spiced veal or beef in hash, coated in
breadcrumbs
lamsvlees lamb
lever liver
ossenhaas tenderloin beef
rookvlees smoked beef
spek bacon
wurst sausages

Fish and seafood

forel trout
garnalen prawns
haring herring
haringsalade herring salad
kabeljauw cod
makreel mackerel
mosselen mussels
oesters oysters
paling eel
schelvis haddock
schol plaice
tong sole
zalm salmon
zeeduivel monkfish

Vegetables

aardappelen potatoes
bloemkool cauliflower

154

LANGUAGE

bonen beans
champignons mushrooms
erwten peas
hutspot mashed potatoes and carrots
knoflook garlic
komkommer cucumber
prei leek
rijst rice
sla salad, lettuce
stampot andijvie mashed potato and endive
stampot boerenkool mashed potato and cabbage
uien onions
wortelen carrots
zuurkool sauerkraut

Sweets and desserts

appelgebak apple tart or cake
gebak pastry
ijs ice cream
koekjes biscuits
pannenkoeken pancakes
pepernoten ginger nuts
poffertjes small pancakes, fritters
(slag)room(whipped) cream
speculaas spice and cinnamon-flavoured biscuit
stroopwafels waffles
vla custard

Fruits

aardbei strawberry

amandel almond
appel apple
appelmoes apple purée
citroen lemon
druiven grape
framboos raspberry
kers cherry
peer pear
perzik peach
pruim plum/prune

Drinks

anijsmelk aniseed-flavoured warm milk
appelsap apple juice
bessenjenever blackcurrant gin
chocomel chocolate milk
citroenjenever lemon gin
droog dry
frisdranken soft drinks
jenever a Dutch/Belgian gin
karnemelk buttermilk
koffie coffee
koffie verkeerd coffee with warm milk
kopstoot beer with a **jenever** chaser
melk milk
met ijs with ice
met slagroom with whipped cream
pils beer
proost! cheers!
sinaasappelsap orange juice
thee tea
tomatensap tomato juice
vruchtensap fruit juice

Flemish specialities

hutsepot a winter warmer consisting of various bits of beef and pork (often including pigs' trotters and ears) casseroled with turnips, celery, leeks and parsnips.
konijn met pruimen rabbit with prunes.
paling in 't groen eel braised in a green (usually spinach) sauce with herbs.
stoemp mashed potato mixed with vegetable and/or meat purée.
stoofvlees cubes of beef marinated in beer and cooked with herbs and onions.
stoverij stewed beef and offal (especially liver and kidneys), slowly tenderised in dark beer and served with a slice of bread covered in mustard.
waterzooi a delicious, filling soup-cum-stew, made with either chicken (*van kip*) or fish (*van riviervis*).

wijn wine
(wit/rood/rosé) (white/red/rosé)

vieux Dutch brandy
zoet sweet

Glossary

Dutch terms

Abdij Abbey

Begijnhof Convent occupied by beguines (*begijns*), members of a sisterhood living as nuns but without vows, retaining the right to return to the secular world.

Beiaard Carillon (set of tuned church bells, either operated by an automatic mechanism or played by a keyboard)

BG (Begane grond) Ground floor ('basement' is K for kelder)

Belfort Belfry

Beurs Stock exchange

Botermarkt Butter market

Brug Bridge

Burgher Member of the upper or mercantile classes of a town, usually with certain civic powers

Geen toegang No entry

Gemeente Municipal, as in Gemeentehuis (Town Hall)

Gerechtshof Law Courts

Gesloten Closed

Gevel Gable: decoration on narrow-fronted canal houses

Gilde Guild

Gracht Canal

Groentenmarkt Vegetable market

(Grote) markt Central town square and the heart of most north Belgian communities, typically still the site of weekly markets

Hal Hall

Hof Courtyard

Huis House

Ingang Entrance

Jeugdherberg Youth hostel

Kaai Quay or wharf

Kapel Chapel

Kasteel Castle

Kerk Church; eg, Grote Kerk – the principal church of the town

Koning King

Koningin Queen

Koninklijk Royal

Korenmarkt Corn market

Kunst Art

Lakenhal Cloth hall: the building in medieval weaving towns where cloth would be weighed, graded and sold

Let Op! Attention!

Luchthaven Airport

Molen Windmill

Noord North

Ommegang Procession

Onze-Lieve-Vrouwekerk or OLV Church of Our Lady

Oost East

Paleis Palace

Plaats/Plein A square or open space

Polder An area of land reclaimed from the sea

Poort Gate

Postbus Post box

Raadhuis Town Hall

Rijk State

Schatkamer Treasury

Schepenzaal Alderman's Hall

Schone kunsten Fine arts

Schouwburg Theatre

Sierkunst Decorative arts

Spoor Track (as in railway) – trains arrive and depart on track (as distinct from platform) numbers

Stadhuis Town Hall

Stedelijk Civic, municipal

Steeg Alley

Steen Stone

Stichting Institute or foundation

Straat Street

Toegang Entrance

Toren Tower

Tuin Garden

Uitgang Exit

VA (Vanaf) 'From'

Vleeshuis Meat market

Volkskunde Folklore

Weg Way

West West

Zuid South

SMALL PRINT

Publishing Information
Second edition 2024

Distribution

UK, Ireland and Europe
Apa Publications (UK) Ltd; sales@roughguides.com
United States and Canada
Ingram Publisher Services; ips@ingramcontent.com
Australia and New Zealand
Booktopia; retailer@booktopia.com.au
Worldwide
Apa Publications (UK) Ltd; sales@roughguides.com

Special Sales, Content Licensing and CoPublishing

Rough Guides can be purchased in bulk quantities at discounted prices. We can create special editions, personalised jackets and corporate imprints tailored to your needs. sales@roughguides.com.
roughguides.com

Printed in Czech Republic

This book was produced using **Typefi** automated publishing software.

A catalogue record for this book is available from the British Library

The publishers and authors have done their best to ensure the accuracy and currency of all the information in **Pocket Rough Guide Bruges and Ghent**, however, they can accept no responsibility for any loss, injury, or inconvenience sustained by any traveller as a result of information or advice contained in the guide.

Rough Guide Credits

Editor: Kate Drynan
Cartography: Katie Bennett
Picture Manager: Tom Smyth
Layout: Pradeep Thapliyal

Original design: Richard Czapnik
Head of DTP and Pre-Press: Rebeka Davies
Head of Publishing: Sarah Clark

Acknowledgements

Phil Lee would like to thank his editor, Kate Dynan, for her efficiency and helpfulness during the preparation of this new edition. Special thanks also to the superbly efficient Anita Rampall of Visit Flanders; Ann Plovie of Visit Bruges for her detailed assistance and suggestions; Melina De Weirdt of Visit Gent for a string of tips and hints; and Erwin van de Wiele, also of Visit Gent, for his hospitality, conversation and enthusiasm.

Help us update

Please send your comments with the subject line "**Pocket Rough Guide Bruges and Ghent Update**" to mail@uk.roughguides.com.

Photo Credits

(Key: T-top; C-centre; B-bottom; L-left; R-right)

Alamy 23T, 23B, 25C, 25B, 27, 32, 41, 44, 58, 59, 63, 80, 81, 82, 87, 90, 103, 105, 106, 114, 117, 118, 122, 124
Anthony De Meyere/Design Museum Gent 18B, 22B
Bistro Pro Deo 86
City Damme/Jan Darthet 93
De Orangerie 128/129
De Stove 35
Diksmuids Boterhuis 33
EKKOW/The Chocolate Line 16T
Galerie St-John, Ghent 112
Getty Images 14B, 19T, 69, 110, 111, 123, 125
iStock 2BL, 16B, 17T, 20C, 28, 57
Jürgen de Witte 25T
Kantcentrum 79
Lio's Bruges 68
Neuhaus 65
OlegAlbinsky 31
Pavlina Photography 115

Public domain 15C
Reddiplomat 29
Rough Guides 45, 84, 85
Sarah Bauwens/Musea Brugge 17B, 20B, 50, 51, 52, 53
Shutterstock 1, 2TL, 2C, 2BR, 4, 5, 12, 13T, 13B, 14T, 18T, 19B, 20T, 21T, 21C, 22T, 22C, 23C, 24T, 24C, 30, 36, 37, 38, 39, 40, 42, 43, 47, 54, 56, 60, 61, 62, 64, 66, 67, 70, 71, 74, 75, 76, 78, 89, 91, 92, 94, 95, 98, 99, 100, 101, 102, 104, 107, 109, 116, 136/137
Stad Brugge 24B, 49
Superstock 119
Toerisme Brugge/Jan D'Hondt 6, 21D, 46, 83
Think Twice 34
Tierenteyn 113
Viernulvier 127
Visit Flanders 14/15B
www.melvinkobe.com 126

Cover Canal in Bruges **Shutterstock**

Index

INDEX

A

accessible travel 141
accommodation, Bruges 130
accommodation, Ghent 134
addresses 141
Adoration of the Mystic Lamb,
 The 110
Adornesdomein 76
airport 138
Arentspark 46
arrival 139
Arrival and information
 Damme 89
ATMs in Bruges and Ghent 144

B

bars and clubs
 Bar Ran
 Bar Rose Red 45
 Bistro du Phare 87
 Café Vlissinghe 87
 Decadance 127
 De Garre 45
 De Trollekelder 117
 De Windmolen 87
 Dulle Griet 116
 Het Brugs Beertje 69
 Het Waterhuis aan de Bierkant
  117
 Hotsy Totsy 117
 L'Estaminet 69
 Lio's 69
 Lokkedize 69
 Missy Sippy Blues & Roots
  Club 117
 Republiek 87
 Rock Circus 127
 't Dreupelkot 116
 Vooruit 127
bars and clubs (by area)
 Central Ghent 116
 North and east of the Markt
  87
 Southern and eastern Ghent
  127
 South of the Markt 69
 The Burg 45
B&Bs in Bruges 133
 Barabas 133
 Het Wit Beertje 133
 Huis Koning 133
 Number 11 133
 Sint-Niklaas B&B 133
B&Bs in Ghent 135
 At Genesis 135
 De Waterzooi 135
 Simon Says 135

beer 84
Begijnhof 63
Belfort 31
Belfort, Ghent 99
bells 31
Bij St-Jacobs 107
boat trips 100
Bosch, Hieronymus 53
Bourgogne des Flandres 43
Breydel, Jan 28
Brouwerij De Halve Maan 63
buses, local 139

C

cafés
 Blackbird 86
 Burger Boutique 126
 Café Labath 114
 De Bron 66
 De Verbeelding 67
 Grand Café Craenenburg 34
 Greenway 126
 Julie's House 114
 Lb DbB 34
 Le Pain Quotidien 66
 Mayana Chocoladebar 126
 Souplounge 114
 Take Five 114
 Tante Marie 93
 Tea-room Laurent 67
 Vero Caffé 44
cafés (by area)
 Central Ghent 114
 Damme 93
 North and east of the Markt
  86
 Southern and eastern Ghent
  126
 South of the Markt 66
 The Burg 44
 The Markt 34
canal boats 139
Charles II in Bruges 83
Charles the Bold 55
Charles the Good 41
children 141
chronology 148
cinema 141
Citadelpark 119
CityCard Ghent 95
climate 5
Coninck, Pieter de 28
crime and personal safety 141
cycle hire 139
cycling 139
Cycling around Damme 92
cycling tours 140

D

Damme 88
David, Gerard 53
Design Museum 103
directory A–Z 141
discount passes 141
drinking 7
Dulle Griet 107

E

eating 7
electricity 142
embassies 142
emergency number 142
Engels Klooster 81
entry requirements 142
Eyck, Jan van 52

F

ferry 139
festivals and events 146
 Cactusfestival (Bruges) 146
 Festival van Vlaanderen
  (Flanders Festival) 146
 Gentse Feesten (Ghent Festival)
  146
 Ghent Film Festival (Ghent)
  148
 Heilig Bloedprocessie
  (Procession of the Holy
  Blood) (Bruges) 146
 Kerstmarkt (Christmas Market)
  (Bruges) 148
 Meifoor (Bruges 146
 Moods (Bruges) 148
 Musica Antiqua (Bruges) 148
 Praalstoet van de Gouden Boom
  (Pageant of the Golden Tree)
  (Bruges) 148
 The Arrival of St Nicholas (aka
  Santa Klaus) (Bruges and
  Ghent) 148
Flemish Primitives 52
Flemish specialities 154
football 142

G

gates 77
gay and lesbian scene 143
Geeraard de Duivelsteen 108
Gerechtshof 40
getting around 139
Ghent 94
glossary 155
Goes, Hugo van der 52

going out 7
Grand Café Craenenburg 30
Graslei 102
Groeninge Museum 49
Groentenmarkt 102
Gruuthuse Museum 48
guided tours 140
Guido Gezellehuis 80
guild houses 102

H

Hallen 32
health 142
Heilig Bloed Basiliek 36
Het Gravensteen 104
Holy Blood 37
horse-drawn carriage 140
hostels in Bruges 133
   Bruges Europa 133
   Snuffel Hostel 133
   St Christopher's Bauhaus 133
hostels in Ghent 135
   Jeugdherberg De Draecke 135
   Uppelink Hostel 135
hotels in Bruges 130
   Adornes 130
   Alegria 130
   Aragon 130
   Augustyn 131
   De Goezeput 131
   De Orangerie 132
   Die Swaene 133
   Fevery 131
   Jacobs 131
   Jan Brito 131
   Monsieur Ernest 132
   Montanus 132
   Navarra 132
   Red Rose 132
   Ter Duinen 133
hotels in Ghent 134
   Boatel 134
   Chamade 134
   Comic Art Hotel 134
   De Flandre 134
   Erasmus 134
   Ghent Marriott Hotel 134
   Ghent River 134
   Harmony 134
   Monasterium Poortackere 134
   NH Gent Belfort 135
   Novotel Gent Centrum 135
   Pillows Grand Boutique Hotel Reylof 135
Huis van Alijn Museum 106

I

insurance 142
international calls 145
itineraries 20

J

Jacob van Artevelde 108
Jan van Eyckplein 71
Jeruzalemkerk 76

K

Kantcentrum 78
Korenlei 103
Korenmarkt 100
Kraanlei 105
Kraanplein 71
Kunsthal Caermersklooster 105

L

Lakenhalle 99
language 150
Lieven Bauwensplein 108
Lobster Pot 67

M

major venues 147
   Concertgebouw 147
   Concertzaal Handelsbeurs 147
   Muziekcentrum De Bijloke 147
   NT Gent Schouwburg 147
   Stadsschouwburg 147
   Vlaamse Opera Gent 147
   Vooruit – Viernulvier 147
maps
   Bruges at a glance 8
   Central Ghent 96
   Cycling around Damme 91
   Damme 88
   Ghent at a glance 10
   North and east of the Markt, Bruges 72
   Southern and eastern Ghent 120
   South of the Markt, Bruges 48
   The Burg, Bruges 38
   The Markt, Bruges 30
Markets 101
Markets in Bruges 48
Mary of Burgundy 55
Memling Collection 58
Minnewater 64
money 143
Monument to Pieter de Coninck and Jan Breydel 28
mosquitoes 140
MSK (Museum voor Schone Kunsten) 122
Museum Onze-Lieve-Vrouw ter Potterie 82
Museum voor Volkskunde 79
Mystic Lamb 110

N

Nepomucenusbrug 43
North and East of the Markt 70

O

Onze-Lieve-Vrouwekerk 54, 91
opening hours 144
Order of the Golden Fleece 61
Oude Civiele Griffie 40
Oude Vismijn 104
Overpoortstraat 124

P

parking 139
Patershol 105
phones 144
post 145
Provinciaal Hof 29
public holidays in Flanders 146

R

Renaissancezaal 't Brugse Vrije 40
restaurants
   Assiette Blanche 45
   Bistro Bruut 45
   Bistro de Pompe 35
   Boem Patat 67
   Boon 114
   Christophe 67
   Chubby Cheeks 114
   De Lamme Goedzak 93
   De Lieve 115
   Den Amand 35
   Den Gouden Karpel 45
   De Raadkamer 116
   De Schaar 68
   De Stove 35
   Domestica 114
   Du Progrès 116
   Franco Belge 86
   Goesepitte 43 67
   Heritage 114
   Le Baan Thai 114
   Lepelblad 115
   Locàle by Kok au Vin 86
   Maison Elza 115
   Martino 127
   Midtown Grill 115
   Réliva 68
   Roots 116
   Sans Cravate 87
   Tanuki 68
restaurants (by area)
   Central Ghent 114
   Damme 93
   North and east of the Markt 86
   Southern and eastern Ghent 127

South of the Markt 67
The Burg 45
The Markt 35

S

Schuttersgilde St-Sebastiaan 80
shopping 7
shops
  2be Beer Wall 44
  Atlas and Zanzibar 126
  Boeken Diogenes 93
  Brugse Boekhandel 65
  Chocolaterie Luc van Hoorebeke 112
  Classics 65
  Dag en Zonne 86
  De Corte 33
  De Reyghere 34
  De Striep 66
  Diksmuids Boterhuis 33
  FNAC 112
  Galerie St-John 112
  Het Mekka van de Kaas 113
  Himschoot 113
  INNO 33
  Interphilia 113
  Kingin 86
  Leonidas 65
  Music Mania 126
  Neuhaus 65, 113
  Olivier's Chocolate Shop 33
  Priem 113
  Proxy Delhaize Noordzand 33
  Quicke 65
  Reisboekhandel 34
  Rombaux 44
  't Apostelientje 86
  The Bottle Shop 44
  The Chocolate Line 65
  The Fallen Angels 112
  Think Twice 34
  Tierenteyn 113
  Worlds' End Comic and Games Centre 113
shops (by area)
  Central Ghent 112
  Damme 93
  North and east of the Markt 86
  Southern and eastern Ghent 126
  South of the Markt 65
  The Burg 44
  The Markt 33
S.M.A.K. (Stedelijk Museum voor Actuele Kunst) 119
Southern and eastern Ghent 118
South of the Markt 46
Spanjaardstraat 75
Spiegelrei canal 74
Stadhuis, Bruges 39
Stadhuis, Damme 89
Stadhuis, Ghent 95
STAM 119
St-Annakerk 76
St-Baafsabdij 124
St-Baafskathedraal 94
St Bavo 95, 125
St-Donaaskathedraal 42
St-Gilliskerk 75
St-Jakobskerk 70
St-Janshospitaal 56
St-Janshospitaalmuseum 57
St-Jorishof 108
St-Michielsbrug 100
St-Michielskerk 100
St-Niklaaskerk 99
St-Pietersabdij 124

St-Salvatorskathedraal 60
St-Veerleplein 103
St-Walburgakerk 75

T

tapestries in Bruges 62
taxis 140
The Battle of Sluys 90
The Burg 36
The disappearance of Sir Frank Brangwyn 47
The Markt 28
The Museum Card 29
time 145
tipping 145
toilets 145
tourist information 145
tours 98
trains 138
trams 139

U

Uilenspiegel Museum 90

V

Van Eyck monument 109
Veldstraat 109
Vismarkt 43
Vooruit 123
Vrijdagmarkt 107

W

walking tours 98
weather 5
windmills 77

CONTENTS

Introduction 4

Best places to explore on two wheels........................ 5
When to visit.. 6
Where to... 7
Copenhagen at a glance 8
Things not to miss..10
Itineraries..18

Places 23

Tivoli and Rådhuspladsen...24
Strøget and the Inner City 30
Slotsholmen..42
Nyhavn and Frederiksstaden....................................48
Rosenborg and around 58
Christianshavn and Holmen......................................68
Vesterbro and Frederiksberg....................................76
Nørrebro and Østerbro 86
Day-trips..94
Malmü 102

Accommodation 107

Essentials 115

Arrival 116
Getting around...116
Directory A–Z 118
Festivals and events 122
Danish 122
Chronology..123
Small print..126

COPENHAGEN

Once a low-key underrated city, for the past decade, the Danish capital has been showered with superlatives, with polls claiming it to have the best quality of life and rating its citizens the happiest people on the planet. If that wasn't enough, accolades for its cuisine, metro, cycling and design have followed, and Danish TV dramas continue to bring its Nordic style, gritty architecture and photogenic inhabitants into millions of living rooms. Despite its new-found glory, Copenhagen remains a relaxed, homely place where visitors quickly feel at ease; and while all this cool contentment doesn't come cheap (for tourists and locals alike) the "great Dane" has quite definitely arrived as one of Europe's outstanding destinations.

Exhibition Hall in Louisiana Museum

Cycling in Copenhagen

Part of Copenhagen's appeal is its hybrid nature, a unique blend of mainland Europe and Scandinavia. The city looks as much to London, Berlin and Amsterdam as it does to Stockholm or Oslo, perhaps a legacy of its swashbuckling seafaring and trading history. Its gregarious English-speaking inhabitants can also seem positively welcoming compared with the icy reserve of their northerly neighbours.

If the city lacks anything you could say it's a true "blockbuster" attraction. Aside from the Little Mermaid and arguably the Tivoli Gardens, Copenhagen doesn't do the "queue round the block" tourism, while its most illustrious former inhabitants (Hans Christian Andersen aside) don't quite make the global pilgrimage hit list. Instead you'll discover a marvellously eclectic range of museums, galleries, designer shops and royal heritage buildings, all easily digestible and perfect for short-break perusing. For an idea of where to begin, turn to our itineraries and "best of" sections.

Whether you're on foot, cycling (see box below) or jumping on the user-friendly transport system you'll also find Copenhagen eminently navigable. You can quickly flit between neighbourhoods, from the cobbled avenues of Frederiksstaden and grand Slotsholmen island to the winding medieval streets of the Latin Quarter and the gritty

Best places to explore on two wheels

Cycling is a way of life in Copenhagen – nearly everyone gets to school and work on two wheels. Pick up a snazzy bike for rent at Københavns Cyklebørs in Indre By, then pedal around Christianshavn's quiet canals, up to Kastellet to see the Little Mermaid or out to Frederiksberg's lush parks. Alternatively, hop on a train (bike in tow) up the coast, then pedal out to see the world-class art of the Louisiana Museum or around Kronborg Castle, one of the most handsome fortresses in the land.

When to visit

Easily Copenhagen's best season is summer, when both locals and visitors stay out nursing their drinks until the wee hours and cultural events such as the ten-day-long Copenhagen Jazz Festival bring live music, dance and art to the streets. Autumn and spring are similarly alluring – especially for cycling – since the afternoons remain warm but the majority of tourists have departed. Still, don't write off winter, a perfectly charming time for drinking *gløgg* (Scandinavian mulled wine) in cosy bars and enjoying the beloved Danish tradition of *hygge* (cosiness). The festive markets of Tivoli and Nyhavn and the Christmas lights make the city an excellent destination for a festive break.

boho chic of Nørrebro. Green space and charming canals are never far away, whether in the landscaped Kongens Have, or postcard-cute Nyhavn. For those schooled in Dansk design and architecture a visit to Christianshavn will reveal the city's more adventurous side: big open skies and sleek glass and chrome modernism. Come nightfall and another Copenhagen emerges – Michelin-star chefs shout out orders, cocktails are shaken and craft beers cracked open (see page 8 for the best neighbourhoods to try).

Given Denmark itself is small, the capital is nearby some other cracking destinations. Half an hour west is medieval Roskilde, home to a superb museum of Viking ships, one of Europe's biggest music festivals, and a museum of rock music, dubbed "the coolest museum in Demark". North of the capital, meanwhile, stands the outstanding modern art museum of Louisiana, the picture-perfect Renaissance castle of Kronborg and – across the iconic Øresund Bridge – the cool, diminutive Swedish city of Malmö, once part of Denmark's regal orbit.

Nyhavn

Where to...

Eat

At the time of writing, the Danish capital boasted a record twenty-four Michelin stars – more than anywhere else in Scandinavia (see page 3). While advance booking at the better-known dining spots is recommended, Copenhagen isn't all haute cuisine: you can also find great local and international spots such as *Christianshavn's Bådudlejning*, *Café* and *Ølhalle* and *Pintxos*. Furthermore, restaurants all over the city often offer affordable lunchtime options, and you can always visit Nørrebro's Torvehallerne market for everything from organic wines to freshly baked goods – especially on Sundays, when many city restaurants close their doors anyway.

OUR FAVOURITES: Aamanns, see page 64. Torvehallerne, see page 66. Alchemist, see page 73.

Drink

Danes, apparently, drink more coffee than anywhere else in the world, and downtown Copenhagen is paradise for caffeine addicts. *Café Europe* is one of Indre By's most popular. Many daytime cafés often morph into cosy and candlelit bars come evening time, and nearly anywhere in Copenhagen you can find music lilting from inside a chilled bar until very late – perfect for enjoying a relaxing pint of Carlsberg or one of Denmark's many excellent microbrews (don't miss Ølfabrikken's traditional stouts). Most recently, the city has acquired some great wine bars, most notably in Vesterbro and Nørrebro.

OUR FAVOURITES: The Coffee Collective, see page 62. Mikkeller, see page 85.

Go out

If you're in the market for late nights out, the trendy meatpacking district of Kødbyen should be your first – or, rather, last – stop. This recently gentrified neighbourhood of lofts and warehouses has become one of Europe's hottest places to party with DJs, live bands and plenty of dancing. For something more mellow, try Sankt Hans Torv and the surrounding streets in Nørrebro, probably the best place in the city for a romantic late-night drink. Don't miss a shot of ice-cold caraway schnapps – a Danish speciality.

OUR FAVOURITES: Bo-Bi Bar, see page 40. Curfew, see page 85. Ruby, see page 41.

Shop

The central cobbled pedestrian Strøget offers large department stores, including Illums Bolighus, a favourite with the Danish queen, plus iconic local brands Royal Copenhagen and Georg Jensen. The nearby streets of Købmagergade and Kompagnistræde have small, independent shops, while the student-filled Latin Quarter is the place to head for secondhand fashion. South, Værnedamsvej in Vesterbro is great for local designers, while northerly Nørrebro (especially Elmegade and Blågårdsgade) offers chic shops with designers on hand to tailor the clothing to fit you perfectly.

OUR FAVOURITES: Designer Zoo, see page 81. Illums Bolighus, see page 36. Royal Copenhagen, see page 36.

Copenhagen at a glance

Nørrebro and Østerbro p.86.
Multicultural Nørrebro gentrified into the hipster epicentre, while the massive Fælledparken in leafy Østerbro is the city most popular park.

Rosenborg and around p.58.
Gorge on art at Denmark's national gallery, then relax in the beautifully landscaped grounds of the Kongens Have (King's Garden).

Strøget and the Inner City p.30.
Hundreds of shops, dozens of cafés and a warren of medieval streets make the Inner City, or "Indre By", the beating heart of the city.

Vesterbro and Frederiksberg p.76.
Once grim and grimy, Vesterbro is now one of the city's hippest quarters – while tree-lined Frederiksberg is one of the most exclusive.

Tivoli and Rådhuspladsen p.24.
All the fun of the fair at Denmark's bigge and most elegant amusement park, plus Copenhagen's main civic square, fringed with refreshment stands.

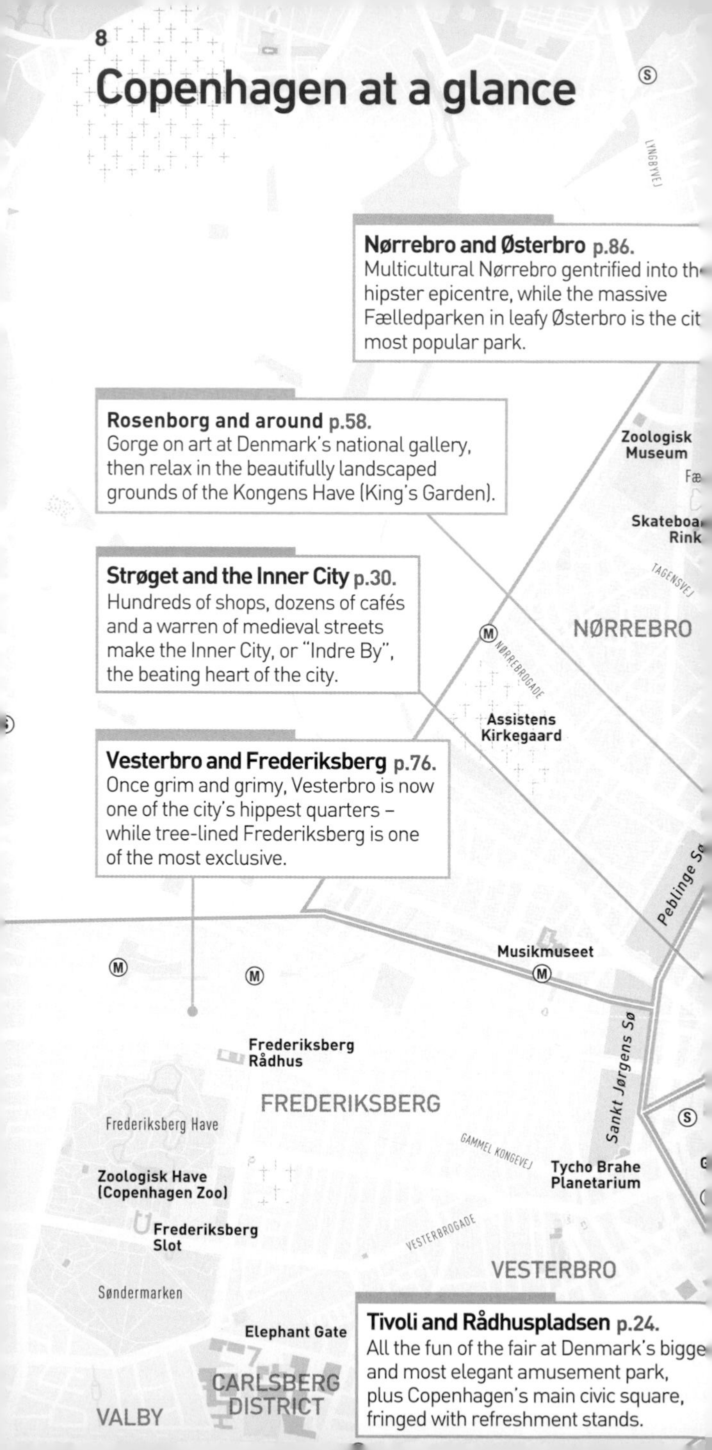

LYNGBYVEJ

Zoologisk Museum

Fæ

Skateboa Rink

TAGENSVEJ

NØRREBROGADE

NØRREBRO

Assistens Kirkegaard

Peblinge Sø

Musikmuseet

Sankt Jørgens Sø

Frederiksberg Rådhus

FREDERIKSBERG

Frederiksberg Have

GAMMEL KONGEVEJ

Tycho Brahe Planetarium

Zoologisk Have (Copenhagen Zoo)

Frederiksberg Slot

VESTERBROGADE

Søndermarken

VESTERBRO

Elephant Gate

CARLSBERG DISTRICT

VALBY

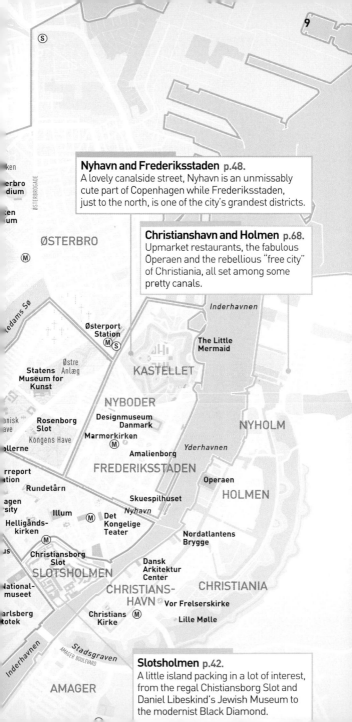

Nyhavn and Frederiksstaden p.48.
A lovely canalside street, Nyhavn is an unmissably cute part of Copenhagen while Frederiksstaden, just to the north, is one of the city's grandest districts.

Christianshavn and Holmen p.68.
Upmarket restaurants, the fabulous Operaen and the rebellious "free city" of Christiania, all set among some pretty canals.

ØSTERBRO

Ⓜ

Inderhavnen

Østerport Station
ⓂⓈ

The Little Mermaid

KASTELLET

Østre Anlæg

Statens Museum for Kunst

NYBODER

NYHOLM

Designmuseum Danmark

nisk ave

Rosenborg Slot

Kongens Have

Marmorkirken
Ⓜ

Yderhavnen

ellerne

Amalienborg

rreport ation

FREDERIKSSTADEN

Rundetårn

Operaen

agen sity

Illum

Ⓜ

Skuespilhuset

Det Kongelige Teater

Nyhavn

HOLMEN

Helligånds-kirken

Ⓜ

us

Nordatlantens Brygge

Christiansborg Slot

SLOTSHOLMEN

Dansk Arkitektur Center

CHRISTIANIA

National-museet

CHRISTIANS-HAVN

Vor Frelserskirke

arlsberg totek

Christians Kirke
Ⓜ

Lille Mølle

Inderhavnen

Stadsgraven
AMAGER BOULEVARD

AMAGER

Slotsholmen p.42.
A little island packing in a lot of interest, from the regal Chistiansborg Slot and Daniel Libeskind's Jewish Museum to the modernist Black Diamond.

15

Things not to miss

It's not possible to see everything that Copenhagen has to offer in one trip – and we don't suggest you try. What follows is a selective taste of the city's highlights, from royal palaces to cutting-edge design.

Den Blå Planet
See page 98
The Blue Planet is a jaw-dropping modern aquarium containing some 20,000 animals across 450 species.

Nationalmuseet
See page 28
World-class collection of historical artefacts, from bog people and fifteenth-century BC sculptures to Viking weapons.

Nyhavn
See page 48
This quaint, much-photographed, harbour is located just alongside a strip of popular bars and restaurants.

< Torvehallerne
See page 66
Beer from Mikkeller, Copenhagen's finest chocolate, and porridge reimagined as dinner are just some of the edible surprises at Denmark's largest food hall.

∨ Tivoli
See page 24
At this magical amusement park, one of the oldest in the world, you'll find hair-raising rides, enchanting gardens, and unforgettable live shows.

< **Designmuseum Danmark**
See page 52
Trace the evolution of Danish design, from Renaissance textiles to Arne Jacobsen chairs – Ikea it ain't.

∨ **Zoologisk Have**
See page 80
Founded in 1859, Copenhagen's zoo is home to 3,000 animals from 264 species. The stand-out sight is the Arctic polar bear habitat.

∧ Rundetårn
See page 31
Instead of stairs, the oldest working observatory tower in Europe has a spectacular 209m spiral pathway.

< Nørrebro
See page 86
Once gritty, now gentrified by creative types, head here for Michelin-stars, superlative coffee, craft beer, and clusters of hip boutiques and vintage furniture shops.

∧ Statens Museum for Kunst
See page 59
Denmark's enormous art museum, with exceptional collections of Danish and international art from the last seven centuries.

∨ Den Sorte Diamant (The Black Diamond)
See page 47
This stunning, reflective piece of waterfront modernism is both a public library and a super spot for people-watching.

∧ Guards at Amalienborg
See page 49
Kids love the royal palace's poker-faced guards, who ceremoniously change their position every day at noon, with marching band accompaniment.

< Frederiksborg Slot
See page 95
Fairy-tale renaissance castle spread out across several small islands, featuring a lake, gardens, Gothic towers and spires.

< **Louisiana Museum of Modern Art**
See page 94
Denmark's most visited art gallery has a beachfront setting nearly as impressive as its collection.

∨ **Kødbyen**
See page 77
Copenhagen's meatpacking district is the hippest area for a night out.

Day One in Copenhagen

Latin Quarter, Inner City. See page 31. Begin the day strolling about this maze of lively medieval streets and squares around Copenhagen University, perfect for losing yourself in history.

Rådhus. See page 27. Climb to the tower of this grandiose, National Romantic city hall, whose fascinating astronomical clock is a destination in itself.

Lunch *Aamanns* (see page 64). This rustic-urban eatery does modern takes on the traditional Danish smørrebrød.

Rosenborg Slot

Canal Tour. See page 121. Join one of the multilingual hourly tours along Copenhagen's centuries-old canals, which offer fascinating insight into important events and sights tied to Denmark's tumultuous history.

Rosenborg Slot. See page 58. Explore your inner royal at this fairy-tale, red-brick Renaissance castle, whose cellar holds the Danish crown jewels and Frederik III's coronation throne, made of gold and narwhal tusk.

Nyboder. See page 63. Make your way out to the multicoloured terraced houses in this relaxed part of town, built in the seventeenth century to house the Danish navy.

Yellow houses in Nyboder district

Dinner *Lumskebugten* (see page 55). Serving traditional Danish cuisine such as smørrebrød in a beautiful setting with a maritime atmosphere, this is the perfect spot for lovers of seafood as well as vegetarians and vegans.

The Little Mermaid. See page 53. Stroll out to Kastellet to catch a glimpse of Copenhagen's mascot and the heroine of Hans Christian Andersen's fairy tale.

Lumskebugten

Day Two in Copenhagen

Ny Carlsberg Glyptotek. See page 26. Start off in this brilliant museum, which holds a vast classical and modern European art collection displayed in opulent rooms.

Krigsmuseet. See page 45. Exhibitions on current and past war battles, including hundreds of seventeenth-century Danish military ships and the 156m arched hall housing the cannon collection.

Christiania. See page 69. Amble along the pretty Christianshavns Kanal, designed by an Amsterdam-born architect, before exploring this renowned hippie "free city" commune.

🍴 **Lunch** *Cofoco* (see page 82). Enjoy a variety of scrumptious "Nordic tapas" from a long and seasonally changing menu at this popular spot.

Frederiksberg Have. See page 79. Pedal out towards Værnedamsvej for a spot of fashionista window shopping, then put down on the open expanses of grass at the city's most wild parklands.

Cisternerne. See page 80. In a city with no shortage of contemporary art spaces, the Cisterns may be the most evocative. Descend the steps from the park into the darkness to check out the ex-reservoir's latest exhibition.

Helsingør. See page 97. Ride the train up the coast to watch the sun set against Kronborg, a fairy-tale fortress and the inspiration for Elsinore Castle in Shakespeare's *Hamlet*.

🍴 **Dinner** *Brasserie Nimb* (see page 29). Great traditional French food with a regularly changing menu in an Asian-style palace, located on the edge of the Tivoli Gardens.

Ny Carlsberg Glyptotek

Christiania

Helsingør

ITINERARIES

Kids' Copenhagen

Families will find plenty to keep the kids happy from amusement parks to swimming pools, science museums to playgrounds.

Tivoli. See page 24. This magical fairground has roller coasters, pantomime theatres and endless helpings of family fun.

Havneparken. See page 72. Combine shopping with swimming at Fisketorvet's Copencabana, popular with children thanks to its two outdoor pools and diving boards built right into the harbour.

Rundetårn. See page 31. This 42m-high stone church tower has an observatory at the top offering great vistas across to the city's numerous spires.

Harbour Bath Fisketorvet

🍽 **Lunch** *Det Lille Apotek* (see page 38). Oldest restaurant in the city with leadlight windows and oil lamps; a great atmosphere for sampling some typical Danish dishes.

Ridebane. See page 43. Visit the Royal Stables, whose regal, marble-clad stables are home to golden carriages and beautiful horses.

Experimentarium. See page 89. This huge science lab lets kids learn about the human body, physics and the natural world, all with hands-on high-energy exhibits.

Training horses at Royal Stables

🍽 **Dinner** *Madklubben* (see page 55). This much-loved Danish chain offers delicious meals at surprisingly affordable prices.

Experimentarium

Budget Copenhagen

Though Copenhagen is one of Europe's most expensive cities, you can save cash by using a discount card, taking harbour bus-boats and visiting free-entry museums.

National Museum. See page 28. Home to Denmark's finest ethnographic artefacts, including an extensive collection of Viking weapons and coins.

Amalienborg. See page 49. A few metres from the harbourfront, soldiers participate in the Changing of the Guard here at noon every day.

Lunch Pick up some bread, cheese and drinks, then picnic on the grass of Kongens Have (see page 59), the city's most popular green space.

Amalienborg

Marmorkirken. See page 51. This marble church was built in 1894 in the image of St Peter's in Rome; join the 1pm tour to ascend the 260 steps to the dome's apogee for some grand city views.

Slotsholmen. See page 42. Descend a narrow stairwell to explore the ruins of two excavated underground castles.

Assistens Kirkegaard. See page 87. Cross the western lakes to take in the final resting place of Danish luminaries such as Hans Christian Andersen and Niels Bohr.

Galerie Asbæk. See page 54. This much-loved gallery represents some of Denmark's best-known painters and photographers and is great for a spot of window shopping.

Dinner *Vespa* (see page 57). This simple, down-at-heel Italian restaurant's four-course set menus are outstanding value for money.

The impressive Marble Church

Kongens Have

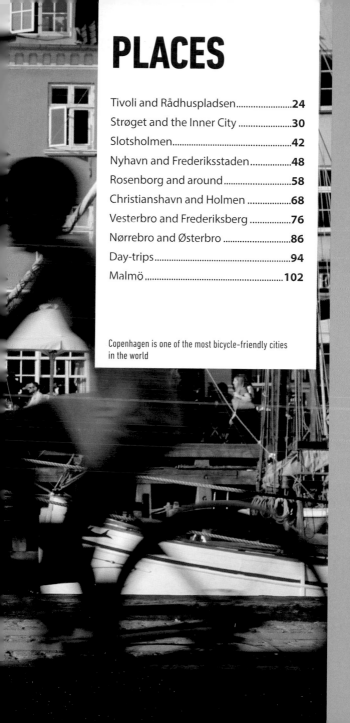

PLACES

Tivoli and Rådhuspladsen........................**24**

Strøget and the Inner City **30**

Slotsholmen......................................**42**

Nyhavn and Frederiksstaden................**48**

Rosenborg and around............................**58**

Christianshavn and Holmen **68**

Vesterbro and Frederiksberg **76**

Nørrebro and Østerbro **86**

Day-trips..**94**

Malmö..**102**

Copenhagen is one of the most bicycle-friendly cities
in the world

Tivoli and Rådhuspladsen

Tivoli, Denmark's most-visited attraction, may appear at first glance every bit as tacky as any other amusement park around the world, but it has much more to offer than just its thrilling set of rides. After taking in the 83,000-square-metre gardens, with their gorgeous flower displays and fountains, romantic boating lake, exotic-looking buildings (from Chinese pagodas to Moorish palaces) and – at night – spectacular illuminations, even the most cynical visitor will have to succumb and agree that it's a magical (albeit expensive) place. A few paces away is the buzzing Rådhuspladsen square, towered over by the grand red-brick nineteenth-century city hall, whose innards hold a fascinating astronomical clock. As well as demarcating the city's geographical heart, the square is the perfect place for a mustard-topped *pølse*.

Tivoli

MAP P.25, POCKET MAP A13
Vesterbrogade 3 Ⓜ København H Ⓦ Tivoli.
dk. March 31 to Sept 24, three weeks
in Oct & mid-Nov to Dec 31 Mon–Thurs
& Sun 11am–10pm, Fri & Sat 11am–
midnight, charge.

Amusement park in Tivoli

Opened in 1843, **Tivoli** was the creation of architect George Carstensen, who had been commissioned by Christian VIII to build a pleasure garden for the masses outside the western gate into the city. It was an immediate success, and – expanded and modernized over the years – was a major influence on Walt Disney for his theme parks a century later. That the gardens continue even today to occupy such a patch of prime real estate, sandwiched between the Hovedbanegården and the Rådhus, is testimony to Tivoli's central place within the city's affections.

Tivoli's principal draw, of course – to children at least – is its twenty-seven-odd **rides**, which include one of the world's oldest still-functioning wooden roller coasters. Still more hair-raising are the Star Flyer, which lifts up and twirls thrill-seekers around some 80m above ground, and Aquila, which thrusts its victims around at the nauseating force of 4G. Music, theatre and panto (mostly free once you're in) are a key part of Tivoli's

What lies beneath: digging up the town

The opening of the orbital metro in late 2019 involved large parts of the old city being excavated, the most extensive building work since Christian IV (aka the builder king) erected most of Copenhagen's defensive works, castles and churches in the sixteenth century. **Archeologists** from the Københavns Museum had a field day (literally) unlocking the city's underground secrets before the diggers were let loose, bringing certain aspects of its history under revision. Data emerged indicating, for example, that a major settlement existed here before Bishop Absalon founded Copenhagen in the twelfth century and that the settlers at the time were much taller than previously thought.

appeal, with several stages and bandstands. Pantomime – in the classic Italian *commedia dell'arte* tradition – is put on throughout the year in the extraordinary Chinese-style **Pantomime Theatre**, and every Friday evening in season at 10pm there's a hugely popular gig (W fredagsrock.dk) at the open-air **Plænen** stage, featuring mainly Scandinavian acts. The gardens

can get crowded but the setting is magical and the atmosphere buzzing – and Tivoli's undulating layout means that you can always find a peaceful and picturesque nook from which to relax and drink in the scene.

Formerly only open during summertime, in recent years Tivoli has extended its season to include three weeks leading up to

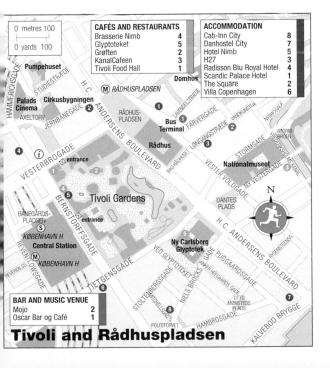

CAFÉS AND RESTAURANTS	
Brasserie Nimb	4
Glyptoteket	5
Grøften	2
KanalCafeen	3
Tivoli Food Hall	1

ACCOMMODATION	
Cab-Inn City	8
Danhostel City	7
Hotel Nimb	5
H27	3
Radisson Blu Royal Hotel	4
Scandic Palace Hotel	1
The Square	2
Villa Copenhagen	6

BAR AND MUSIC VENUE	
Mojo	2
Oscar Bar og Café	1

Tivoli and Rådhuspladsen

Ny Carlsberg Glyptotek

Halloween, when the gardens are bestrewn with smiley pumpkins and clingy cobwebs, and a six-week **Christmas market**, when the best of Danish Yuletide traditions are on show.

Central Station

MAP P.25, POCKET MAP A14

Designed by station builder extraordinaire Heinrich Wenck as a *Gesamtkunstwerk* (total work of art), the hulking yet elegant **Hovedbanegården** (Central Station) is one of the country's most noteworthy National Romantic buildings. Dating from 1911, it's built predominantly in red brick, slate and granite, as dictated by the style, with abundant decorative detail – all of which Wenck was responsible for. Note in particular the large wood-beamed (rather than cast-iron) arches supporting the roof structure above the central hall and platforms, and the magnificent chandeliers.

The station is home to the studio of a national television channel, TV2. Journalists from the daily *Go'morgen Danmark* ("Good Morning Denmark") breakfast show often canvass opinions on the issues of the day from passing travellers, so don't be surprised if you're suddenly stopped for a quick interview.

Ny Carlsberg Glyptotek

MAP P.25, POCKET MAP B14
Dantes Plads 7 Ⓜ Rådhuspladsen
Ⓦ glyptoteket.dk, Tues, Wed & Fri–Sun 10am–5pm, Thurs 10am–9pm, charge; free on the last Wed of every month.

Impossible to miss with its opulent red-brick Venetian Renaissance facade, the exquisite **Ny Carlsberg Glyptotek** was established by brewing magnate Carl Jacobsen (1842–1914) to provide a public home for his vast private art collection. The building and collection have since been extended and expanded several times, the gallery's richly decorated rooms providing as captivating a spectacle as the remarkable haul of ancient and modern works on display.

The main entrance takes you into the museum's original building (1897), designed by Danish architect **Vilhelm Dahlerup**.

Housed within its two floors of extravagantly colourful friezes, marble pillars and mosaic floors are sculptures and paintings from the **Danish Golden Age**, including Bertel Thorvaldsen's evocative *The Three Graces* relief, and a fine collection of **French sculpture**, with particular emphasis on Rodin – the largest collection of his work outside France. The undoubted highlight of the Dahlerup section, however, is the tranquil, glass-domed **Winter Garden** around which it centres, filled with palm trees, statues and a fountain.

On the opposite side of the Winter Garden, the large marble-pillared Central Hall of the elaborate **Kampmann** extension (1905) leads to an extensive **Ancient Mediterranean** collection, which starts around 6000 BC and traces the development of the Greek, Etruscan and Roman empires. From the Central Hall a set of stairs leads up to a newer wing designed by Henning Larsen (of the Opera House; see page 71), a courtyard infill housing a fantastic collection of **French post-impressionist** paintings including noteworthy pieces by Degas, Manet and Gauguin.

The Rådhus
MAP P.25, POCKET MAP B13
Rådhuspladsen Ⓜ Rådhuspladsen
ⓣ 33 66 33 66, Mon–Fri 9am–4pm, Sat 9.30–1pm; access to Jens Olsen's World Clock Mon–Fri 9am–4pm, Sat 9.30am–1pm; tours in English Mon–Fri 1pm, Sat 10am, charge.

Dominating Rådhuspladsen, the city's bustling cobbled main square (much of it currently cordoned off by metro building works), is the grand **Rådhus** (City Hall) from 1905, a great example of the National Romantic style with beautiful and intricate decorative detail throughout. Just past the entrance, the stately main hall has walls of layered polished red brick and limestone (a reference to the national flag) and an impressive arched gallery, beneath which a limestone strip is inscribed with key moments in Copenhagen's history. As a working public building the City Hall is open to visitors, though the informative **tours** are the best way to capture its full detail. Tours include access to **Jens Olsen's world clock** – an extraordinary astronomical timepiece from 1955 with hundreds of ticking dials tracking

Axeltorv Square: circus friezes and multicoloured facades

Vesterport, once the western gate into the city, has some notable architectural landmarks. Cirkusbygningen ("the Circus Building") was built in the 1880s; note the elaborate horse-racing frieze that still encircles the building. Now a venue for dinner shows, in its heyday the adjoining stables stretched as far as Studiestræde and housed circus horses, giraffes and elephants. On the other side of Axeltorv, 17-screen Palads cinema opened in 1912, its brightly coloured facade added in 1989 by Danish abstract artist Poul Gernes. In 2017, plans to level the building sparked outrage among Copenhageners, who proved quite protective of the landmark pink theatre. The protests were successful, and as of the time of writing the city council is considering a trio of new project proposals – for expansion rather than demolition. Each of the proposed plans incorporates the historic structure, though no winner has yet emerged.

the planetary movement with astounding accuracy – and a climb to the top of the 105m **tower** (closed at the time of research but set to reopen in 2024), offering stunning views of the city.

Nationalmuseet

MAP P.25, POCKET MAP C13
Ny Vestergade 10 Ⓜ Rådhuspladsen
Ⓦ natmus.dk, June–Sept daily 10am–6pm,
Oct–May Tues–Sun 10am–5pm, charge.

Housed in an eighteenth-century Rococo palace, formerly the Danish Crown Prince's residence, the immense **National Museum**'s vast collection, which stretches from prehistory to the present day via the Viking period and Middle Ages, could easily take days to go through. If you're short of time, head straight for the second floor and the captivating **Inuit** part of the vast **Ethnographic** collection, the most extensive of its kind in the world. There's a wealth of

detail on their hunting techniques and exhibits include dog sledges and some amazing hand-carved kayaks. It also provides a succinct account of the events leading to Denmark's colonization of Greenland. Standout among the exhibits in the **Danish prehistory** section are the magical gold-plated Trundholm Sun Chariot, dating from around 1400 BC, which has featured on many a Danish stamp since its discovery in 1902, and – above all – the bog-preserved **Egtved Girl** (1370 BC), who still has her clothes, hair and jewellery intact. Finally, a detour to the **Viking exhibition** will categorically banish the perception that all Vikings did was rape and pillage. Room 23 gives an insight into the remarkable distances they travelled – as far as present-day Iran and Afghanistan – on their trade and diplomatic missions to gather silver, the main currency of the era.

Nationalmuseet

Cafés and restaurants

Brasserie Nimb

MAP P.25, POCKET MAP A13
Bernstorffsgade 5 ⓦ nimb.dk.
One of four restaurants within
the lavish *Nimb Hotel*, Tivoli's
romantic fairy-tale *Arabian Nights*-
style palace (though also accessible
from outside the gardens), the
ground-floor *Brasserie* is a temple
to traditional French cuisine. Open
throughout the year. €€€

Glyptoteket

MAP P.25, POCKET MAP B14
Dantes Plads 7 ⓦ glyptoteket.dk.
Even if the Ny Carlsberg
Glyptotek's art and sculpture don't
grab you, it's worth visiting the café,
occupying a beautiful position in
the glass-domed Winter Garden, for
exquisite smørrebrød and cake. €

Grøften

MAP P.25, POCKET MAP A13
Tivoli ⓦ groeften.dk.
Historic restaurant with seating
outdoors on a large open terrace,
popular with celebs of a certain
vintage. The overloaded prawn
sandwich and the all-you-can-eat
skipperlabskovs (Danish goulash)
are legendary, as is the *stjerneskud*
(the "shooting star" is comprised of
shrimp and both a poached and a
fried fish fillet on toast). €

KanalCafeen

MAP P.25, POCKET MAP C13
Frederiksholms Kanal 18 ⓦ kanalcafeen.dk.
Founded in 1852, this cosy, historic
lunchtime restaurant opposite
Christiansborg serves outstanding,
good-value smørrebrød. Inside,
the decor is all heavy tablecloths
and period oil paintings, while
outside there's canal side seating in
summer. €

Tivoli Food Hall

MAP P.25, POCKET MAP A13

Grøften, restaurant in Tivoli

Bernstorffsgade 3 ⓦ tivoli.dk.
A great option for a meal between
rides, this food court of over a dozen
stalls has something for everyone,
from burgers and sour dough pizzas
to sushi, tacos and curries. Squeezed
along the park's edge, it's also
accessible from outside, with entry
just opposite the train station. €

Bar

Oscar Bar og Café

MAP P.25, POCKET MAP B13
Regnbuepladsen 9 ⓦ oscarbarcafe.dk.
Set just next to the Rådhus, this
very popular gay bar is lively and
well lit, and has DJs pumping tunes
out until late on weekends. Happy
hour (4–9pm) has 40kr Carlsbergs,
and there are good sandwiches and
burgers too.

Music venue

Mojo

MAP P.25, POCKET MAP C13
Løngangstræde 21C ⓦ mojo.dk.
This authentic, smoky bar with
sticky beer-stained tables is a must
for blues aficionados. The live
gigs (most nights from 10pm) are
usually free, though chargeable
when bigger names are playing.

Strøget and the Inner City

Indre By ("inner city") is Copenhagen's heart and hub, its compact warren of narrow streets and cobbled squares home to the capital's principal shopping district and countless bars and restaurants. For centuries, Indre By was Copenhagen, springing into life with the arrival of Bishop Absalon in 1167, and fortified with stone walls until the nineteenth century. Historic buildings rub shoulders with modern but the area, bisected by the bustling pedestrianized thoroughfare of Strøget, is at its most atmospheric around the Latin Quarter, original home to the university, and pretty, colourful Gråbrødre Torv.

Strøget

MAP P.32, POCKET MAP B12–D11

The principal artery of the city's main shopping district, **Strøget** is a series of five interconnecting pedestrian streets, over 1km in length, which runs from Rådhuspladsen to Kongens Nytorv (see page 34). One of the world's first pedestrian strips when it was created in 1962, it's abuzz with life 24/7 from the constant flow of shoppers during the day and revellers at night. Street entertainers and fruit and snack sellers also ply their trade – the weeks before Christmas are especially lively, with carol singers, shoppers galore and delicious treats – such as *æbleskiver* (sweet pancake balls) and *gløgg* (mulled wine) on sale.

Amagertorv

The Rådhuspladsen end
of Strøget, beginning with
Frederiksberggade, is fairly tacky
but the strip gradually goes more
upmarket, running past some of the
city's oldest buildings and squares.
On **Gammeltorv** (Old Square),
look out for the **Caritas Fountain**,
which predates the (much more
famous) Manneken Pis in Brussels,
and features a woman spraying
water from her breasts as a small
boy pees into the basin.

From here, Strøget continues
past Amagertorv (see page 33),
culminating in a line of exclusive
designer stores as it reaches
Østergade and Kongens Nytorv
(see page 34).

Rundetårn

MAP P.32, POCKET MAP C11
Købmagergade 52A Ⓜ **Nørreport**
Ⓦ rundetaarn.dk, Tower: April–Sept 10am–
8pm; Oct–March Thurs–Mon 10am–6pm,
Tues–Wed 10am–9pm; Observatory: Oct–
March 6pm–9pm, charge.

Built by Christian IV in the
mid-seventeenth century, the
42m-high **Rundetårn** (Round
Tower) originally formed part of a
larger complex, functioning both as
church tower and **observatory**. The
observatory, at the top of the tower,
is still operational – the oldest of
its kind still in use in Europe – and
can be visited in wintertime, while
the ascent, along a wide, cobbled
walkway, is straightforward even for
vertigo sufferers. As you make your
way up, you can catch your breath
at the **modern art gallery** in the
former university library hall, and
at the various other quirky exhibits
en route, including Christian IV's
toilet. The view from the top,
across the city's many towers and
spires, is fabulous.

The Latin Quarter

MAP P.32, POCKET MAP B11
Frue Plads Ⓜ **Nørreport**
In one of the city's most historic
areas, the buildings of the so-called
Latin Quarter around Fiolstræde

Rundetårn

date back to the foundation of
Scandinavia's earliest university
in 1475. Hailing from 1836, the
grand neo-Gothic **university**
building across Frue Plads from
Vor Frue Kirke serves a primarily
administrative purpose today –
most of the university departments
have relocated outside the city
centre. On one side a row of
busts of the university's rationalist
scholars – including Nobel prize-
winning Niels Bohr – faces off
against busts of religious men
lining the cathedral wall opposite.

Helligåndskirken

MAP P.32, POCKET MAP C12
Amagertorv Ⓜ **Gammel Strand**
Ⓦ helligaandskirken.dk, Mon–Fri
noon–4pm, Sat 11am–1pm (plus services
on Sun).

One of the city's oldest churches,
dating back to the thirteenth
century, the **Helligåndskirken**
(Church of the Holy Ghost)

Vor Frue Kirke

was originally part of a Catholic monastery. Following the Reformation it became a Lutheran church, and although repeatedly destroyed (by fire and bombardment), an evocative section of the monastery, the **Helligåndshuset**, survives in the church's west wing (to the left of the entrance) as the city's largest and most intact medieval building. It's not hard to imagine its past incarnation as a medieval hospital, beds crammed in between the slender granite columns that hold up the heavy vaulted ceiling. Today it houses regular flea markets, concerts and exhibitions.

Vor Frue Kirke

MAP P.32, POCKET MAP B11
Frue Plads Ⓜ Nørreport Ⓦ domkirken.dk,
daily 8am–5pm, except during services.
The plain, rather sombre-looking **Vor Frue Kirke** (Church of Our Lady) dates from 1829 and has

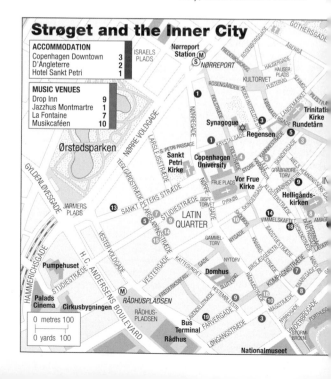

Strøget and the Inner City

ACCOMMODATION	
Copenhagen Downtown	3
D'Angleterre	2
Hotel Sankt Petri	1

MUSIC VENUES	
Drop Inn	9
Jazzhus Montmartre	1
La Fontaine	7
Musikcaféen	10

Nørreport Station Ⓜ
Ⓢ NØRREPORT

ISRAELS PLADS

Synagogue
Regensen
Trinitatis Kirke
Rundetårn

Ørstedsparken

Sankt Petri Kirke
Copenhagen University
Vor Frue Kirke
Helligånds-kirken

JARMERS PLADS

LATIN QUARTER

Pumpehuset

Domhus

Palads Cinema
Cirkusbygningen
Ⓜ RÅDHUSPLADSEN
RÅDHUS-PLADSEN

Bus Terminal
Rådhus

0 metres 100
0 yards 100

Nationalmuseet

unctioned as Copenhagen's athedral since 1923, though there's een a church on this site since he eleventh century. It's not until ou're through the heavy Doric-illared portal into the whitewashed Neoclassical interior that its more elegant features are revealed. A imple carved frieze above the altar accentuates a magnificent statue of Christ by Bertel Thorvaldsen see page 45); the statue's hand positioning gave Thorvaldsen much grief before he finally decided on the open downward-facing position appreciated by both Catholics and Protestants alike. In 2004, the cathedral briefly hit the international spotlight as the venue for the wedding of Crown Prince Frederik and his Tasmanian wife Mary.

Amagertorv and Højbro Plads

MAP P.32, POCKET MAP C12–D12

Højbro Plads ⑩ Gammel Strand

If Strøget has a focal point, it's the L-shaped interconnecting squares of **Amagertorv** and **Højbro Plads**. On the direct route between the once royal residence of Christiansborg and Vor Frue Kirke these two squares have borne witness to numerous coronation parties, royal weddings and (prior to the Reformation) religious processions. They're especially bustling in summertime when the cafés set up outside and snack vendors and bicycle-rickshaw operators ply their trade. Tourists seem perpetually drawn to pose by the two artworks by sculptor Vilhem Bissen: an equestrian statue of Bishop Absalon and the *Storkespringvandet* (Stork Fountain), while a more recent addition is the beautiful mosaic paving by Bjørn Nørgaard (see page 43).

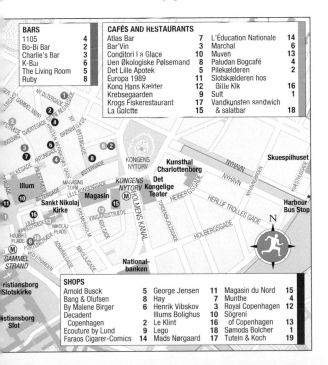

BARS	
1105	4
Bo-Bi Bar	2
Charlie's Bar	3
K-Bar	6
The Living Room	5
Ruby	8

CAFÉS AND RESTAURANTS			
Atlas Bar	7	L'Éducation Nationale	14
Bar'Vin	3	Marchal	6
Conditori la Glace	10	Muven	13
Den Økologiske Pølsemand	8	Paludan Bogcafé	4
Det Lille Apotek	5	Pilekælderen	2
Europa 1989	11	Slotskælderen hos	
Kong Hans Kælder	12	Gitte Kik	16
Krebsegaarden	9	Sult	1
Krogs Fiskerestaurant	17	Vandkunsten sandwich	
La Galette	15	& salatbar	18

SHOPS					
Arnold Busck	5	George Jensen	11	Magasin du Nord	15
Bang & Olufsen	8	Hay	7	Munthe	4
By Malene Birger	6	Henrik Vibskov	3	Royal Copenhagen	12
Decadent		Illums Bolighus	10	Sögreni	
Copenhagen	2	Le Klint	16	of Copenhagen	13
Ecouture by Lund	9	Lego	18	Sømods Bolcher	1
Faraos Cigarer-Comics	14	Mads Nørgaard	17	Tutein & Koch	19

Købmagergade and around

MAP P.32, POCKET MAP D11

On the corner of Strøget and the busy pedestrianized side street of **Købmagergade**, the Illum department store is one of the city's top places to shop, full of labels including Acne and Paul Smith. Running off Købmagergade to the east is a super-trendy knot of lanes – most notably **Pilestræde** – littered with exclusive designer shops.

Kongens Nytorv

MAP P.32, POCKET MAP E11

The city's grandest square, **Kongens Nytorv** was for years the main entrance to the royal part of the city. The "King's New Square" was laid out in 1670 by Christian V as part of a large urban expansion project. A 1688-era bronze statue of him thus stands at its centre – the oldest equestrian statue in Scandinavia, in fact. You'll also come across a

copper-clad Baroque telephone kiosk from 1913.

Det Kongelige Teater

MAP P.32, POCKET MAP E11

Kongens Nytorv Ⓜ Kongens Nytorv Ⓦ kglteater.dk.

Somewhat confusingly, **Det Kongelige Teater** (the Royal Theatre) comprises three buildings: the main building on Kongens Nytorv, the Opera House on Holmen (see page 71) and the Skuespilhuset (see page 51). Built in 1874, the Kongens Nytorv theatre is by far the oldest of the three, and for years was the country's main national performance venue, hosting opera, ballet and drama under one roof – though today it is primarily used for ballet. As a fourteen-year-old, Hans Christian Andersen is known to have tried his luck as a ballet dancer here though the audition was, by all accounts, a disaster. To fully experience the theatre's grandeur you'll have to watch a performance.

The Royal Danish Theatre

Shops

Arnold Busck
MAP P.32, POCKET MAP C11
Købmagergade 49 ⓦ arnoldbusck.dk.
Large, central bookstore with a
sizeable English collection as well
as souvenir trinkets, postcards and
stamps. There's also a cosy café
where you can rest your legs after
climbing Rundetårn, just opposite
the bookstore to the north.

Bang & Olufsen
MAP P.32, POCKET MAP D11
Østergade 18 ⓦ bang-olufsen.com.
At B&O's sleek flagship store you
can check out their latest top-of
the-range sound and vision kit:
good to look at even if it might
stretch beyond your holiday
budget. Attention to detail and
built with high quality materials,
B&O's wide variety of headphones
will satisfy any customer willing to
open their wallet.

By Malene Birger
MAP P.32, POCKET MAP D11
Antonigade 10 ⓦ bymalenebirger.com.
Exclusive international designer
store with a bohemian twist to
classic Scandinavian minimalism.

Decadent Copenhagen
MAP P.32, POCKET MAP D11
Store Regnegade 3
ⓦ decadentcopenhagen.com.
Flagship store of this Danish line,
which began making high-quality,
trendy yet practical leather women's
handbags, and has since branched
out into shoes. Bags start around
2000kr.

Ecoture by Lund
MAP P.32, POCKET MAP C11
Gråbrødretorv 7 ⓦ ecouture.dk.
You can find the glamorous
women's clothing line with organic/
socially responsible stance (hence
the "eco" in the name) and a vintage
feel in a central location – although
opening hours remain restricted.

Hay

Faraos Cigarer-Comics
MAP P.32, POCKET MAP C12
Vimmelskaftet 47-49 ⓦ faraos.dk.
This sprawling, three-storey comic
bookstore is among the largest in
Scandinavia, stocked with both
new and used floppy comics and
graphic novels. There's a vast
selection of classics alongside
all the newest DC, Image and
Marvel titles.

George Jensen
MAP P.32, POCKET MAP D12
Amagertorv 4 ⓦ georgejensen.com.
Silverware designed in the
spirit and style of the celebrated
silversmith Georg Jensen, who
first became known for his Art
Nouveau-style jewellery in the early
twentieth century. A small museum
inside tells his story.

Hay
MAP P.32, POCKET MAP D11
Pilestræde 29-31 ⓦ hay.dk.
Colourful, funky household
accessories, including furniture
and rugs, mostly by cutting-
edge Danish designers. A Hay
candleholder would make a great
souvenir or gift.

Illums Bolighus

Henrik Vibskov

MAP P.32, POCKET MAP C11
Gammel Mønt 14
Ⓦ henrikvibskovboutique.com.
Weird and wonderful (and pricey) gear from Copenhagen's *enfant terrible* clothes designer. Henrik, also an artist and drummer, is notorious for his colourful, flamboyant and über-trendy men's and women's wear.

Illums Bolighus

MAP P.32, POCKET MAP D12
Amagertorv 10 Ⓦ illumsbolighus.dk.
A Copenhagen institution, this gorgeous design department store sells everything from top-of-the-range clothes to furniture and kitchenware from global designer icons. It's also the place to go year-round for beautiful Christmas decorations.

Le Klint

MAP P.32, POCKET MAP D12
Store Kirkestræde 1 Ⓦ leklint.com.
Originally started by famous furniture designer Kaare Klint, Le Klint's lamps are now a globally sought-after brand. The current in-house designers have maintained his simple, aesthetic style.

Lego

MAP P.32, POCKET MAP C12
Vimmelskaftet 37 Ⓦ stores.lego.com.
A must for Lego connoisseurs of all ages, the flagship store even provides building tips and tricks, and can get you replacement pieces for those crucial ones you've lost from the colourful and never-ending Pick-a-Brick wall.

Mads Nørgaard

MAP P.32, POCKET MAP C12
Amagertorv 13–15 Ⓦ madsnorgaard.com.
Good-quality, own-design everyday wear for women and children (at no. 13) and men (no. 15) in cheerful, often stripy colours. The #101, a comfortable, long sleeve t-shirt is a modern Danish classic, with more than 3 million sold since 1967.

Magasin du Nord

MAP P.32, POCKET MAP E12
Kongens Nytorv 13 Ⓦ magasin.dk.
This age-old department store is still going strong, selling top-notch clothes and homeware. Head to the basement for the gourmet food hall, well stocked with organic and fair-trade foodstuffs and wines. You'll also find magazines and newspapers from around the globe down here.

Munthe

MAP P.32, POCKET MAP D11
Store Regnegade 2 Ⓦ dk.munthe.com.
Pricey and exciting – bordering on grungy – women's clothing, designed by Naja Munthe. Known for its exquisite details, feminine lines and high-quality materials, the collection is completely renewed every three months.

Royal Copenhagen

MAP P.32, POCKET MAP C12
Amagertorv 6 Ⓦ royalcopenhagen.com.
Flagship store for the Royal Porcelain Factory's famous china, distinguished by its blue patterning. The beautiful gabled store building, from 1616, is one of the city's oldest, having survived countless

city-centre fires. Prices start at 249kr for a decorated egg cup.

Sögreni of Copenhagen

MAP P.32, POCKET MAP A12
Sankt Peders Stræde 30A
Ⓦ sogrenibikes.com.

Sögreni's beautiful handmade bikes are assembled in store, though with prices starting at around 12,000kr they don't come cheap. It's a great place to come and buy bike accessories, such as chain guards and lights, which are also designed and crafted in-house. Items begin at around 320kr for a pretty little copper bike bell.

Sømods Bolcher

MAP P.32, POCKET MAP B11
Nørregade 36 Ⓦ soemods-bolcher.dk.

Dinky little confectioner that uses age-old methods – dating back to its establishment in 1891 – to produce beautiful boiled and hand-rolled candy in myriad colours and flavours. Visitors are invited to watch the process of shaping globs of scorching hot sugar into candies.

Tutein & Koch

MAP P.32, POCKET MAP B13
Farvergade 8 Ⓦ tuteinogkoch.dk.

Copenhagen's favourite stationery store, stocked with an exhaustive range of paper supplies, markers, paints, inks and pens.

Cafés and restaurants

Atlas Bar

MAP P.32, POCKET MAP B12
Larsbjørnsstræde 18 Ⓦ atlasbar.dk.

Informal café-cum-restaurant serving affordable dishes from around the globe in a charming, laidback setting. There is an extensive plant-based menu (including delicious nut burgers made with hazelnuts, carrots and celeriac) with a good range of freshly made salads, and lots of freshly squeezed juices, too. €

Bar'Vin

MAP P.32, POCKET MAP C11
Skindergade 3 Ⓦ barvin.dk.

The menu at this rustic, relaxed wine bar changes to match the wine (rather than the other way around), though the delicious charcuterie and cheese platters always remain a good bet. €€

Conditori La Glace

MAP P.32, POCKET MAP B12
Skoubogade 3 Ⓦ laglace.dk.

A must-visit for any sweet tooth, this Copenhagen institution first opened its doors in 1870 long serving as the most respected patisserie in a country that prides itself on cakes and pastries. The famous (and ironically named) "Sportskage" consists of crushed nougat, whipped cream, a macaroon bottom and caramelized choux pastry – well worth the calories and the somewhat upmarket price. €€

Den Økologiske Pølsemand

MAP P.32, POCKET MAP C12
Amagertorv 31 Ⓦ døp.dk.

This unassuming hotdog stand offers a delicious rendition of the

Peter Beier Chokolade

Danish hotdog, a national staple and point of pride, serving all-organic sausages (with vegan and gluten-free alternatives available). The classic *ristet med det hele* ("roasted with everything") comes with pickles, raw and fried onions, mustard and ketchup. €

Det Lille Apotek

MAP P.32, POCKET MAP C11

Store Kannikestræde 15 ⓦ detlilleapotek.dk.
Dating back to 1720, the city's oldest restaurant was once one of Hans Christian Andersen's favourite haunts, and with its leadlight windows and hanging oil lamps it still retains plenty of old-time atmosphere. Highlights on the menu of traditional Danish dishes include *parsiserbøf* (a beef patty fried onto a slice of white bread and served with capers, onions, horseradish, pickled beets and a raw egg yolk) and *flæskesteg* (pork roast with crackling, sugar-glazed potatoes, pickled red cabbage and a thick, creamy sauce). €€

Europa 1989

MAP P.32, POCKET MAP D12

Amagertorv 1 ⓦ europa1989.dk.
Large, fancy café on bustling Højbro Plads serving excellent coffee and cake, good breakfasts and brunch (daily until 2pm). It's also a popular after-work spot, mostly for the drinks (the beer selection is good) and their excellent nibbles; try the lobster-dog or the beef tartare. €€

Kong Hans Kælder

MAP P.32, POCKET MAP D12

Vingårdstræde 6 ⓦ konghans.dk.
Set in the cellar of a medieval merchant's house with gothic arches, this two-Michelin-starred restaurant has a setting as dramatic as it is romantic. The picture-perfect food is French-inspired with a twist. The many-course menu will set you back 2300kr, excluding wine, while an à la carte main starts at 655kr. Advance booking highly recommended. €€€

Det Lille Apotek

Europa 1989

Krebsegaarden

MAP P.32, POCKET MAP B12

Studiestræde 17 ⓦ krebsegaarden.dk.
Named for the historic building
in which it is housed (dating to
1803), this arty restaurant in the
Inner City centre is uniquely
dependent on the gallery to
which it's attached: the menu,
which changes around eight times
per year, is always linked to the
current exhibition. Menus are
thus inspired by the nationality
or favourite foods of the featured
artist, a selection of whose works
will naturally adorn the restaurant's
walls. €€

Krogs Fiskerestaurant

MAP P.32, POCKET MAP C12

Gammel Strand 38 ⓦ krogs.dk.
Though hidden behind the metro
building chaos, the *grande dame* of
the city's seafood restaurants – all
high ceilings and meticulously
dressed tables – is worth the hassle
to get to. Choose between elegant
indoor or streetside seating and try
the French oysters or lobster with
all the trimmings. €€

La Galette

MAP P.32, POCKET MAP B12

Larsbjørnsstræde 9 ⓦ lagalette.dk.
Informal place serving French-style
buckwheat pancakes with both sweet
and savoury fillings. Specialities
include the Menez-Hom, filled with
goat's cheese, walnuts and salad,
and the Normande with calvados-
flambéed caramelized apples. In
summer there's outdoor seating in
the back yard. €

L'Éducation Nationale

MAP P.32, POCKET MAP B12

Larsbjørnsstræde 12 ⓦ leducation.dk.
Authentic and cosy, French-style
bistro with tightly packed tables and
French-speaking waiters. Lunchtime
standards, such as omelette and
moules marinières, are reasonably
priced. The evening menu is pricier
but still good value, and there's an
excellent selection of wines. €€

Marchal

MAP P.32, POCKET MAP E11

Kongens Nytorv 34 ⓦ dangleterre.com.
Appropriately located within the
venerable Hotel D'Angleterre,

opened in 1755 and dominating Kongens Nytorv, Michellin-starred Marchal serves Nordic-inspired cuisine with a classic French twist. €€€

Maven

MAP P.32, POCKET MAP D12
Nikolaj Plads 10 ⓦ restaurantmaven.dk.
Inside the massive, red-brick Skt Nikolaj Kirke, a deconsecrated church that also hosts temporary exhibitions, *Maven* ("stomach") offers excellent French/Italian-inspired lunch and dinner menus as well as traditional lunchtime smørrebrød. Also a popular spot for evening drinks. €€

Paludan Bogcafé

MAP P.32, POCKET MAP B11
Fiolstræde 10–12 ⓦ paludan-cafe.dk.
With its free wi-fi and great-value meals – chicken tagliatelle, the Paludan burger or spinach and salmon pasta, for example – this bookshop-cum-café is a great student hangout. There's also good coffee and cheap beer. €

Pilekælderen

MAP P.32, POCKET MAP D11
Pilestræde 48 ⓦ pilekaelderen.dk.
Authentic, traditional lunchtime restaurant with thick stone walls and a low wood-beamed ceiling. It specializes in stunning smørrebrød, such as herring marinated in elderberry aquavit – all home-made, of course. €€

Slotskælderen hos Gitte Kik

MAP P.32, POCKET MAP D12
Fortunstræde 4 ⓦ slotskaelderen.dk.
Cosy basement restaurant serving excellent traditional smørrebrød. Choose from the vast selection at the counter, such as delicious *rullepølse* (rolled pork with parsley and pepper), and the food will be brought to your table. €

Sult

MAP P.32, POCKET MAP C10
Vognmagergade 8B ⓦ restaurantsult.dk.
Occupying a high-ceilinged dining hall in the same building as the Danish Film Institute, *Sult* is an excellent buffet-style restaurant with very reasonable prices. The weekend brunch buffet is especially impressive and the price includes drinks. €€

Vandkunsten sandwich & salatbar

MAP P.32, POCKET MAP C12
Rådhusstræde 17 ⓦ vsandwich.dk.
Excellent place to grab a sandwich on the go, with lots of yummy vegetarian options (avocado mousse, grilled aubergine and self-styled salads, for example) and freshly baked, crisp Italian rolls. €

Bars

1105

MAP P.32, POCKET MAP D11
Kristen Bernikows Gade 4 ⓦ 1105.dk.
Cool, elegant, low-lit cocktail bar, where the mixologists wear crisp white lab coats. *1105* has made a name for itself with the creation of the Copenhagen cocktail, a delicious mix of genever (Dutch gin), cherry liqueur, lime juice and a host of secret ingredients.

Bo-Bi Bar

MAP P.32, POCKET MAP C11
Klareboderne 4 ⓣ 33 12 55 43.
This Baroque, red hole-in-the-wall is one of the city's most authentic watering holes. Opened in 1917, it sports Copenhagen's oldest bar counter and attracts a refreshingly boho clientele of writers, students and intellectuals – great for people-watching. Serves cheap bottles of great Danish and Czech beers as well as local schnapps.

Charlie's Bar

MAP P.32, POCKET MAP D11
Pilestræde 33 ⓣ 33 32 22 89.
Small and packed, Copenhagen's only UK-style pub – even boasting Casque Mark accreditation – draws

in the crowds night after night for its ever-changing range of British ales and ciders.

K-Bar
MAP P.32, POCKET MAP D12
Ved Stranden 20 Ⓦ k-bar.dk.
Tucked round the corner from Højbro Plads square, this funky cocktail bar has deep, cosy sofas into which punters can happily sink as they sip the beautiful concoctions of owner Kirsten – hence the K. Try the unusual and moreish Rissitini, made with gin, sake, lychee liqueur and ginger.

The Living Room
MAP P.32, POCKET MAP D12
Larsbjørnsstræde 17 Ⓦ thelivingroom.dk.
Laidback corner bar on chilled Larsbjørnsstræde, with tables outside and soft sofas in the basement. It's a great place to go for freshly squeezed juices, organic wines, coffee and affordable cocktails.

Ruby
MAP P.32, POCKET MAP C12
Nybrogade 10 Ⓦ rby.dk.
Set in what appears to be for all the world an unassuming ground-floor apartment, with comfy leather armchairs and no obvious signage, this is possibly the city's best cocktail bar. Try the signature Rapscallion – a Scottish take on the Manhattan, with Talisker over a sweet PX sherry.

Music venues

Drop Inn
MAP P.32, POCKET MAP B12
Kompagnistræde 34 Ⓦ drop-inn.dk.
Small folk, blues and rock venue, with tables spilling onto the pavement during hot summer months and a good selection of international beers. Music from about 10pm most nights; it's often free to get in during the week but there may be a small charge at the weekend.

Jazzhus Montmartre
MAP P.32, POCKET MAP D11
Store Regnegade 19A
Ⓦ jazzhusmontmartre.dk.
Intimate, not-for-profit jazz club, which reopened in 2010 after having placed Copenhagen firmly on the international jazz map in the 1950s when it hosted legends such as Dexter Gordon and Stan Getz. Concerts two to three nights a week.

La Fontaine
MAP P.32, POCKET MAP C12
Kompagnistræde 11 Ⓦ lafontaine.dk.
As Copenhagen's oldest jazz venue, *La Fontaine* has for decades been where jazz musicians make for on their nights off. It's small and packed, with live gigs at the weekend (from 9pm; expect an entry fee).

Musikcaféen
MAP P.32, POCKET MAP C12
Rådhusstræde 13 Ⓦ facebook.com/musikcafeenihuset.
On the third floor of the Huset cultural centre, this is the place to hear up-and-coming bands before they become famous. Gigs most nights, starting at 8 or 9pm.

Bo Bi Dar

Slotsholmen

Encircled by Indre By on three sides and abutting the Inner Harbour on the fourth, the flat, diminutive island of Slotsholmen has been the country's seat of power for almost a thousand years. It was here, in 1167, that Bishop Absalon founded a castle to protect the village's herring traders from Wendish pirates. The area is anchored by the commanding and glum-looking Christiansborg Slot; home to the Danish parliament and the royals' reception rooms, it's the fifth incarnation of a royal dwelling on this site. Other highlights within the palace complex include the extravagant Royal Stables and riding ground, the elegant Palace Chapel and, next door, the colourful Thorvaldsens Museum, while on the opposite side of Christiansborg the Daniel Libeskind-designed interior of the Danish Jewish Museum and, on the waterfront, the gleaming Black Diamond extension to the Royal Library provide more modern architectural draws.

Folketing (Danish Parliament)

MAP P.44, POCKET MAP D13
Christiansborg ⓜ Gammel Strand ⓦ the danishparliament.dk. Free tours can be booked online; sittings roughly Oct to mid-June Tues & Wed from 1pm, Thurs & Fri from 10am.

Royal Reception Rooms

Occupying the southern half of the three-winged palace of Christiansborg, the **Folketing** (Danish parliament) is a must for fans of the cult TV political drama series *Borgen*, set in and around the palace. You can watch the debates in the principal parliamentary chamber, the **Folketingssal**, when in session – ring the visitors' entrance bell, and, if spaces are available, you'll be taken through security checks to the public galleries – though bear in mind that debates are not nearly as animated as the UK equivalent. Alternatively the Sunday English-language **tours** cover the history of Danish democracy as well as the palace's colourful history, taking you down the long Vandrehal where the much revered original Danish constitution from 1849 is displayed in a silver chest.

Royal Reception Rooms

MAP P.44, POCKET MAP D12
Christiansborg ⓜ Gammel Strand ⓦ christiansborg.dk. April–June and Sept daily 10am–5pm, July and August daily 10am–6pm, Oct–March Tues–Sun

Royalty Danish style

The Danish Royal Family stands as one of the oldest monarchies in the world. The current monarch, Her Majesty Queen Margrethe II, traces her lineage all the way back to Harald Bluetooth, the famous Viking chieftain and first king of a united Denmark over a thousand years ago. The Royal Family remains an extremely popular institution in Denmark. Crown Prince Frederik has been regularly voted "Dane of The Year", while his Tasmanian-born wife Princess Mary is both vaunted style icon and global advocate of women's health. Rarely the centre of public controversy, the Royal Family stole headlines in September 2022, when the Queen decided to strip certain grandchildren – those born to her second son Joachim – of their Princely titles, downgrading their titles to those of mere counts and countesses.

10am–5pm; closed during royal functions, charge (combined ticket with Ruins Under Christiansborg and Royal Stables); tours at 3pm.

Although it was built as a royal palace, the royals have never actually lived at Christiansborg, favouring the slightly more open and accessible Amalienborg. A section of the northern wing of the palace is, however, still in royal use for official functions as the **Royal Reception Rooms** (Det Kongelige Repræsentationslokaler) accessed via the Inner Courtyard. Sure to impress any visiting dignitaries, all the rooms are beautifully adorned. An intricate marble frieze depicting Alexander's march into Babylon by Thorvaldsen (see page 45) was recovered from the previous Christiansborg and following skilful restoration is on display in the Alexander Hall. The marble walls in the oval Throne Room are clad in delicate silks from Lyon, while on the ceiling a magnificent painting depicts the origins of the national flag. Best of all, however, is the long Great Hall, lined with seventeen magnificent tapestries by Bjørn Nørgaard (also famous for the mosaics on Strøget; see page 30). A fiftieth birthday present for the current Queen, they depict the country's history from the Viking Age to the present. See if you can spot The Beatles and Mao Zedong.

Ruinerne Under Christiansborg (castle ruins)

MAP P.44, POCKET MAP D12
Christiansborg Ⓜ Gammel Strand
Ⓦ christiansborg.dk. April–June and Sept daily 10am–5pm, July and Aug daily 10am–6pm, Oct–March Tues–Sun 10am–5pm, charge (combined ticket with Royal Reception Rooms and Royal Stables). The **ruins** of Slotsholmen's two earliest castles have been excavated and now form part of an underground **exhibition** beneath Christiansborg, accessed via a stairwell from the main entrance portal. A walkway tracks the foundations of Bishop Absalon's original castle, while the extant highlight of its successor, Københavns Slot, which was put up in the late fourteenth century, is the foundations of its notorious Blue Tower prison where King Christian IV's favourite daughter Leonora Christine was kept captive for nearly 22 years, paying for the crimes of her husband, Corfitz Ulfeldt, who was convicted of treason.

Ridebane (Royal Stables)

MAP P.44, POCKET MAP C13
Christiansborg Ridebane 12 Ⓜ Gammel Strand Ⓦ christiansborg.dk. April–June and Aug–Sept daily 1.30–4pm, July daily 10am–6pm, Oct–March Tues–Sun 1:30–4pm; English tours Sat at 2pm, charge (option for combined ticket with Royal Reception

Rooms and Ruins under Christiansborg). Beyond the Inner Courtyard, the **Ridebane** (Royal Stables) and surrounding riding ground are all that's left of the opulent Baroque palace that stood here from 1738 until it burnt to the ground 56 years later. If you arrive around mid-morning you stand a good chance of seeing the Queen's horses being exercised either in the outdoor riding arena, or, if you poke your head in discreetly, in the lavish Riding Hall.

The **Museet Kongelige Stalde og Kareter** (Museum of Royal Stables and Coaches), in the southern flank, houses the extravagant marble-clad stables where a few lucky horses are still kept, alongside the royal collection of gilded carriages plus the previous king's beautiful old Bentley.

To the west as you exit the museum, the Baroque **Marmorbroen** (Marble Bridge) linking Slotsholmen with mainland Indre By was the original palace's main approach.

Christiansborg Slotskirke (Palace Chapel)

MAP P.44, POCKET MAP D12
Prins Jørgens Gård 1 Ⓜ Gammel Strand
Ⓦ christiansborg.dk. July daily 10am–6pm; Aug–June Sun 10am–5pm.

Fully restored following a catastrophic fire in 1992 the Neoclassical **Palace Chapel** is all that remains of the second Christiansborg palace, which like its predecessor also burnt to the ground some fifty-odd years after completion (in 1833). The palace was said to be the most lavish of all the Christiansborg incarnations, though the church's elegant and light interior – topped by a vast white dome with four angels in relief seemingly floating beneath – is exquisite Classical simplicity itself. Still put to use for the opening

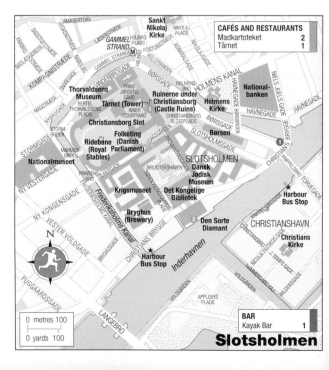

Slotsholmen

Royal Stables

of parliament service and for the occasional royal event, the church is also used for organ practice by the Danish Music Conservatory.

Thorvaldsens Museum

MAP P.44, POCKET MAP C12
Bertel Thorvaldsens Plads 2 Ⓜ Gammel Strand Ⓦ thorvaldsensmuseum.dk.Tues–Sun 10am–5pm, charge; free admission on Wednesdays.

Dedicated to Denmark's most internationally celebrated sculptor, the **Thorvaldsens Museum** is an absorbing place to while away a few hours. You certainly won't miss the grand Neoclassical edifice, overlooking the picturesque Frederiksholms Kanal, within which it's housed: with its striking ochre facade, and unusual slanting doors and window frames, it stands out as one of the city's most original buildings.

Having trained in Copenhagen, **Bertel Thorvaldsen** (1770–1844) spent forty years fulfilling high-profile commissions in Rome before returning triumphantly in 1839 – an event depicted on the huge frieze painted on the canal-facing side of the building. Thorvaldsen spent the last few years

of his life fulfilling commissions in Copenhagen, and his work can be seen in both Vor Frue Kirke and Christiansborg Slotskirke.

Inside, richly decorated walls and mosaic floors provide a fitting backdrop for the vast collection of Thorvaldsen's works on the ground floor, from huge marble sculptures to sketches and grubby plaster casts with the sculptor's own original marks. Highlights include the intimate *Cupid and Psyche* and Thorvaldsen's own self-portrait in stone. Upstairs, the sculptor's fine collection of Greek, Roman and Egyptian antiquities is on display.

Krigsmuseet

MAP P.44, POCKET MAP F8
Tøjhusgade 3 Ⓜ Gammel Strand Ⓦ natmus.dk.Tues–Sun 10am–5pm, charge; under 18s free.

Part of the National Museum (see page 28), the **Danish War Museum** showcases both famous battles from the past and more recent battles, most remarkable, though, is the 156m arched hall housing the cannon collection, said to be the longest such hall in Europe. The exhibitions range form a walk-through relaying the Danish

Thorvaldsens Museum

experience in war-torn Afghanistan, to Cold War posters. Most remarkable, though, is the 156m arched hall housing the cannon collection, said to be the longest such hall in Europe. The former Orlogsmuseet (Royal Danish Naval museum) closed down in 2015; as a result the Krigsmuseet houses incredibly detailed, to-scale ship models from sixteenth-century galleons, modern submarines play and other historical warships from the Danish navy.

Børsen

MAP P.44, POCKET MAP D13
Børsgade Ⓜ Gammel Strand.

A fanciful riot of gables, pinnacles and grey-green copper, the red-brick **Børsen** building is one of the more remarkable monuments of Christian IV's reign. It's for its wonderfully whimsical spire – made up of the intertwined tails of four sculpted dragons – that the building is best known. The dragons supposedly protect the Børsen from attack and fire, and seem to be fulfilling their duties quite successfully as the building has survived many a skirmish as those around it have burnt to the ground. Although ownership of

the building has long since passed to the Chamber of Commerce (it's not open to the public), the dragon spire remains the official symbol of the Danish stock exchange.

Dansk Jødisk Museum

MAP P.44, POCKET MAP D13
Proviantpassagen 6 Ⓜ Gammel Strand
Ⓦ jewmus.dk. June–Aug Tues–Sun 10am–5pm; Sept–May Tues–Sun noon–5pm, Sat & Sun noon–5pm, charge; under 18s free.

Opened in 2004 and designed by Daniel Libeskind, architect of the new World Trade Center site in New York, the **Danish Jewish Museum** retells the story of Jewry in Denmark from their arrival in the seventeenth century at the invitation of Christian IV up to the gruesome wartime period. Housed in the Galajhus (Royal Boat House), the building gives no indication from the outside of its subtly disorientating interior, a labyrinth of fractured passageways and sloping floors reminiscent of Libeskind's more famous Jewish Museum in Berlin. The museum's layout corresponds to the interlocking characters of the Hebrew word *Mitzvah* ("good deed"), a reference to the Danes' smuggling of seven thousand Jews hidden away in fishing boats across to sanctuary in Sweden during World War II (see page 53).

The exhibition itself is divided into five sections, focusing on different aspects of Danish-Jewish life. The most captivating of these is the Mitzvah section itself, which recounts the plight of Danish Jews during Nazi occupation. There are some heartfelt and touching letters and photos from refugees in Sweden on show, and hand-drawn sketches of horrible episodes at the Theresienstadt concentration camp (in what's now the Czech Republic), where 481 Danish Jews were sent.

Den Sorte Diamant (The Black Diamond)
MAP P.44, POCKET MAP D13
Søren Kierkegaards Plads 1 ⓦ Gammel Strand ⓦ kb dk. Mon–Sat 8am–9pm; tours Sat 3pm, charge.
Den Sorte Diamant (The Black Diamond), a monumental slab of black Zimbabwean granite and glass that leans over (and glitters magically in) the waters of the Inner Harbour below, is one of the city's great modern architectural icons.

Cafés and restaurants

Madkartoteket
MAP P.44, POCKET MAP D13
Søren Kierkegaards Plads 1
ⓦ madkartoteket.dk.
A popular venue among the city's studious, this café, located in the light and airy foyer of the Black Diamond, serves sandwiches, excellent coffee and a tempting array of mouth-watering cakes. There are deckchairs on the Inner Harbour quayside in summer, too. €

Tårnet
MAP P.44, POCKET MAP D12
Christiansborg Slotsplads ⓦ Meyers.dk.
Set within the beautiful, historic rooms of the Parliament Building,

Completed in 1999, the building is an extension to the Italian-inspired **Kongelige Bibliotek** (Royal Library) (1906), to which it is connected by a futuristic glass-enclosed bridge.

The building houses an auditorium with outstanding acoustics, museums dedicated to photography and cartoon art, and a changing display of works from the Royal Library's collection. You're free to wander about the building at will, though some of the exhibitions do charge an entrance fee. Among its attractions are the National Museum of Photography, which – in addition to some 50,000 photos in its collection, dating back to the birth of photography in 1839 – hosts interesting changing exhibitions of both modern and historical photographers (Mon–Sat 10am–7pm; charge).

The old library building behind is less accessible to the general public and best experienced on the **guided tours**. Highlights include several of the atmospheric old study halls, one which features the city's earliest grid-powered electric lamps.

Tårnet ("the Tower") serves topnotch smørrebrød and other Danish classics with a refined modern twist. Try the open-faced sourdough sandwich with eggs and anchovy créme. The restaurant also offers access to the building's tower, affording fantastic views of the city. €€

Bar

Kayak Bar
MAP P.44, POCKET MAP E13
Børskaj 12 ⓦ kayakbar.dk.
This low-key bar is tucked away from the road, pressed up against the canal on the waterside. Sit back and enjoy a cold beer or a mountain of shrimp while watching the boats slip by. This is also the launching point for canal kayak tours.

Nyhavn and Frederiksstaden

Packed with busy bars and restaurants, canalside Nyhavn attracts thousands of visitors thanks to its pretty postcard setting. To its north are the elegant Rococo houses and immaculately straight streets of Frederiksstaden, built as a grand symbol of Frederik V's reign. The huge dome of the Marmorkirken dominates the skyline, while three main north–south streets divide the area: Store Kongensgade, lined with galleries, restaurants and high-end shops; quieter Bredgade; and partially cobbled Amaliegade, which bisects the palaces of Amalienborg – the royals' official winter residence. All three streets lead up to Christian IV's impressive defensive fortress, the grass-bastioned Kastellet, close to which is a pair of inspirational museums. Finally, perched on a lonely rock off the Kastellet's northern edge, is the city's most famous icon – the diminutive Little Mermaid.

Nyhavn

MAP P.50, POCKET MAP E11–F11
Ⓜ Kongens Nytorv.

Picturesque **Nyhavn** is perhaps the city's most popular tourist hangout. The "new harbour" was created in 1671 to link Kongens

Nyhavn

Nytorv to the sea – the earliest of the townhouses, no. 9, dates from this period – and has been home to some famous residents – Hans Christian Andersen lived for a while at no. 67. The area has not always been so salubrious, however: Nyhavn went through a long period as the city's most disreputable red-light district before its transformation into the welcoming visitor haunt of today. On a sunny summer's evening (there are outdoor heaters in winter) it's easy to see the attraction of sipping a beer while gazing over the historic yachts (usually) moored in the harbour. Be warned, though: food and drink do not come cheap.

Kunsthal Charlottenborg

MAP P.50, POCKET MAP E11
Nyhavn 2 Ⓜ Kongens Nytorv
Ⓦ charlottenborg.dk. Sat–Sun 11am–5pm, charge; free admission on Wednesdays after 5pm.

Located between Kongens Nytorv and Nyhavn (and with entrances on both) the **Kunsthal Charlottenborg** is housed in one

Amalienborg

of the least prepossessing palaces in Copenhagen. Built for the illegitimate son of Frederik III, it has since 1754 been home to the Royal Danish Academy of Fine Arts. There are no permanent displays but changing exhibitions of modern art are put on in the newer building (added in 1883) behind. One such exhibition in 1971, about the new hippie movement, triggered the founding of Christiania (see page 71).

Amalienborg

MAP P.50, POCKET MAP F10
Amalienborgmuseet (Amalienborg Museum) Ⓜ Marmorkirken Ⓦ amalienborg museet.dk, roughly April–Aug daily 10am–4pm; Sept–March daily 10am–3pm; check website for precise scheme as hours vary from week to week, charge.

The winter residence of the Danish royal family, **Amalienborg** is made up four almost identical Rococo palaces, arranged symmetrically around an octagonal courtyard that centres on a statue of Frederik V on horseback. Designed by royal architect Nicolai Eigtved in 1750, the palaces were originally built for (and funded by) wealthy Danish nobles, though the royals commandeered them following the devastating fire at Christiansborg in 1794. Today all four palaces are named both after their original benefactor and a subsequent resident royal. The Queen lives in Christian IX's Palæ – or Schacks Palæ – with her husband Prince Henrik, while Frederik VIII's Palæ (Brockdorffs Palæ) is home to Crown Prince Frederik and family; both are completely off-limits.

Note too that **Christian VII's Palæ** (also known as Moltkes Palæ), whose fabulous Great Hall is considered to be one of the finest Rococo rooms in Europe, is unfortunately no longer open to the public.

You can, however, visit Christian VIII's Palæ (Levetzaus Palæ), the first floor of which contains the **Amalienborgmuseet** (Amalienborg Museum), devoted to more recent royal history. The studies of each of the last three kings have been fully reconstructed (complete with vast pipe collections and family portraits), giving a flavour

Nyhavn and Frederiksstaden

	metres	200
0		
	yards	200
0		

CAFÉS AND RESTAURANTS

Buka Bakery	12
Café Oscar	5
Cap Horn	15
Emmerys	13
Hyttefadet	16
Kafferiet	2
Kokkeriet	3
Lumskebugten	1
Madklubben	7
MASH	11
Mormors	8
Nyhavn 17	14
Punk Royale	9
Rebel	10
Taste	6
Vespa	4

SHOPS

DesignMuseum Danmark shop	2
Galerie Asbæk	3
Løgismose	1
Peter Beier Chokolade	4

BAR

Den Vandrette	1

ACCOMMODATION

71 Nyhavn	3
Admiral Hotel	2
Babette Guldsmeden	1
Hotel Bethel	4

of their modern if by no means luxurious lifestyles.

Outside on the courtyard, the **changing of the guard** ceremony at noon each day is a great hit with kids.

Skuespilhuset

MAP P.50, POCKET MAP F11

Sankt Annæ Plads 36 Ⓜ Kongens Nytorv Ⓦ kglteater.dk. Check website for guided tour times, charge.

The **Skuespilhuset** (Playhouse), around the corner from Nyhavn, is unanimously agreed to be one of the city's most elegant new buildings. It has a stunning position on the Inner Harbour, with a projecting upper storey that appears to be balancing precariously over the water's edge. A copper-clad tower thrusts skyward from within, while a wooden promenade encircles the building and doubles as an outdoor café. To see the inside, either join one of the irregular tours or take in a performance – although productions here are almost exclusively staged in Danish.

The Royal Danish Playhouse

Marmorkirken

MAP P.50, POCKET MAP E10

Frederiksgade 4 Ⓜ Marmorkirken Ⓣ 33 15 01 44. Mon–Thurs & Sat 10am–5pm, Fri & Sun noon–5pm, free.

Modelled on St Peter's in the Vatican, the **Marmorkirken** (Marble Church), which is properly called Frederiks Kirke, took almost 150 years to complete. Originally commissioned by Frederik V in 1749, the church's construction was halted twenty years later due to lack of funds, and only with financial support from a leading Danish industrial magnate, C.F. Tietgen, was it completed – using cheaper marble – in 1894, having languished in ruins for more than a century. You can join a tour to climb the 260 steps to the top of the **dome** (charge), from which there are spectacular views down over diminutive Copenhagen beneath you and towards the Swedish coastline in the distance. Note too how the relatively new Operaen across the harbour has been aligned perfectly with the Marmorkirken and Amalienborg.

Designmuseum Danmark

MAP P.50, POCKET MAP G6

Bredgade 68 Ⓜ Marmorkirken

Ⓦ designmuseum.dk. Tues–Sun 10am–6pm, Thurs 10am–8pm, charge.

Formerly the Kunstindustrimuseet, and not to be confused with the (now closed) Danish Design Center, this temple to (predominantly Danish) design occupies the four wings of the old Frederiks Hospital. Pride of place among the permanent exhibitions goes to the section on twentieth-century **Danish applied art and craft**, which takes in the full range of the iconic designs that have given Denmark its international reputation – from Arne Jacobsen's Ant chair to Kaj Bojesen's classic wooden toy monkey and Ole Kirk Christiansen's Lego brick. Elsewhere, the collection traces the history of European and Asian applied and decorative art, with the emphasis on how it relates to the development of Danish design. The Asian collection is particularly strong – ranging from Japanese sword paraphernalia to Chinese Ming vases. Check out the selection in the museum shop (see page 54) if you fancy taking any pieces home with you.

Frihedsmuseet

MAP P.50, POCKET MAP G6

Esplanaden 13 Ⓜ Marmorkirken

Ⓦ natmus.dk. Daily 10am–5pm (Sept–April: closed Mon), charge; under 18s free.

The original Frihedsmuseum ("Museum of Freedom" or Museum of Danish Resistance) was sadly destroyed by fire in 2013. Fortunately, no archival records or artefacts – such as Himmler's eye patch, taken off him by the Allies as he was captured trying to flee in disguise – were lost in the 2013 blaze. Its replacement, inaugurated in 2020, resembles a bunker, with most of its World War II-era exhibits situated underground. Though small, the museum is well worthwhile, presenting the personal stories of five historical witnesses to the war which represent both sides of the struggle in Denmark. Audio-guide highly recommended.

Kastellet

MAP P.50, POCKET MAP G5

Ⓜ Østerport Ⓜ Marmorkirken. Daily 6am–10pm.

Designmuseum Danmark

The Danish Resistance

Despite pledging to remain neutral during World War II Denmark was occupied by German forces from April 9, 1940 until May 1945. While the occupation was not the bloodbath that unfurled elsewhere in Europe, **resistance groups** nonetheless sprung up, among them the "Churchill Club", a group of schoolboys who sabotaged German vehicles, and the Hvidsten Group (subject of a hit 2012 Danish film) who distributed British weapons from secret airdrops. One of the proudest moments of this period was the clandestine evacuation in October 1943 of the vast majority of Denmark's seven thousand Jews to safety in neutral Sweden; almost everyone seems to have an uncle or grandfather who was somehow involved.

Surrounded by grassy ramparts and a series of moats, Copenhagen's quaint **Kastellet** (Citadel) is one of the best-preserved star-shaped fortresses in northern Europe. Brainchild of Christian IV and completed by Frederik III, it was constructed to defend the city from all sides, including from the city itself in case of rebellion. Its terraced rows of immaculate, mansard-roofed barracks, painted in warm red hues, are still occupied by troops, making this also one of Europe's oldest functioning military bases. The granite war memorial in its southwest corner, dedicated to the many Danish soldiers who have been lost in action around the world since 1948, was unveiled in 2011.

The Little Mermaid

MAP P.50, POCKET MAP G5
Ⓜ Østerport, Ⓜ Marmorkirken.

Sitting on a boulder in the Inner Harbour off the northern edge of Kastellet, looking forlornly out to sea, **The Little Mermaid** (*Den lille havfrue*) is the city's most famous symbol. The embodiment of Hans Christian Andersen's fairy-tale character, she was created by Danish sculptor Edvard Eriksen in 1913 and paid for by Carlsberg brewery magnate Carl Jakobsen. Considering her diminutive size and somewhat vacant facial expression, the cynical observer might find it difficult to fathom her appeal to the busloads of tourists that visit her 24 hours a day,

though her tragic tale of doomed love for her dream prince still has a powerful hold on the Danish imagination. The statue has not had an easy life, either. She's been the frequent victim of radical groups, covered in paint several times and beheaded twice.

A more recent addition a few hundred metres to the north along the waterfront at Langeliniekaj, the Little Mermaid's iconoclastic "ugly sister" is far more entertaining. Part of Bjørn Nørgaard's sculpture garden **The Genetically Modified Paradise**, she sits like her older sister on a boulder in the water, but with body and limbs grotesquely elongated and contorted – perhaps a truer rendition of Andersen's Little Mermaid's suffering than the original statue.

Medicinsk Museion

MAP P.50, POCKET MAP G6
Bredgade 62 Ⓜ Marmorkirken Ⓦ museion. ku.dk. Tues-Fri 10am–4pm, Sat-Sun 12pm–4pm, charge.

Not for the faint of heart, the **Medical Museum** presents a fascinating tour of the Danish history of medicine. The ample collection of rare items – from dissected body parts to conjoined babies encased in glass – may leave some visitors somewhat queasy, though it will certainly impress upon all a greater appreciation for the hard-fought advances in modern medicine.

Shops

DesignMuseum
Danmark shop

MAP P.50, POCKET MAP G6
Bredgade 68 ⓦ designmuseum.dk.
The Design Museum's shop is a
great place for industrial design,
and to pick up ceramics, glass,
textiles and jewellery, all Danish-
made. Check out Kaj Bojesen's
wooden animal toys and the
beautiful glassware by Holmegaard.

Galerie Asbæk

MAP P.50, POCKET MAP E11
Bredgade 23 ⓦ asbaek.dk.
This well-known art gallery sells
works by some of the country's
leading contemporary artists,
including CoBrA painter Carl
Henning-Pedersen (aka the
"Scandinavian Chagall") and
photographer Niels Bonde.

Løgismose

MAP P.50, POCKET MAP G5
Nordre Toldbod 16 ⓦ loegismose.dk.

A cornucopia of fabulous wines and
spirits is on sale at this deli on the
Innerhavnen, as well as delicious
cheeses and charcuterie from
France, Spain and Italy. It's also an
outlet for heavenly Summerbird
chocolate (see page 81).

Peter Beier Chokolade

MAP P.50, POCKET MAP E11
Store Kongensgade 3
ⓦ pbchokolade.dk.
Wonderful selection of handmade
chocolates, made with the finest
ingredients. The cocoa comes
from their own plantation in the
Caribbean.

Cafés and
restaurants

Buka Bakery

MAP P.50, POCKET MAP E11
Store Kongensgade 18
ⓦ buka-bakery.com.
Part of a recent (and very welcome)
wave of upscale bakeries aimed at

Cap Horn

upholding Denmark's proud pastry tradition, this bakery-cum-café offers delightful, filled croissants (try the pistachio) and usually has a fruity, seasonal spandauer – the Danish "Danish". €

Café Oscar

MAP P.50, POCKET MAP G6
Bredgade 58 ⓦ cafeoscar.dk.

Upmarket corner café a short walk from Amalienborg, serving a selection of excellent smørrebrød, sandwiches and salads, plus an evening menu of café classics like Moules Frites. Fabulous food aside, it's to be seen hobnobbing with the rich and famous that most people come. €€

Cap Horn

MAP P.50, POCKET MAP E11
Nyhavn 21 ⓦ caphorn.dk.

The best choice among the long row of overpriced restaurants along Nyhavns Kanal, *Cap Horn* serves largely organic fare, including juicy burgers and always one or two seafood options. €€

Emmerys

MAP P.50, POCKET MAP E11
Store Strandstræde 21 ⓦ emmerys.dk.

Part of an ever-expanding chain of café-bakeries, *Emmerys* is famous for its slow-risen organic bread, which you sample in sandwiches or as part of a breakfast platter. It's a great coffee stop, too, and treat yourself to a superb gooey brownie while you're at it. €

Hyttefadet

MAP P.50, POCKET MAP F11
Nyhavn 25 ⓦ hyttefadet.dk.

One of Nyhavn's older restaurants, purportedly dating back to the 1720s, *Hyttefadet* serves smørrebrød for lunch and traditional Danish fare for dinner – try the *wienerschnitzel med dreng* (lit. "with boy", a slice of lemon artfully topped with anchovies, capers and fresh grated horseradish). Embrace the touristy vibes and enjoy the postcard view of Nyhavn. €€

Kafferiet

MAP P.50, POCKET MAP G6
Esplanaden 44 ⓦ kafferiet.net.

Colourful and cosy little coffee shop across from Kastellet with a few tables inside and a couple outside on the street, too. There's delightful coffee and home-made cakes, plus interesting Italian confectionery: sweets from Pastiglie Leone and strong Amarelli liquorice. A little gem in an otherwise café-barren area. €

Kokkeriet

MAP P.50, POCKET MAP F6
Kronprinsessegade 64 ⓦ kokkeriet.dk.

Located on a quiet street in the heart of Copenhagen, this Michelin-starred restaurant offers traditional Danish and wider Scandinavian cuisine at its best. Set tasting menus paired with excellent wines are available. Advance bookings recommended. €€€

Lumskebugten

MAP P.50, POCKET MAP G5
Esplanade 21 ⓦ lumskebugten.dk.

A small and exclusive restaurant by Churchill Park near the Little Mermaid statue, with fine food and excellent wine. While known for its seafood, vegetarians can delight in their own three-course menu – a joy in such a meat-and-fish-oriented city. Vegans are well-catered for too. Reservations are essential. €€

Madklubben

MAP P.50, POCKET MAP E10
Store Kongensgade 66
ⓦ madklubben.dk.

Branch of the wildly popular restaurant chain that offers simple, tasty food with fast and efficient service. €

MASH

MAP P.50, POCKET MAP E11

Bredgade 20 Ⓦ mashsteak.dk.
MASH stands for Modern American Steak House, which is exactly what you get – juicy steaks in a US diner setting. Starters range from carpaccio to half a grilled lobster and the steaks come in all shapes and sizes – from Uruguayan tenderloin to American bone-in ribeye, via Japanese A5 Wagyu. €€

Mormors

MAP P.50, POCKET MAP E10
Bredgade 45 Ⓦ mormors.dk.
A homely pit stop, *Mormors* ("Grandma's") easily lives up to its name with its warm and welcoming feel. There's hot soup for the cold winter months, a range of freshly made juices, sandwiches galore and a counter full of delicious cakes. Park yourself in one of the window seats inside and enjoy the quirky aesthetics, or soak up some rays on the pavement tables out front.€

Nyhavn 17

MAP P.50, POCKET MAP E11
Nyhavn 17 Ⓦ nyhavn17.dk.
Housed in a 17th-century building with a big red neon sign on the front, it's hard to miss. Inside it's French bistro-meets old-fashioned bar, decorated with vintage photographs and nautical ornaments. The *stegt flæsk* (fried pork belly served with white parsley gravy) is a favourite. €€

Punk Royale

MAP P.50, POCKET MAP E10
Dronningens Tværgade 10
Ⓦ punkroyale.se/punk-royale-copenhagen
Edgy to the extreme, this highly unconventional restaurant combines fine dining with a range of surprises, from appetizers served in ash trays to latex gloves replacing silverware for certain dishes. Expect a wild ride of a meal with fire, glitter, a rave aesthetic and a fair bit of alcohol. Set menus. €€€

Nyhaven 17

Vespa

Rebel

MAP P.50, POCKET MAP E10
Store Kongensgade 52
Ⓦ restaurantrebel.dk.
Compact restaurant spread over
two floors serving elegant French-
inspired tapas. It's especially
renowned for its beef tartare,
served with rhubarb, herbed
mayonnaise and vinaigrette,
and turbot served with escargot,
lobster glaze and tarragon. 'The
little rebel' meal is a great variety
of flavours if you are undecided.
€€

Taste

MAP P.50, POCKET MAP E10
Store Kongensgade 80–82
Ⓦ taste-bistro-patisserie.dk.
This fabulous deli (with a few
tables out front) serves gorgeous
home-made salads, sandwiches
plus a range of exquisite cakes –
though as everything is of tip top
quality nothing comes cheap. Try
the tarte aux citron and the grilled
goat's cheese, beetroot and walnut
sandwich, with a honey and
rosemary dressing. €

Vespa

MAP P.50, POCKET MAP F6
Store Kongensgade 90 Ⓦ cofoco.dk.
Part of the Cofoco "food empire",
which follows a simple no-frills
concept. What's on offer is a
well-prepared four-course Italian
menu, consisting of four antipasti,
a secondo of your choice and a
dessert. Restrictive perhaps, but
excellent value for money. €€

Bar

Den Vandrette

MAP P.50, POCKET MAP F12
Havnegade 53A Ⓦ denvandrette.dk.
Wine cellar next to Copenhagen's
newest harbour bridge, with
a bare decor of brick and oak,
soft lighting and a range of
lesser-known biodynamic and
organic wines behind the counter.
Charcuterie and cheeses available.

Rosenborg and around

Christian IV's Renaissance summer palace, the Rosenborg Slot, provides a regal contrast with the crowded streets of the inner city to the east. To its west, running from Østerport station in the north to Vesterport in the south is an almost continuous string of attractive parks and gardens. Apart from being lovely places to explore, they also house a couple of significant art museums: the Statens Museum for Kunst and Hirschsprungske Samling, and the city's Botanical Gardens. It was thanks to visionary town planner Ferdinand Meldahl that the ring of ramparts and bastions encircling the city here were maintained as a green belt in 1857. The area between the ramparts and the lake later developed into sought-after residential areas and streets such as Nansensgade have a strong neighbourhood feel.

Rosenborg Slot

MAP P.60, POCKET MAP E6
4A Østervoldgade Ⓜ Nørreport
Ⓦ rosenborgslot.dk. Opening times vary;
check website for details. Castle, charge;
gardens, free.

A Disney-esque fairy-tale palace, the **Rosenborg Slot** was originally built as a summer residence for Christian IV, a retreat from the rabble at Christiansborg. Completed in 1634, it's a grand red-brick Renaissance edifice decorated with spires and towers and ornate Dutch gables. The palace remained a royal residence until 1838, when it was opened to the public.

Rosenborg Slot

Park life

Based around the Rosenborg Slot, the beautifully manicured **Kongens Have** (King's Garden) is Copenhagen's oldest park. Visitors come to see the famous statue of Hans Christian Andersen and watch live music and puppet-theatre performances during the summer (June–Aug daily except Mon 2 & 3pm; free; Ⓦ marionetteatret.dk). Stretching north from the Botanisk Have (Botanical Gardens), the undulating hills of **Østre Anlæg** are part of the old fortifications and house a number of different children's playgrounds including one in front of the National Museum of Art. **Ørstedsparken**, with its rolling hills and rampart lake, is a popular place to go in winter for skating and downhill sledging. There are also two innovative playgrounds here, one with staff at hand to show you the ropes. The parks offer a tranquil escape from the hustle and bustle of the city for a moment of peace and quiet.

The star exhibit inside is the **crown jewels**, chief among them the Crown of the Absolute Monarch which weighs in at a hefty two kilos and sports two massive sapphires. The jewels are kept locked in the basement Treasury, behind thick steel doors. Also downstairs are the priceless wines of the Royal cellar, only cracked open at very special occasions. Before heading down here it's worth taking in Frederik III's lavish marble room with its extravagant stucco ceiling and a chess set made up of Danish and Swedish pieces (in reference to the war he lost to Karl Gustav in 1658). Another highlight of the palace is the magnificent **Long Hall** on the second floor with its gilded coronation throne, made from narwhal tusk, and three silver lions standing guard.

Botanisk Have

MAP P.60, POCKET MAP E6
Gothersgade 128 Ⓜ Nørreport Ⓦ botanik. snm.ku.dk. Daily April–Sept 8.30am–6pm, Oct–March 8.30am–4pm, free.

Relocated in 1874 from a small park behind Charlottenborg palace the **Botanisk Have** (Botanical Gardens) packs in pretty much every plant you'll find in Denmark together with several exotic species. It's a pleasant and peaceful place to wander, with its long squiggly pond clearly showing the area's previous incarnation as the city ramparts. Among the many greenhouses in the gardens, the grand Palm House overshadows them all. It was donated by brewing magnate Carl Jacobsen who was deeply involved in its design and various ingenious temperature and humidity controls. You will also find houses for cacti, orchids, alpine plants, and a new greenhouse for endangered species (check the website for their specific opening times). Guided tours are available in English; days vary, so check the website.

The Botanical Museum, part of the gardens, is currently closed. A brand new National Natural History Museum, complete with innovative underground architecture, is due to open in 2020 at the northern end of the gardens.

Statens Museum for Kunst

MAP P.60, POCKET MAP E5
Sølvgade 48–50 Ⓜ Nørreport, Ⓜ Østerport Ⓦ smk.dk. Tues & Thurs–Sun 10am–6pm, Wed 10am–8pm, charge.

Found in the southeastern corner of Østre Anlæg park, the vast **Statens Museum for Kunst** (National Museum of Art) houses the bulk of Christian II's extensive collection of European paintings and sculptures. Housed in an 1896 building by Dahlerup (see also Ny Carlsberg Glyptotek, page 26) and complemented by a modern extension in 1998, the collection is divided into European art from the fourteenth to the eighteenth century, Danish and Nordic Art from 1750 to 1900, French art from 1900–1930, and modern art from the twentieth century. Trying to see it all in one day is almost impossible. Instead, if you're interested in Danish art, head straight for the second floor where works from the so-called Golden Age – the nineteenth century – are displayed in largely chronological order. Look out especially for the beautifully lit paintings of the Skagen school – among them P.S. Krøyer and Anna Ancher. Look out too for the stark almost photographic scenes of Copenhagen in the nineteenth century by Vilhelm Hammershøi. On the second floor you'll also find

work from the twentieth-century CoBrA movement (a collection of artists from Copenhagen, Brussels and Amsterdam). Contemporary international art is displayed in the museum's new extension. Recent temporary exhibits have included Matisse and Miró.

Hirschsprungske Samling

MAP P.60, POCKET MAP F5
Stockholmsgade 20 Ⓜ Nørreport,
Ⓜ Østerport Ⓦ hirschsprung.dk. Wed–Sun 10am–6pm, charge.

More manageable than the Statens Museum, the **Hirschsprung Collection** focuses on art from the Danish Golden Age (1800–1850), donated by Heinrich Hirschsprung, a second-generation German Jew who had made his fortune in tobacco. Housed in a beautiful Neoclassical pavilion, paintings are displayed in small intimate rooms (a condition Hirschsprung set before handing over his collection to the

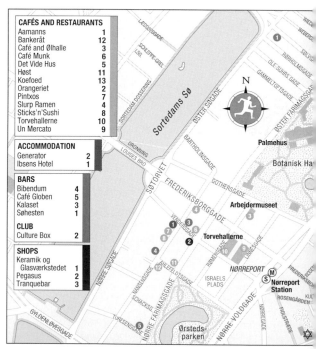

CAFÉS AND RESTAURANTS	
Aamanns	1
Bankeråt	12
Café og Ølhalle	3
Café Munk	6
Det Vide Hus	5
Høst	11
Koefoed	13
Orangeriet	2
Pintxos	7
Slurp Ramen	4
Sticks'n'Sushi	8
Torvehallerne	10
Un Mercato	9

ACCOMMODATION	
Generator	2
Ibsens Hotel	1

BARS	
Bibendum	4
Café Globen	5
Kalaset	3
Søhesten	1

CLUB	
Culture Box	2

SHOPS	
Keramik og Glasværkstedet	1
Pegasus	2
Tranquebar	3

state). As at the Staten Museum, the work of the Skagen artists P.S. Krøyer and Anna Ancher particularly stands out. Tranquil bucolic landscapes by P.C. Skovgaard and Johan Lundbye are also worth noting. More entertaining are the gossip-magazine-like paintings by Kristian Zahrtmann who depicted eighteenth-century royal scandals such as English-born Queen Caroline Mathilde's affair with court physician Johann Friedrich Struensee.

Arbejdermuseet

MAP P.60, POCKET MAP A10
Rømersgade 22 Ⓜ Nørreport
Ⓦ arbejdermuseet.dk. Daily 10am–4pm, Thurs until 8pm, charge.

Dedicated to the Danish workers movement, **Arbejdermuseet** is housed in the group's old meeting house from 1878 and covers the cultural history of the Danish working class from 1850 onwards. Although it's probably more of

Statens Museum for Kunst

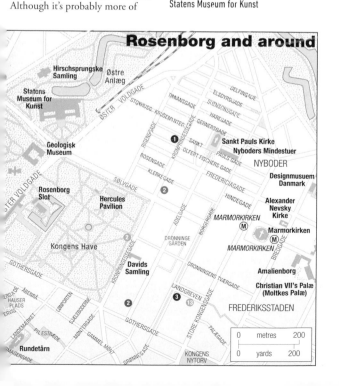

A taste of Torvehallerne

A few of Torvehallerne's best stalls (⑩ torvehallernekbh.dk) are listed below and should be visited in their own right.

The Coffee Collective – the best coffee in town.

Grød – sells porridge, risotto and anything else eaten with a spoon, exclusively.

Hallernes Smørrebrød – great smørrebrød selected from a large display cabinet; Mikkeller on draught.

Hija de Sanchez – the city's best tacos, brought to you by a former *Noma* chef (see page 82).

Souls – excellent plant-based burgers and sides.

Summerbird – chocolate made in heaven.

Tapa del Torro – delicious home-made tapas.

Unika – retail outlet for Danish-made, upmarket cheeses, some more experimental and adventurous than others.

interest to Danes, the historic assembly hall is worth a peek. Its tranquil bucolic decor witnessed some of the movement's most significant gatherings, not least the Socialist World Congress of 1910 which had Lenin himself in attendance (there's a Russian-made statue of him in the foyer dating from the late 1980s). The children's section, although mostly in Danish, is also popular, and often noisy, featuring doll's houses, dressing-up gear, colouring-in books and even a small pretend brewery. There's also a museum shop selling iconic workers' posters from the old Soviet Union and Kaffebaren, a 1950s workers' café serving coffee both with or without Rich's – a Chicory-based coffee replacement made popular during World War II, when coffee supplies were extremely scarce in Denmark.

Davids Samling

MAP P.60, POCKET MAP D10
Kronprinsessegade 30 ⑩ Marmorkirken
⑩ davidmus.dk. Thurs–Tues 10am–5pm,
Wed 10am–9pm, free.

Spread over all five floors of an eighteenth-century apartment building, the captivating **Davids Samling** comprises the remarkable collection of one C.L. David (1878–1960), a Danish lawyer who devoted

his life to the acquisition of fine and applied art. It's a labyrinth of rooms, and the museum plan handed out on arrival will prove essential. The highlight without doubt is the extensive exhibition of Islamic art on the third and fourth floors. One of the most important in the West, it includes delicate Persian miniatures, striking blue Ottoman mosaics and beautifully decorated glass bowls from Egypt and Syria. David's collections of eighteenth- and nineteenth-century porcelain and furniture and twentieth-century art (look out for the evocative landscape paintings by Vilhelm Hammershøi and the extravagant French ceramics) are also impressive but don't match the heights of the Islamic finds.

Torvehallerne and Israels Plads

MAP P.60 POCKET MAP B10
Market halls: Frederiksborggade 21
⑩ Nørreport ⑩ torvehallernekbh.dk. Mon–
Fri 10am–7pm, Sat–Sun 10am–6pm.

The **Torvehallerne** food hall (see page 66) is Copenhagen's most popular marketplace, attracting 115,000 visitors a week to its artisan stalls and restaurants. **Israels Plads** square next door, traditionally known for its flower stalls, reopened after two years of renovation, and this busy square fills with people in the summer, where its "flying carpet" architecture merges with neighbouring Ørstedsparken. The square was given its current name in 1968 in memory of Jewish persecution in Denmark during World War II.

Nyboder

MAP P.60, POCKET MAP F6.
Nyboder Mindestuer, 24 Sankt Paulsgade
Ⓜ Østerport Ⓦ nybodersmindestuer.dk.
Sun 11am–2pm, charge.

Standing out in contrast to the area's grand regal mansions, the colourful and quaint **Nyboder** district is made up of a series of rows of cute, predominantly ochre-coloured terraced houses. The area was originally built in the 1630s to provide housing for Christian IV's ever-expanding naval fleet, though most of the current buildings date from the eighteenth century – all except for a single row of houses along Sankt Paulsgade, where the **Nyboders Mindestuer** (Nyboder

The Coffee Collective, Torvehallerne

Memorial Rooms) has been largely kept intact and functions as a museum, with tours available by appointment. Diminutive though Nyboder's houses may be, this has always been a sought-after place to live, with its own private school and hospital, and demand remains high, particularly these days priority is no longer given to military personnel.

Dining with the Danes

The "New Nordic Cuisine" scene burst onto the global stage in 2010 when Copenhagen's *Noma* (see page 92) was named the world's best restaurant – a title it has claimed four more times since. The double-act behind it, restaurateur Claus Meyer and chef René Redzepi, blazed a trail by taking inspiration from, instead of being restricted, by the limited produce of Nordic countries. Seasonal, ethically sourced ingredients (often foraged or homegrown), are prepared using methods rooted in Nordic traditions - marinated, smoked or salted for example.

In 2022, the restaurant stole global headlines and shook the world of fine dining when it announced that it will close its doors at the end of 2024. The reason given was that cooking at such a high level is "financially and emotionally unsustainable", sparking an ongoing debate about the working environment and culture of the world's most respected kitchens. *Noma* won't disappear from the world entirely, however: it is set to reopen in 2025 as *Noma 3.0*, a "giant experimental food lab" that will return to serving guests.

Meanwhile, the Danish capital continues to garner far more Michelin stars than anywhere else in Scandinavia. Alternatively, to sample the Nordic kitchen while leaving your bank balance intact, you can head to Copenhagen Street Food (see page 92) or Torvehallerne food market (see page 66) to shop where the chefs do.

Shops

Keramik og Glasværkstedet

MAP P.60, POCKET MAP F6
Kronprinsessegade 43
Ⓦ keramikogglasvaerkstedet.dk.
Funky workshop-cum-gallery
selling delicate and minimalist
ceramics and glassware made on
the premises by four independent
artists.

Pegasus

MAP P.60, POCKET MAP A10
Nørre Farimagsgade 53 Ⓦ pegasus.dk.
Nerdy basement store selling
a huge selection of comics
and graphic novels (new and
secondhand) from around the
globe with an especially good
selection of American comics.

Tranquebar

MAP P.60, POCKET MAP E10
Borgergade 14 Ⓦ tranquebar.net.

Aamanns

Well-stocked book and music
shop with a vast selection of travel
literature and world music (and,
of course, a good range of Rough
Guides). There's good coffee
and delicious croissants – made
by well-known Copenhagen
chef Daniel Letz – in the
bookstore café.

Cafés and restaurants

Aamanns

MAP P.60, POCKET MAP E5
Øster Farimagsgade 10-12
Ⓦ aamanns.dk.
This stylish ode to traditional
Danish open sandwiches makes
hands-down the city's best
smørrebrød. Head chef Adam
Aamanns ensures everything is
free range and sourced from local
Danish farmers. It's perfect for a
visit with children, too, who love

the bite-sized portions. You can either eat in or take away in smart little picnic-friendly boxes. €

Bankeråt

MAP P.60, POCKET MAP A10
Ahlefeldtsgade 27–29 ⓦ bankeraat.dk.
Oldie but goodie Nansensgade café which is just as popular now as when it opened in the 80s with its largely unchanged quirky decor. Its signature breakfast/brunch Morgenkomplex comes in lots of different variations including "Full Engelsk". Turns into a popular bar come evening. €

Café and Ølhalle

MAP P.60, POCKET MAP B10
Rømersgade 22 ⓦ cafeogoelhalle.dk.
You may find the traditional nineteenth-century worker's fare served here a little heavy, but it is authentic and very tasty. Known for their natural ingredients and attention to detail, try the popular buffet which serves up a variety of smørrebrød and cakes. €

Café Munk

MAP P.60, POCKET MAP A10
Nørre Farimagsgade 55
ⓦ facebook.com/CafeMunk.
Easily spotted by its colourful outdoor seating, *Café Munk* is a quirky, laid-back restaurant serving Indian food (particularly renowned for its butter chicken), burgers and cocktails. Many of their dishes are suitable for vegans and vegetarians. Unlike many restaurants and bars in Copenhagen, Café Munk is above ground level. Convenient central location and affordable prices. €

Det Vide Hus

MAP P.60, POCKET MAP C10
Gothersgade 113
ⓦ facebook.com/detvidehus.
Cosy café serving favourites such as banana bread and avocado on toast with excellent coffee - all just a six-minute walk from Rosenborg Slot. The staff are friendly and there's

more seating upstairs to enjoy a relaxing pit stop. €

Høst

MAP P.60, POCKET MAP A10
Nørre Farimagsgade 41 ⓦ cofoco.dk.
The word *Høst* means harvest in Danish, so it's no surprise this award-winning restaurant's dishes are based around seasonal Nordic ingredients. Housed in a typical Copenhagen building, the interior is relaxed and stylish with exposed brick walls and Danish furniture. You can go for a three or five course menu with meals such as baked cod with tomatoes or fried Norwegian lobster. €€

Koefoed

MAP P.60, POCKET MAP E10
Landgreven 3 ⓦ restaurant-koefoed.dk.
Elegant *Koefoed* is an ode to the gourmet island of Bornholm, famous for its slow-food ethos and quality produce. The lunchtime smørrebrød has won awards - try *sol over gudhjem*, Bornholm's "national dish", served with smoked herring, radishes, chives and a raw egg yolk. Eat in the atmospheric, vaulted, stone-walled interior or outside on streetside tables. €€

Un Mercato

MAP P.60, POCKET MAP B10
Torvehallerne, Frederiksborggade 19
ⓦ unmercato.dk.
No-nonsense Italian rotisserie on the first floor of Torvehallerne, run by the people behind *Cofoco* restaurants. The lunchtime flame-grilled chicken or veggie sandwiches are mouthwatering. €

Orangeriet

MAP P.60, POCKET MAP D10
Kronprinsessegade 13
ⓦ restaurant-orangeriet.dk.
Atmospheric glass-encased café-restaurant located along the western wall of Kongens Have, with great views of the gardens, serving excellent smørrebrød for

lunch and more substantial meals for dinner. €€

Pintxos

MAP P.60, POCKET MAP A10
Nansensgade 63 ⓦ pintxostapas.dk.
Genuine Spanish restaurant with genuine Spanish waiters, and tapas galore in a romantic courtyard. The atmosphere is warm, cosy and inviting. €

Slurp Ramen

MAP P.60, POCKET MAP A10
Nansensgade 90 ⓦ slurpramen.dk.
Small, scrumptious Tokyo-style noodle joint with a menu to match: there are five kinds of ramen served here, including an excellent vegetarian option cooked in a mushroom-based broth. €

Sticks'n'sushi

MAP P.60, POCKET MAP A10
Nansensgade 59 ⓦ sushi.dk.
Copenhagen's original purveyors of sushi to the masses. Starting out some twenty years ago, they now have branches across the city (and in London). They can still make a mean sushi and also specialize in

yakitori sticks (marinated skewers of meat and fish) as well as an outstanding array of salads, best of which is the scrumptious Jungle Fish salad. €€

Torvehallerne

MAP P.60, POCKET MAP B10
Frederiksborggade 21
ⓦ torvehallernekbh.dk.
Denmark's biggest and best food market. It's split into two long open-sided halls, one featuring meat, cheese and fish and a non-smelly section where you'll find chocolate, bread and the like. In between are plenty of outdoor benches at which to eat. Restaurants and takeaways stay open an hour after the market closes. A great way to explore Torvehallerne is to join the city's new Food Tours (see page 121). €

Bars

Bibendum

MAP P.60, POCKET MAP A10
Nansensgade 45 ⓦ bibendum.dk.

Torvehallerne indoor food market

Kalaset

Small cosy basement wine bar with a huge selection of wine, all of which are sold by the glass as well as by the bottle. Also good nibbles to soak up the alcohol such as such as tartar or cured hake.

Café Globen

MAP P.60, POCKET MAP A11
Turesensgade 2b ⓦ cafegloben.dk.
Laidback travellers' haunt halfway between a club and a café with lots of guidebooks lying around and people keen to talk about their latest adventures, offering a good range of brews from both home and abroad.

Kalaset

MAP P.60, POCKET MAP A10
Vendersgade 16 ⓦ kalaset.dk.
Quirky shabby-chic basement café which spills out onto the pavement during summer when it's excellent to enjoy a cold drink.

Søhesten

MAP P.60, POCKET MAP E5
Sølvgade 103 ⓦ soehestenbar.dk.
Cosy, 80s-style bar with pub quizzes on Tuesdays, live jazz on Wednesdays and DJ dance nights on Fridays and Saturdays, typically featuring a classic, nostalgic soundtrack.

Club

Culture Box

MAP P.60, POCKET MAP F6
Kronprinsessegade 54
ⓦ culture-box.com.
Among Copenhagen's best-loved electronic music venues, this bar-club is spread over two floors with a Berlin-style industrial decor, hosting local and international names in house and techno. Carries on until the wee hours of the morning.

Christianshavn and Holmen

With its tight network of narrow canals and cobbled streets, Christianshavn – sometimes known as Little Amsterdam – is one of the city's most charming areas. Water is omnipresent, perhaps not surprising given that the island was constructed from reclaimed land in the sixteenth century to form a defensive arc around the city. For the most part the attractions here are low-key, though Christianshavn's principal source of tourist intrigue – the unique "Freetown" of Christiania, home to one of the world's most famous alternative communities – pulls in almost a million visitors a year. To the north, former naval base Holmen and its neighbouring islands have been re-energized after decades of disuse with post-industrial developments like the national opera house and an old shipyard, B&W Hallerne, that was rebuilt to host 2014's Eurovision Song Contest. To the south, Islands Brygge quay stretches along the harbourfront of Amager, and is worth visiting for its waterside park and lively cultural centre.

Christianshavns Kanal

MAP P.70, POCKET MAP E14–F14
Ⓜ Christianshavn.

Lined on both sides by cobbled streets and colourful merchant's houses, the tranquil **Christianshavns Kanal** originally provided the main way of accessing the island. This picturesque area is redolent of old Amsterdam, and indeed was designed by a Dutch architect, Johan Semp, who was commissioned in the early seventeenth century by Christian IV to plan the district.

Then as now, Christianshavn's main square, **Christianshavn Torv**, was the focal point of public transport to the island – today there's a metro station (underground) and constant flow of buses, as well as a canal-boat stop. A notable exception to the imposing historic buildings around the square is the modernist **Lagkagehuset** (Layercake House) at Torvegade

45. It created riotous debate when it was built in 1931 as it was felt it didn't blend in to its historic surroundings but today is deemed a national treasure.

Christians Kirke

MAP P.70, POCKET MAP E14
Strandgade 1 Ⓜ Christianshavn
Ⓦ christianskirke.dk. Tues–Fri 11am–5pm.

Surrounded by modern offices and apartments, Eigtved's Rococo **Christians Kirke** (1759) looks oddly out of place. It was originally built for the city's German congregation and still functions as a church, though its theatre-like interior makes it an excellent music venue.

Vor Frelserskirke

MAP P.70 POCKET MAP F13
Skt Annæ Gade 29 Ⓜ Christianshavn
Ⓦ vorfrelserskirke.dk. Church daily 11am–3.30pm; Tower June to mid-Sept daily 9am–8pm; mid-Sept to May daily 10am–4pm (Sun opens at 10.30am);

subject to closures for rain, snow or very windy weather. Church, free; Tower, charge.

Capped by an iconic church tower, its soaring spire wrapped in a gilded spiral external staircase which culminates in a globe carrying a flag-waving Jesus, **Vor Frelserskirke** (Our Saviour's Church) is an unmissable feature of the Christianshavn skyline. Constructed in the late 1600s, the church owes its opulence to Christian V, whose status as Denmark's first absolute monarch is underlined by some lavish Baroque flourishes. Inside, look out especially for the two stucco elephants holding up the gigantic three-storey organ, though the real highlight is the ascent of the **tower**, accessed by a separate entrance. There are 400 steps to the top, 150 of which are external – quite a challenge on a busy summer's day – but the stupendous views across the city are ample reward.

Freetown Christiania

MAP P.70, POCKET MAP G8
Main entrance on Prinsessegade

Christianshavn. Infocaféen daily noon–6pm; guided tours (starting at the main entrance) Sat & Sun 3pm.

A self-proclaimed autonomous enclave with its own governance and rules, **Freetown Christiania** is Copenhagen's main alternative claim to fame. Ever since 1971, when a group of homeless Copenhageners first occupied the disused Bådsmandsstræde army barracks, Christiania has attracted controversy, its very existence perennially threatened (see box). Today, thanks in no small part to its open cannabis trade, it's one of the city's most visited tourist attractions. Despite its dishevelled look and whacked-out feel, it's a remarkable place. Egalitarian, creative and ecologically minded, the ideals of its thousand-or-so residents have resulted in some truly unique self-built homes, imaginative businesses, and a host of artistic venues.

Extending for around 1km along the bastions that straddle Christian IV's picturesque defensive moat, there is quite a lot

CHRISTIANSHAVN AND HOLMEN

Mural, Christiania

CHRISTIANSHAVN AND HOLMEN

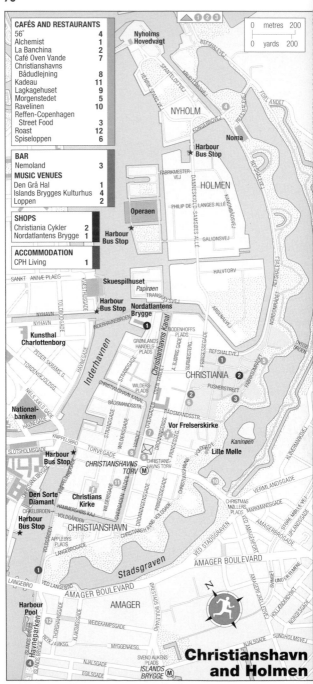

CAFÉS AND RESTAURANTS
56°	4
Alchemist	1
La Banchina	2
Café Oven Vande	7
Christianshavns Bådudlejning	8
Kadeau	11
Lagkagehuset	9
Morgenstedet	5
Ravelinen	10
Reffen-Copenhagen Street Food	3
Roast	12
Spiseloppen	6

BAR
Nemoland	3

MUSIC VENUES
Den Grå Hal	1
Islands Brygges Kulturhus	4
Loppen	2

SHOPS
Christiania Cykler	2
Nordatlantens Brygge	1

ACCOMMODATION
CPH Living	1

0 metres 200
0 yards 200

Nyholms Hovedvagt

REFSHALEVEJ
SPANTELOFTVEJ
KRUDTLØBSVEJ
HENRIK SPANS VEJ
FORLANDET

NYHOLM

KONGEBROVEJ

Noma

Harbour Bus Stop

FABRIKMESTER-VEJ

HOLMEN

DANNESKIOLD-SAMSØES ALLÉ

PHILIP DE LANGES ALLÉ

KANDBRUSVEJ

Operaen

GALIONSVEJ

Harbour Bus Stop

HALVTORV

Skuespilhuset
Papirøen
TRANGRAVSVEJ

SANKT ANNÆ PLADS
KVÆSTHUSGADE

Harbour Bus Stop

Nordatlantens Brygge

NYHAVN
TOLDBODGADE
INDERHAVNSBROEN

BODENHOFFS PLADS

ARSENALVEJ

NORDRE RUNDDEL

Kunsthal Charlottenborg

NYHAVN
PEDER SKRAMS G.
TORDENSKJOLDSG.
NIELS JUELS GADE
HAVNEGADE

Inderhavnen

Christianshavns Kanal

GRØNLANDS HANDELS PLADS

BURMEISTERS GADE
A. BARING GADE
PRINSESSEGADE

REFSHALEVEJ

STRANDGADE
WILDERS-PLADS

DYSSE-BROEN

National-banken

KNIPPELSBRO

STRANDGADE
BÅDSMANDSSTR.
CHRISTIANSHAVNS KANAL
WILDERSGADE
OVERGADEN

BÅDSMANDSSTR.

CHRISTIANIA

PUSHERSTREET

FABRIKSGRAVEN

Vor Frelserskirke

SLOTSHOLMSGADE
Harbour Bus Stop

TORVEGADE
WILDERSGADE
DRONNINGENSGADE
PRINSESSEGADE
CHRISTIANSHAVNS TORV

CHRISTIANS-HAVNS TORV

VOLDGADE

Kaninøen
Lille Mølle
KLINTEGÅRDEN

KLINGBERGGADE

Den Sorte Diamant

CIRKELBROEN

Harbour Bus Stop

CHRISTIANS BRYGGE
KNIPPELSBRO

Christians Kirke

HAMMERSHØIS KAJ
WILDERSGADE
DRONNINGENSGADE
PRINSESSEGADE

CHRISTIANSHAVN

CHRISTIANS VOLDGADE

VERMLANDSGADE

CHRISTMAS MØLLERS PLADS

STORE MØLLE VEJ
MARKMANDSGADE
AMAGERBROGADE
UPLANDSGADE

VOLDGÅRDEN
APPLEBYS PLADS
LANGEBROGADE

VED STADSGRAVEN

Stadsgraven

LANGEBRO
VED LANGEBRO

AMAGER BOULEVARD

AMAGER BOULEVARD
ØRESTADS BOULEVARD

N

AMAGER

LUND OG ELMERE
AMAGER FÆLLEDVEJ
HOLLÆNDERDYBET
NØRREGÅRDS

Harbour Pool

Havneparken

ISLANDS BRYGGE
THORSHAVNSGADE
REYKJAVIKSG.
WEIDEKAMPSGADE
KLAKSVIGSG.

MYGGENÆSG.

NJALSGADE
EGILSGADE

SVEND AUKENS PLADS
ISLANDS BRYGGE (M)

NJALSGADE
SUNDHOLMSVEJ

Christianshavn and Holmen

Christiania: reinventing itself to survive

Since its inception half a century ago, residents have struggled to defend Christiania's existence. Clashes over the residents' occupation (for free) of prime city real estate, past non-payment of taxes, with police over the drug trade and finally, the government's plans for redevelopment, forced temporary closure in 2011. Residents managed to broker a remarkable deal with the government, however, to buy back the buildings at sub-market rates (still 76 million kroner), and to pay annual rent of 6 million kroner for the rest, issuing so-called People's Shares (ⓦchristianiafolkeaktie.dk) as a way for outside supporters to fund its survival. Pusher Street in particular has been threatened repeatedly with closures over recent decades; the latest commotion is unfolding at the time of this writing, with authorities doubling penalties for drug-related crimes, presented as a first step to finally bringing the street's drug trade to an end.

of Christiania to see, and the best way to experience it is to join one of the immensely informative (if inevitably one-sided) guided tours. Housed within Loppebygningen, a former artillery magazine, are the **Gallopperiet** art gallery (ⓦgallopperiet.dk), *Spiseloppen* restaurant (see page 75) and Loppen music venue (see page 75).

Continuing along the main artery, you reach **Carl Madsens Plads**, lined with stalls selling knick-knacks and fast food, which marks the beginning of **Pusherstreet** – impossible to miss from its unmistakeable aroma. Lining the street are rows of well-stocked shacks selling everything from pre-rolled joints to smoking paraphernalia. A couple of basic rules apply on Pusherstreet: don't run (or the stallholders will think there's a police raid) and don't take photos. Also remember that the use of hash is still a criminal offence in Denmark.

Following the edge of the moat around from *Nemoland* (see page 75) leads you into the quieter, greener and more residential area. Here you will find some of Christiania's most ingenious alternative dwellings. A pedestrian bridge crosses the moat at the next bastion, or you can continue along past four bastions to the public road at the end, and follow the moat path back on the opposite side.

Operaen

MAP P.70, POCKET MAP G6
Holmen, Harbour Bus: Operaen
ⓦoperaen.dk. Tours most Wed, Sat & Sun, charge.

Occupying a prominent position on the compact island of Holmen diametrically across the water from the Marmorkirken, the Henning Larsen-designed **Operaen** (Opera House) is visible from almost any point along the harbour. It's a striking building, surmounted by an enormous flat roof that delicately overhangs the water's edge, while the no-expense-spared interior features gigantic outlandish lighting globes, designed by Danish-Icelandic artist Olafur Eliasson, in the foyer; note too the Jura sandstone walls inset with masses of tiny fossils. To gain access, though, you'll need either to see a performance (doors open 2hr beforehand) or join a guided tour.

Søren Kierkegaard

The top-hatted figure of Søren Kierkegaard (1813–55) was a familiar sight to Copenhageners as he took his daily walk along the city's cobbled streets. Regarded as one of the founders of Existentialism, Kierkegaard's philosophy developed out of personal anguish and his distaste for organised religion. A 1918 bronze statue of the Danish poet and philosopher can be found in the garden of the Royal Danish Library. Kierkegaard's manuscripts are part of the Royal Library collection and have on occasion been displayed for the general public.

Islands Brygge

MAP P.70, POCKET MAP F9

Just south of Christianshavn, on the island of Amager, the **Islands Brygge** development is fast becoming one of the city's most happening areas. Much of this former industrial harbour strip has been converted into a waterfront park, the **Havneparken** – popular with people from all walks of life, from parents with prams to parkour enthusiasts – with cultural

activity focused around the Islands Bryggges Kulturhus (see page 75). Best of all, however, is the innovative, council-run **harbour pool** (daily 6am–10pm, lifeguards on duty June–Aug 10am–6pm; free), the perfect place to cool off in the summer.

The quayside walkway extends south to the bicycle and pedestrian bridge, officially the **Bryggebroen** ("Quay bridge"), which gives access to Fisketorvet and Vesterbro.

Operaen

Shops

Christiania Cykler

MAP P.70, POCKET MAP G8
Mælkeven 83A, Christiania
🔟 christianiabikes.dk.

Classic, sturdy and super-cool,
Christiania Bikes' hand-crafted
three-wheel cargo cycles are one
of the city's icons. Prices start at
10,100kr.

Nordatlantens Brygge

MAP P.70, POCKET MAP G7
Strandgade 91 🔟 nordatlantens.dk.

Housed in an enormous
eighteenth-century warehouse,
Nordatlantens Brygge promotes
artistic and cultural links between
Denmark, Greenland, Iceland
and the Faroe Islands. A small
store at the back sells regional
music and crafts such as Icelandic
knitwear and sealskin slippers from
Greenland.

Cafés and restaurants

56°

MAP P.70, POCKET MAP H6
Krudtløbsvej 8 🔟 56grader.dk.

Housed in an old armoury dating
back to 1744, this reasonably
priced, high-end restaurant offers
a wonderful 4-course meal, with
the option to have a wine pairing
experience along with it too. In
the summer you can enjoy your
meal in the garden. €€€

Alchemist

MAP P.70, POCKET MAP H5
Refshalevej 173C 🔟 alchemist.dk.

Located slightly to the north of
Noma on Refhalesøen, *Alchemist*
too is a dining experience to
remember, its inventive and
provocative founding chef Rasmus
Munk determined to climb to
new culinary heights. A meal here
not for the faint of heart; it will
last between four and six hours
and will be divided into dramatic
acts, comprised in total of some
50 "impressions" paired with
plenty of choices of beverage. €€€

La Banchina

MAP P.70, POCKET MAP H5
Refshalevej 141 🔟 labanchina.dk.

It's worth the trip out to this tiny,
low-key waterside restaurant, café
and wine bar. There's an on-site
sauna and the sprawling wooden
deck outside becomes packed in
summertime with Copenhageners
soaking up the sun. €

Café Oven Vande

MAP P.70, POCKET MAP F13
Overgaden Oven Vandet 44
🔟 cafeovenvande.dk.

With tables and chairs spilling
out onto the pavement, this
Christianshavn institution is a
fine place to enjoy an excellent
lunchtime smørrebrød platter by
the canal. Catching the sunset, it's
also hugely popular in the evening
when there's a French-inspired
menu. €€

Sauna at La Banchina

Christianshavns Bådudlejning

MAP P.70, POCKET MAP F14
Overgaden Neden Vandet 29
W baadudlejningen.dk.

Formerly a boat rental point, this partially covered floating pontoon, moored at the Torvegade bridge, is now a trendy lunch spot, serving a few sandwich options and light snacks. In summer it's open for dinner too. €

Kadeau

MAP P.70, POCKET MAP E14
Wildersgade 10B W kadeau.dk.

Inspired by the Baltic isle of Bornholm – in both its seafood focus and the art on display – *Kadeau* has two Michelin stars for good reason. Its inventive dishes include locally sourced octopus, beetroot and pork belly, as well as indigenous grains and berries. €€€

Kadeau

Lagkagehuset

MAP P.70, POCKET MAP F14
Torvegade W lagkagehuset.dk.

The original *Lagkagehuset* (there are now branches across the country and even in the UK under the name "Ole & Steen"), "Layercake House" (see page 68) is a decent bakery-cum-patisserie serving beautiful pastries. €

Morgenstedet

MAP P.70, POCKET MAP H8
Fabriksområdet 134, Christiania
W morgenstedet.dk.

Small, welcoming plant-based place set in a cute little cottage that once belonged to the army, with tables outside in a peaceful garden. Inexpensive organic food includes a hot meal of the day, such as bean stew or potato gratin, and a selection of salads. €

Ravelinen
MAP P.70, POCKET MAP G8
Torvegade 79 ⓦ ravelinen.dk.
This long-time local favourite offers a classic Danish menu in a down-to-earth setting with a wonderful view of the water dividing Christianshavn and Amager. The building dates back to 1728, when it was built to house toll collectors at the outer edge of the 16th-century city. €€

Reffen – Copenhagen Street Food
MAP P.70, POCKET MAP H5
Refshalevej 167 ⓦ reffen.dk.
This hugely popular food market has a more casual feel than Torvehallerne, where edible goodies from all around the world are sold from the waterfront food trucks, most of it organic and sustainable. €

Roast
MAP P.70, POCKET MAP F8
Vestmannagade 4 ⓦ roast.com.
Expertly crafted coffees by passionate and knowledgeable baristas. The delicious smelling roastery is on site. €

Spiseloppen
MAP P.70, POCKET MAP G8
Bådsmandsstræde 43, Christiania
ⓦ spiseloppen.dk.
Considering the ramshackle staircase leading up to it, the high quality of the cuisine offered by this rustic Christiania collective comes as quite a surprise. The global reach of the menu reflects the wide origins of its chefs. €

Bar

Nemoland
MAP P.70, POCKET MAP G8
Fabriksområdet 52 ⓦ nemoland.dk.
This lively café-bar with a large outdoor space is a popular place for visitors to sample purchases from Pusher Street undisturbed.

There are free gigs on a rickety stage outside on summer Sundays, featuring well-known Danish artists and lesser-known international acts.

Music venues

Den Grå Hal
MAP P.70, POCKET MAP G8
Refshalevej 2 ⓦ dengraahal.dk.
Den Grå Hal, translating to 'The Grey Hall', is an alternative cultural and music venue in Freetown Christiania. The graffiti-covered warehouse dates back to 1891 and was originally used for military cavalry training before becoming a concert hall and event space. The site can accommodate 1500 people and has hosted major musicians such as Bob Dylan, Metallica and Bonnie Tyler. The venue is also used for art exhibitions, community events and theatre performances, enriching the city's cultural calendar.

Islands Brygges Kulturhus
MAP P.70, POCKET MAP E9
Islands Brygge 18
ⓦ kulturhusetislandsbrygge.kk.dk.
The waterfront *Islands Brygges Kulturhus* puts on a packed programme of gigs, activities, flea markets and film nights. There's also a café-bar-restaurant with a large water-facing terrace out front.

Loppen
MAP P.70, POCKET MAP G8
Christiania ⓦ loppen.dk.
On the first floor of the warehouse that also houses *Spiseloppen* this usually tightly packed venue hosts superb live gigs five nights a week. Music ranges from Danish folk to hardcore punk; there is sometimes an admission fee, and sometimes its free to enter depending on the event. There are gigs most days of the week starting from 8.30pm.

Vesterbro and Frederiksberg

The two neighbouring districts of Vesterbro and Frederiksberg couldn't be more contrasting. Vesterbro was until recently a solidly working-class area. Urban regeneration projects over the past fifteen years have smartened it up, inflating the value of property, and attracting more affluent residents. They have also brought with them a slew of edgy art galleries, restaurants and bars such as those in the über-trendy, newly converted Kødbyen meat-packing area. Conservative Frederiksberg combines elegant tree-lined avenues, beautiful parks and grand villas – a stroll down Frederiksberg Allé to the romantic seventeenth-century Frederiksberg Have (gardens) and palace gives a flavour of its well-heeled opulence. The quaint little street of Værnedamsvej links the two districts with some superb places to eat and drink, exclusive shops and a neighbourly, outgoing feel.

Vesterbrogade and Istedgade

MAP P.78, POCKET MAP B8–E8

As one of the main arteries leading into the city, **Vesterbrogade** has been lined with restaurants and inns since the sixteenth century. Today, it offers access to the hugely popular nightlife of Kødbyen, and retains a bohemian atmosphere thanks to the large number of artists and musicians who still live here. Running roughly parallel,

Værnedamsvej

The Carlsberg Quarter

Exciting developments are well underway on the site of the old Carlsberg Brewery, which moved its production to a new, modern complex in Jutland. After lengthy public consultation it was decided to develop the site into a vibrant new cultural and residential quarter, **Carlsberg Byen**.

The project is still ongoing, as new businesses, shops and restaurants keep opening up in the quarter. One of these ventures is the Hotel Ottilia (w brochner-hotels.com/hotel-ottilia) with a stunning Italian rooftop restaurant, *Tramonto Rooftop*, boasting a perfect 360-degree view of the Carlsberg City District and the rest of Copenhagen. Other points of interest include **Dansehallerne** (w dansehallerne.dk), a modern dance performance venue at Tap E; **Encoded** (w encoded.dk), a Danish handcrafted furniture and interior design store; and a variety of restaurants including famous burger joint **Gasoline Grill** (w gasolinegrill.com). You could easily spend a half-day exploring the complex. Landmark sights include the iconic **Elephant Gate**, the glorious winding Lotus Chimney, the Lime Tower lighthouse and the Star Gate, the original main entrance to the brewery. Many of Carlsberg's luscious green spaces are opened up to the public, including J.C. Jacobsen's tranquil garden.

Istedgade is all that is left of the city's once infamous red-light district which flourished after the legalization of pornography in the 1960s. Today a handful of hookers and the occasional porn shop near Central Station is all that remains.

Tycho Brahe Planetarium

MAP P.78, POCKET MAP D8
Gammel Kongevej 10 w København H,
Train station: København H, Vesterport
w planetariet.dk. Mon noon–8pm,
Tues–Thurs and Sat 9.30am–8.30pm, Fri
9.30am–9.30pm, Sun 9.30am–7pm, charge.
Housed in a massive and unmissable yellow-brick cylinder at the foot of Sankt Jørgens lake, the city's **planetarium** is named after sixteenth-century Danish astronomer Tycho Brahe. For many visitors – especially the local schoolkids who overrun the place during the week – the main attraction is the enormous 3D IMAX screen in the planetarium's central Space Theatre, which shows science and nature films.

Kødbyen

MAP P.78, POCKET MAP D9
w København H.
Once Copenhagen's former meat-packing district, **Kødbyen** is now one of the trendiest areas in the city. It encompasses cutting-edge galleries and arty cocktail bars, rustic-chic restaurants and grungy nightclubs, with a vibe that changes through the day. Until noon the feel is cold industrial, with life emanating only from the few remaining food-processing plants. After lunch, the galleries begin to open and a colourful, trendsetting crowd moves in. Come evening the restaurants pack out with diners and then partygoers who continue the evening milling from bar to bar, and later on into the nightclubs.

Kødbyen's earliest buildings – the eastern, "brown" part of the site – date back to the late nineteenth century when the city's slaughterhouses were focused on one site in a bid to improve hygiene. The original indoor cattle market has now been

Elephant Gate, Carlsberg Quarter

converted into the **Øksnehallen** exhibition centre, an interesting building with a vast vaulted ceiling that hosts regular photography exhibitions as well as trade fairs for food and fashion, most of them open to the public. In the 1930s the district was extended with the so-called "white" section to the west, whose functionalist blue-and-white-tile-covered buildings are now protected as an industrial monument.

Carlsberg Visitor Centre

MAP P.78, POCKET MAP B9
Gamle Carlsbergvej 11, Train station: Carlsberg Ⓦ visitcarlsberg.dk, charge.

Set to open at the end of 2023, Carlsberg's slick new visitor centre will take you through the history of the brewery, providing insight into the interlinked history of Danes and beer. Highlights include the world's largest collection of beer bottles

CAFÉS AND RESTAURANTS

Anarki	1	Famo	6	Hija de Sanchez		Paté Paté	10
Bento	9	Frk. Barners		Taqueria	13	Riccos Kaffebar	15
Café Viggo	2	Kælder	7	Kødbyens Fiskebar	14	Spuntino	4
Chicky Grill		Granola	3	Mad & Kaffe	16	Sticks'n'Sushi	17
Bar	11	Hansens Gamle		Mother	12		
Cofoco	8	Familiehave	5				

MUSIC VENUE

Vega	9

BARS

Bang & Jensen	8
Curfew	3
Falernum	2
Märkbar	5
Mesteren & Lærlingen	10
Mikkeller	6
Salon 39	1
Vinbaren Vesterbro Torv	7

SHOPS

Designer Zoo	5
Donn Ya Doll	6
Meyers Bageri	1
Samsøe og Samsøe	3
Stig P	2
Summerbird	4

Elephant House
Frederiksberg Have
Danske Haveselskabs Have
Frederiksberg Kirke
FREDERIKSBERG ALLÉ

Zoologisk Have (Copenhagen Zoo)
Frederiksberg Slot
ROSKILDEVEJ

Hippo House
Søndermarken
Cisternerne

Elephant Gate
NY CARLSBERG VEJ

Jakobsens Brewhouse
Dansehallerne
CARLSBERG DISTRICT
Carlsberg Visitor Centre

Vesterbro and Frederiksberg

SØNDER BOULEVA

over 20,000) and a wonderful assortment of old advertising campaigns. Although it lacks the noise and excitement of a large working brewery, you do get the opportunity to sample (alongside regular Carlsberg) some interesting beers from the on-site microbrewery, the **Jacobsen Brewhouse**, at the end of your visit.

Frederiksberg Have and Slot

MAP P.78, POCKET MAP A8
Roskildevej Ⓜ Frederiksberg Allé, Frederiksberg Ⓦ kongeligeslotte.dk. Gardens sunrise–sunset; Palace guided tours Jan–Aug & Aug–Nov last Sat of the month 11am & 1pm. Gardens, free; Palace, charge.
One of the city's most beautiful and romantic spots, **Frederiksberg Have** was originally laid out in the late seventeenth century as gardens for the recently completed royal palace. The gardens' Baroque formality was remodelled in the English landscape style a century later, with winding paths weaving across undulating lawns, boating canals and numerous follies hidden among the trees. The park can be accessed from all sides, but arriving from the *slot* gives you the best overview of its layout. Hugely popular for picnicking and lounging, the gardens also host music and theatre performances in summer (check the website for details).

Frederiksberg Slot itself, built in Baroque style, was the royal family's main summer residence until the mid-1800s, and now houses the Danish Officers Academy – it's therefore off-limits except for the infrequent guided tours. The interior is awash with intricate stuccowork and bold and colourful ceiling paintings; grandest of all is the elaborately

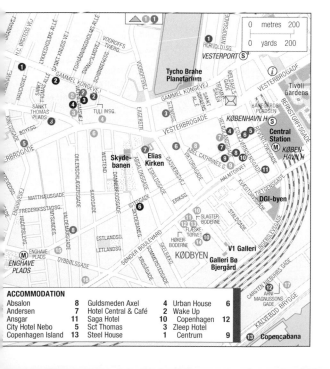

ACCOMMODATION					
Absalon	8	Guldsmeden Axel	4	Urban House	6
Andersen	7	Hotel Central & Café	2	Wake Up	
Ansgar	11	Saga Hotel	10	Copenhagen	12
City Hotel Nebo	5	Sct Thomas	3	Zleep Hotel	
Copenhagen Island	13	Steel House	1	Centrum	9

Zoologisk Have

decorated chapel, which you may
find a little over the top.

Zoologisk Have

MAP P.78, POCKET MAP A8
Roskildevej 32 Ⓜ Frederiksberg Allé,
Ⓜ Frederiksberg Ⓦ zoo.dk. Nov–April from
10am, May–Oct from 9am; closing times
vary, check website for details, charge.
Founded in 1859, Copenhagen's
zoological gardens encompass
everything you'd expect from a
zoo with over 2500 animals from
around the globe. Aside from
the wooden 44m observation
tower (1905), two recently added
structures stand out: Foster &
Partners' etched-glass-domed
Elephant House, complete with
underfloor heating, and Danish
architects Dall & Lindhardsen's
Hippo House, where you
can watch the animals frolic
underwater. Both are easily
visible from neighbouring parks
(Frederiksberg Have for the
elephants and Søndermarken for

the hippos), so – should you wish
– you can avoid forking out the
entrance fee to view them.

Cisternerne

MAP P.78, POCKET MAP A8
Roskildevej 25A Ⓜ Frederiksberg
Allé, Ⓜ Frederiksberg
Ⓦ frederiksbergmuseerne.dk/da/
cisternerne. April–Nov Tues–Sun
11am–6pm, Thurs until 8pm, charge.
Buried beneath the greenery
of Søndermarken is one of
Copenhagen's most captivating
spaces for contemporary art.
Descend a flight of steps from
the park to enter a network of
Cisterns, carved into the ground
in the mid nineteenth century to
serve as the capital's drinking water
supply. Drained in the 1980s, the
damp, dripstone cave left behind
– complete with decades-old
stalactites – was converted into a
venue for art exhibitions in 1996,
making the most of the evocative,
ghostly space.

Shops

Designer Zoo

MAP P.78, POCKET MAP B8

Vesterbrogade 137 ⓦ designerzoo.dk.
Welcoming store run by eight
designers selling own-made
furniture, jewellery, knitwear,
pottery and glass. A great place for
that elusive Christmas gift.

Donn Ya Doll

MAP P.78, POCKET MAP D8

Istedgade 55 ⓦ donnyadoll.dk.
Charming if slightly chaotic multi-
brand fashion store offering a great
range by Danish and international
designers.

Meyers Bageri

MAP P.78, POCKET MAP C7

Gammel Kongevej 107
ⓦ meyersmad.dk.
The very first branch of Meyer's
bakeries, with a great selection
of breads and pastries as well as
baking tools and specialty flours
for the adventurous home baker.
The now-ubiquitous *kanelsnurre*
is said to have been the brainchild
of the popular chain's namesake,
Claus Meyer, so be sure to try the
original here.

Samsøe og Samsøe

MAP P.78, POCKET MAP C8

Værnedamsvej 12 ⓦ samsoe.com.
Cool own-brand designer wear for
men and women, plus a few items
from other labels. They're known
for their simple, loose-fitting style
and punchy colours.

Stig P

MAP P.78, POCKET MAP C8

Gl. Kongevej 91C ⓦ stig-p.com.
This colourful women's clothing
store was the first to be opened
on trendy Kronprinsensgade back
in 1969. Now having relocated
to Gl. Kongevej, it offers a range
of designer wear including Stella
McCartney, Calvin Klein and Stig
P's own label.

Summerbird

MAP P.78, POCKET MAP C8

Værnedamsvej 9 ⓦ summerbird.dk.
Dinky little chocolatier selling
arguably the world's best chocolate.
Try the otherworldly *flødeboller*
("cream buns") – fluffy, chocolate-
coated marshmallow treats.

Cafés and restaurants

Anarki

MAP P.78 POCKET MAP D7

Vodroffsvej 47 ⓦ restaurant-anarki.dk.
Chef Rune Sauer Sonnichsen
draws inspiration from all corners
of the world and a multi-page
global wine list attracts oenophiles
to this bistro. The retro decor,
such a vintage maps and low-lit
green lamps, creates an intimate
mood. €€

Summerbird gift box

VESTERBRO AND FREDERIKSBERG

Bento

MAP P.78, POCKET MAP D8
Helgolandsgade 16 ⓦ uki.dk.
Family-run Japanese restaurant
with a traditional minimalist
interior that transports visitors
instantly to Tokyo. Famous for
its *makunouchi* (bento) boxes,
and features a well-stocked
Japanese cocktail bar. Takeaway
available. €€

Café Viggo

MAP P.78, POCKET MAP C8
Værnedamsvej 15 ⓦ cafeviggo.com.
Named after Belgian comic-book
character Gaston (Vakse Viggo
in Danish), this French-style
café-bistro is packed both day
and night. Apart from good,
solid bistro dishes such as quiche
forestière or steak haché, the
chef excels in genuine Breton
galettes. €€

Chicky Grill Bar

MAP P.78, POCKET MAP D8
Halmtorvet 21 ⓣ 33 22 66 96.
No-nonsense bar with booth
seating that serves substantial
portions of national classics – the
perfect place for a *flæskesteg* (pork
roast) with potatoes and gravy.
Wash it down with a bottled
Carlsberg to complete the genuine
Danish experience. €

Cofoco

MAP P.78, POCKET MAP D8
Abel Cathrines Gade 7 ⓦ cofoco.dk.
Bright and modern, *Cofoco* is the
very first branch (opened in 2004)
of what has become a restaurant
empire. Dishes are superb but
small, the idea being that you
sample a range: a menu of snacks
and five courses costs 500kr. €€

Famo

MAP P.78, POCKET MAP C8
Saxogade 3 ⓦ famo.dk.
Small, cheerful, no-frills Italian
restaurant serving a four-course
menu, prepared by a pair of
Michelin-starred chefs who have
decided to go it alone. Flavour-
packed delicacies might include
panzanella (Florentine bread-
and-tomato salad, crammed with
anchovies and herbs) and *ribolita*
(Tuscan bean soup). €€

Frk. Barners Kælder

MAP P.78, POCKET MAP D8
Helgolandsgade 8 ⓦ frkbarners.dk.
With outdoor seating on a
streetside terrace and a cosy
cavern-like atmosphere inside,
this traditional restaurant –
complete with red-and-white-
check tablecloths – serves
time-honoured Danish classics
such as herring platters at lunch,
and veal liver in cream sauce at
dinnertime. €€

Granola

MAP P.78, POCKET MAP C8
Værnedamsvej 5 ⓦ granola.dk.
Retro-style milkshake bar whose
decor – including genuine
1930s ceiling lamps from the
Rover factory – shows staggering
attention to detail. Breakfast,
smoothies and juices are served
from early morning, while later
on the menu centres on well-
prepared home-made dishes such
as quiches, salads, sandwiches
– and delicious milkshakes, of
course. €

Hansens Gamle Familiehave

MAP P.78, POCKET MAP B8
Pile Alle 10 ⓦ hansenshave.dk.
In a pretty garden (with a
retractable winter roof) around
the corner from Frederiksberg
Slot this popular place excels in
smørrebrød. There's also a good
range of traditional hot dishes
such as fried eel with parsley
sauce, and roast pork with pickled
red cabbage. €€

Hija de Sanchez Taqueria

MAP P.78, POCKET MAP D8
Slagterboderne 8
ⓦ lovesanchez.dk.

Mother

Launched by a former pastry-
chef at *Noma*, this tiny restaurant
in the Meat Packing District is
a delight, serving a small but
excellent selection of tacos along
with delicious *esquitas* (Mexican
street corn). Weather permitting,
enjoy a margarita outside – a
great option for soaking up the
Kødbyen coolness. €

Kødbyens Fiskebar

MAP P.78, POCKET MAP D9
Flæsketorvet 100
Ⓦ fiskebaren.dk.

Located in the former meat-
packing district, this super-trendy
fish restaurant in hip Kødbyen
offers sustainably sourced fresh
fish and seafood, from oysters
to Norwegian scallop, the menu
varying according to the season
and catch. With whitewashed
walls and shiny black floors, it
oozes cool industrial chic. €€

Mad & Kaffe

MAP P.78, POCKET MAP C9
Sonder Blvd 68 Ⓦ madogkaffe.dk.

With various locations across the
city, each café has its own stylish
and homey feel which resemble
the local areas. You can create
your own breakfast platters of 3,
5 or 7 items, with great vegetarian
and vegan options. If you're not
a brunch person, try the falafel
burger with homemade fries.
Excellent coffee and cakes are
available all day. €

Mother

MAP P.78, POCKET MAP D8
Høkerboderne 9 Ⓦ mother.dk.

Organic sourdough pizza served
in a long, rustic butcher's hall in
industrial-hip Kødbyen. *Mother*'s
chipper Italian proprietor, who
also mans the door, is kept busy
throughout the day as hungry
diners arrive in droves. There is a

small but select wine list as well as full-flavoured Menabrea beer on draught. €

Paté Paté

MAP P.78, POCKET MAP D8
Slagterboderne 1 Ⓦ patepate.dk.
On-trend Kødbyen wine bar-cum-restaurant housed in a former meat pâté factory. Apart from a vast selection of great wines, *Paté Paté* also offers good, solid French food, with lighter bites on offer at lunchtime and dinner mains, which include pan-fried cod and steak tartare. €€

Riccos Kaffebar

MAP P.78, POCKET MAP C9
Istedgade 119 Ⓦ riccos.dk.
Riccos coffee shops have spread throughout the city but this is where it all started, and their unfaltering passion for good organic coffee is still in evidence. Packed into a tight space with only a few tiny tables and a long communal bench along the wall, coffee aficionados cram together

here every morning for their caffeine fix. €

Spuntino

MAP P.78, POCKET MAP C8
Vesterbrogade 68 Ⓦ cofoco.dk.
Part of the excellent Cofoco chain, no-frills *Spuntino* offers Italian classics such as *arancini*, braised lamb shank and *panna cotta*. Mix and match as you wish or go for the recommended seven-course menu. €€

Sticks'n'sushi

MAP P.78, POCKET MAP D9
Arni Magnussons Gade 2 Ⓦ sushi.dk.
Great-tasting sushi, seafood salads and Japanese dishes on the top floor of the twelve-storey *Tivoli Hotel*, with great views of Kødbyen and beyond. €€

Bars

Bang & Jensen

MAP P.78, POCKET MAP C8
Istedgade 130 Ⓦ bangogjensen.dk.

Mikkeller

Housed in an old nineteenth-century chemist with high stucco ceilings, *Bang & Jensen* is a cosy neighbourhood café by day and a heaving bar at night, featuring definite hipster vibes and an excellent selection of beers.

Curfew

MAP P.78, POCKET MAP D8

Stenosgade 1 ⓦ curfew.dk.

Lavish cocktail bar inspired by the speakeasy culture of the 1920s and 1930s, run by flamboyant Portuguese-born cocktail aficionado, Humberto Marques. Seasonally-changing menu with literature-inspired cocktails.

Falernum

MAP P.78, POCKET MAP C8

Værnedamsvej 16 ⓦ falernum.dk.

This snug wood-panelled wine bar offers most of its wines by the glass, with friendly and knowledgeable waiters on hand to share tasting notes. There's a wide range of food served throughout the day, such as croquettes and an outstanding charcuterie platter.

Märkbar

MAP P.78, POCKET MAP C8

Vesterbrogade 106A ☏ 33 21 23 93.

Dark, grungy, Berlin-inspired rock bar with an industrial feel and a dependable crowd of regulars nodding their heads to the rhythm. A good range of beer at affordable prices that won't make you wince.

Mesteren & Lærlingen

MAP P.78, POCKET MAP D9

Flæsketorvet 86 ☏ 32 15 24 83.

Small, worn corner dive in Kødbyen with a disc-juggling DJ on Friday and Saturday nights. Based in what used to be the meat-packing district, the music ranges from Pink Floyd to African Soul and the vibe is unpretentious and welcoming. Smoking is permitted inside. Open seven days a week.

Mikkeller

MAP P.78, POCKET MAP D8

Viktoriagade 8 ⓦ mikkeller.dk.

Increasingly popular and enjoying global reach, Mikkeller burst onto the microbrewery scene in 2006. For the next decade or so, its name was whispered in hushed reverential tones among cognoscenti. It's now an unquestioned authority when it comes to beer while this intimate basement bar is a worthy adjunct to the serious business of brewing. A self-declared Carlsberg-Free Zone, it offers a superb range of innovative microbrewery ales, including twenty on tap.

Salon 39

MAP P.78, POCKET MAP D7

Vodroffsvej 39 ⓦ salon39.dk.

Frederiksberg's first cocktail bar, this stylish, elegant place is now also popular for the meals that accompany the cocktails.

Vinbaren Vesterbro Torv

MAP P.78, POCKET MAP C8

Svendsgade 1

ⓦ vinbarenvesterbrotorv.dk.

Cosy, intimate wine bar with top notch selection of wine from across the world. Enjoy the occasional live jazz music and the piano for guests to play some tunes. If you've enjoyed your wine from the bar, you're in luck – the bottles are available to take home from their store.

Music venue

Vega

MAP P.78, POCKET MAP C9

Enghavevej 40 ⓦ vega.dk.

One of the city's top live music venues, housing three stages with sublime sound featuring well-established artists and bands through the week. The attached *Ideal Bar* offers a slightly lower-key (and much smaller) venue for catching local bands and DJs.

Nørrebro and Østerbro

Beyond the city ramparts, the two neighbouring mid-nineteenth-century districts of Nørrebro and Østerbro are sometimes difficult to tell apart. This is despite deeply contrasting histories – Nørrebro's one of deprivation and social struggle followed by more recent immigration and gentrification, and Østerbro's characterized by traditional wealth and privilege. Aside from Copenhagen's most famous cemetery they lack standout tourist sights. They do, however, have plenty to offer when it comes to going out and having a good time with the locals. Squares such as trendy Sankt Hans Torv and multicultural Blågårds Plads in Nørrebro, and laidback Bopa Plads in Østerbro, are alive and kicking day and night, as is the once grimy Jærgersborgsgade, now one of the city's most hyped streets, thanks mostly to the presence of a Michelin-starred restaurant.

SHOPS	
Accord	3
Isoteket	1,6
Karamelleriet	2
Lakor	5
Prag	7
Ravnsborggade Antique Stores	8
Spidsroden	9
Wilgart	4

CAFÉS AND RESTAURANTS	
Ali Bageri	1
Bevar's	7
Cafe 22	6
Grillen	8
Kaffesalonen	9
Mirabelle	2
Nørrebro Bryghus	4
Sebastopol	3
Søpromenaden	5

BARS	
The Barking Dog	3
Blågård's Apotek	7
BRUS	1
ØlBaren	5
Props Coffee Shop	6
Vivant	4

MUSIC VENUE	
Rust	2

Sankt Hans Torv

Assistens Kirkegaard

MAP P.86, POCKET MAP C5
Nørrebrogade; entrances on Nørrebrogade,
Jagtvej and Kapelvej ⓜ Nørrebros Runddel.
April–Sept daily 7am–10pm, Oct–March
7am–7pm.

The tranquil leafy cemetery of
Assistens Kirkegaard was first
established in 1760 as a burial
place outside the city walls for its
poor and destitute. Since then, and
especially in the nineteenth century
during Copenhagen's Golden Age
of art and culture, it became the
city's most prestigious and famous
burial place. Most of the graves are
of the key movers and shakers in
the city's past. Pick up one of the
colourfully dotted maps at one of
the many entrances, each colour
representing a profession, and
you can make your way around to
find graves of luminaries such as
author Hans Christian Andersen,
philosopher Søren Kirkegaard,
Nobel-prize-winning physicist
Niels Bohr and many, many more.

While burials still occasionally
take place here, Assistens
Kirkegaard has more in common

with a regular park with its
wide tree-lined cycle paths and
picnickers and sunbathers lounging
about on warm days, some using
the tombstones as back rests.

Fælledparken

MAP P.88, POCKET MAP E3–4
Vibenshus Runddel ⓜ Trianglen.
Fælledparken is at half a square
kilometre the city's largest park used
by over 11 million visitors each
year. It started life as a common
used to graze the city's livestock.
Later it became the favoured
haunt for the city's gentlefolk on
their Sunday afternoon strolls.
Today you'll find all walks of life
here, many of them kicking a ball
around one of the six demarcated
football pitches. At the corner
near Trianglen a tranquil scent
garden has been designed for the
visually impaired, while across
Edel Sauntes Allé, you'll find the
4600sq m Fælledparken Skatepark.
On sunny days the park becomes a
patchwork of sunbathers' blankets
and it's often difficult to find a spare
patch of grass to settle on. Various

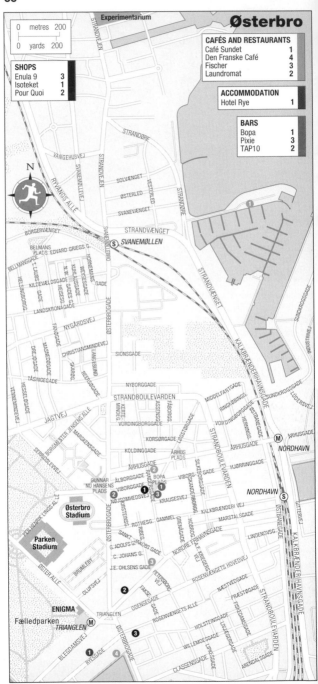

Østerbro

CAFÉS AND RESTAURANTS

Café Sundet	1
Den Franske Café	4
Fischer	3
Laundromat	2

ACCOMMODATION

Hotel Rye	1

BARS

Bopa	1
Pixie	3
TAP10	2

SHOPS

Enula 9	3
Isoteket	1
Pour Quoi	2

NØRREBRO AND ØSTERBRO

events take place in Fælledparken throughout the year. Highlights include May Day and the annual carnival which both culminate here with lots of partying. In front of the park's small café there are also occasional gigs during summer, as well as weekly free Salsa lessons.

ENIGMA

MAP P.88, POCKET MAP E4
Øster Allé 1 Ⓜ Trianglen Ⓦ enigma.dk. Daily 10am–5pm, charge.

ENIGMA, formerly the Enigma Post & Telemuseum, opened in its current form and location in 2023. Filled with fascinating, interactive displays, it has an entire section devoted to kids, though it's also an excellent place for adults to while away the time. Exhibitions tackle the history of communication, starting with the establishment of the Danish postal service in 1624. There's also a portion devoted to the rise of the internet and the current (and future) societal debates it has sparked. The name *ENIGMA* comes from the cipher machines

that were used for commercial and military communication. The oldest such machine in the world is on display here, one of just three to have survived to this day.

Experimentarium

MAP P.88, POCKET MAP F1
Tuborg Havnevej 7, Train station: Hellerup Ⓦ experimentarium.dk. Daily 9.30am–5pm, charge.

Worth a detour if you have kids, **Experimentarium** is a giant hands-on science lab where you can test all sorts of things. The large permanent exhibit looks at the human body (avoid the section on sound waves if you don't like loud noises), how soap bubbles work, energy generation and much more. A large temporary exhibitions space often features blockbuster attractions on loan from other museums. Staff are at hand to show you what to do, if needed. Most children are worn out after a day of running around, pulling on ropes, pushing barrels, leaving parents free to do what they want afterwards.

NØRREBRO AND ØSTERBRO

Experimentarium

Shops

Accord

MAP P.86, POCKET MAP C5
Nørrebrogade 90 ⓦ accord.dk.
This secondhand music store buys
and sells vinyl records, and is a
popular weekend hangout among
forty-something nostalgists, though
there's plenty here for younger
folk too.

Enula 9

MAP P.88, POCKET MAP F4
Rosenvængets Allé 6 ⓦ enula9.dk.
Tiny shop selling beautiful clothes
and accessories for pregnant
women and babies.

Isoteket

MAP P.88, POCKET MAP C4/D5/F3
Randersgade 43 ⓦ isoteket.dk.
The best ice cream in Copenhagen,
with all organic ingredients and
amazingly inventive flavour
combinations, amongst them
coffee and lemongrass ice cream,
passionfruit and marzipan gelato,
and pear and ginger sorbet. The
selection is ever-changing, with
vegan options always available.

Fischer

Karamelleriet

MAP P.88, POCKET MAP C5
Jægersborggade 36 ⓦ karamelleriet.com.
The sweet, smoky smell of burning
sugar lures innocent passersby into
this candy lair, where staff hand-pull
caramel before your eyes. Flavours
range from salty liquorice to toffee.

Lakor

MAP P. 88, POCKET MAP D5
Elmegade 17 ⓦ lakor.dk.
Hip, gorpcore store selling
own-brand men's clothing. Shop
here and you'll fit right in with
Copenhagen's coolest.

Pour Quoi

MAP P.88, POCKET MAP F4
Nordre Frihavnsgade 13 ☎ 35 26 62 54.
Cool clothes for women sold in
a compact three-storey shop with
heaps of fabulous dangly, glittering
accessories. Perfect for those lusting
after leopard-print leggings or a
unique T-shirt.

Prag

MAP P.88, POCKET MAP D5
Nørrebrogade 45 ⓦ prag.dk.
One of three of its kind in
Copenhagen, this wonderfully
chaotic vintage store is jam-packed
with hand-picked pieces from
Denmark and abroad, along with a
few new accessories.

Ravnsborggade
Antique Stores

MAP P.86, POCKET MAP D6
The Nørrebrogade end of
Ravnsborggade is famous for its
antique stores. Perusing these has
become a popular Saturday morning
treat and the prices have skyrocketed
as a consequence. You may still be
able to find some bargains if you dig
around long enough.

Spidsroden

MAP P.88, POCKET MAP D6
Prins Jørgens Gade 14 ⓦ spidsroden.dk.
This small, basement co-op is great
for all your organic health store
needs, but also a ideal spot to pic'

up a coffee or sandwich to enjoy in the adjacent Folkets Park while your kids exhaust their jitters on the sizeable playground.

Wilgart

MAP P.88, POCKET MAP C5
Jægersborggade 4 Ⓦ wilgart.dk.
Not to be confused with a hatter, Wilgart is a cap-maker, entirely specialized in the endangered craft of handmade caps and hats. If you are searching for a one-of-a-kind six-pence, here's your stop.

Cafés and restaurants

Ali Bageri

MAP P.86, POCKET MAP C3
Heimdalsgade 39 Ⓦ alibageri.dk.
A Copenhagen institution (with a second branch near Nørrebro Station), this is the go-to place for a big, traditional Lebanese breakfast platter. Chaotic at first glance, the restaurant is a well-oiled machine pumping out delicious *manakish*, *fatte* and some of the best hummus outside of the Levant. Save room for a piece of baklava and prepare to skip lunch. €

Bevar's

MAP P.86, POCKET MAP D5
Ravnsborggade 10B Ⓦ bevars.dk.
Relaxing retreat if you want to hide away and enjoy a good selection of drinks in a very comfortable armchair. A popular spot for students and workers, at night it transforms into a candlelit diner with live music. €

Cafe 22

MAP P.86, POCKET MAP D5
Sortedams Dosseringen 21 Ⓦ cafe22.dk.
Tucked away on a quiet corner, *Café 22* is a cosy basement café-restaurant with a string of popular lakeside tables with blankets available when the air gets chilly. Busy all day, from breakfast onwards; the good-value

menu includes a mouthwatering veggie or meaty brunch. €

Café Sundet

MAP P.88, POCKET MAP F1
Svaneknoppen 2, Svanemøllen
Ⓦ cafesundet.dk.
On the first floor of the Svanemøllen sailing clubhouse with wonderful views of Øresund, *Café Sundet* is the perfect place for a leisurely lunch. The focus is naturally on seafood – such as grilled salmon with saffron sauce. The menu features a kids' menu including lasagna and fried fish. €€

Den Franske Café

MAP P.88, POCKET MAP E4
Sortedams Dosseringen 101
Ⓦ denfranskecafe.dk.
At the posh Østerbro end of the lake, this delightful café with outdoor seating on the lakeside promenade features French-style decor and a few Gallic touches on the menu – freshly baked croissants for example. You'll also find classic Danish rye-bread sandwiches plus some very tasty burgers served with home-made *frites*. €

Fischer

MAP P.88, POCKET MAP F4
Victor Borges Plads 12 Ⓦ hosfischer.dk.
Compact, romantic trattoria in the heart of Østerbro, just off Nordre Frihavnsgade, offering flavour-packed Roman dishes – such as *guancia di maiale con fagioli* (pork cheeks stuffed with cowberries) – a result of the chef's many years of training in Rome. Dinners are served family style, with five antipasti, two pasta dishes and a dessert. €€

Grillen

MAP P.86, POCKET MAP D6
Nørrebrogade 12 Ⓦ grillenburgerbar.dk.
If you are in need of a juicy burger with a good portion of fries, this is a decent pick. Choose among six different burgers and four different kinds of fries and dips. €

Kaffesalonen

MAP P.86, POCKET MAP D6

Peblinge Dosseringen 6 ⓦ kaffesalonen.com.
An old lakeside favourite which
started life as a breakfast/coffee
shop for workers on their way home
from the nightshift and now offers
delicious meals throughout the day,
including grilled goat's cheese salad
and ribeye steak served with all the
trimmings. Weather permitting,
service extends to a lakeside pontoon
with a lively bar – especially worth
dropping by on Midsummer's Eve. €

Laundromat

MAP P.86, POCKET MAP F3

Århusgade 38 ⓦ thelaundromatcafe.com.
Hugely successful Icelandic
concept café which combines
laundromat, library and café in
one. Their weekend brunch comes
recommended, having won several
awards, but the place is busy all day
with students sipping coffee and
people making use of the free wi-fi. €

Mirabelle

MAP P.86, POCKET MAP D5

Guldbergsgade 29 ⓦ mirabelle-spiseria.dk.
Blending Scandinavian and Sicilian
flavours in gorgeous surrounds,
the Sicilian-owned, former bakery
Mirabelle is best known for its
breakfast and brunch, the options
including homemade yoghurt with
blood-orange and almond granola
and toasted brioche with smoked
ham, cheese and a fried egg. Boasting
an all-Sicilian wine list, it also serves
a la carte lunches and dinners,
inspired by southern Italian cuisine
and making the most of a limited list
of ingredients. €€

Nørrebro Bryghus

MAP P.86, POCKET MAP D5

Ryesgade 3 ⓦ noerrebrobryghus.dk.
Microbrewery-cum-restaurant with
an ever-changing menu and long,
wood-beamed tables that are packed
most nights. It also hosts regular beer
tastings that include a recounting of
the brewery's story. Events include
beer yoga and sing-alongs. €€

Sebastopol

MAP P.86, POCKET MAP D5

Sankt Hans Torv 32 ⓦ sebastopol.dk.
A Copenhagen fixture since 1994,
Sebastopol offers a touch of Parisian
café chic on trendy Sankt Hans Torv.
It's often packed with arty Nørrebro
types indulging in a leisurely
brunch. Later in the day the French
bistro menu includes dishes such as
steak tartare or *moules frites*. With
south-facing seating outside on the
square, *Sebastopol* is also a popular
place for a sundowner drink. €€

Søpromenaden

MAP P.86, POCKET MAP D5

Sortedam Dosseringen 103
ⓦ søpromenaden.dk.
With checked tablecloths and a
lovely lakeside setting, *Søpromenaden*
emanates rural charm even though
it's at the lake's busy and chic
Østerbro end. Menu highlights
include an extensive lunchtime
smørrebrød list and all-time Danish
classics such as *frikadeller* and *rødkål*
– meatballs served with pickled red
cabbage. €

Bars

The Barking Dog

MAP P.86, POCKET MAP D5

Sankt Hans Gade 19 ⓦ thebarkingdog.dk.
When you've had enough of the
city's uber-stylish offerings this
relaxed neighbourhood pub may
come in handy. Featuring a small
selection of beers (including a few
from Nørrebros Bryghus) and wine,
The Barking Dog also makes a mean
Power's Sour cocktail; ask the waiter
for the story.

Blågård's Apotek

MAP P.86, POCKET MAP D6

Blågårds Plads 2 ☏ 35 37 24 42.
Known as *Kroteket* ('The Barmacy')
to locals, this café – turned bar at
night – used to be an old pharmacy.
If you look closely you can still
see some old pharmacy details like
the old pharmacist's desk. This

non-profit café hosts many social events and showcases local arts but besides that it's best known for the wide selection of beers, amazing atmosphere and knowledgeable staff.

Bopa

MAP P.88, POCKET MAP F3
Løgstørgade 8 @ cafebopa.dk.
Cosy café-bar which gets packed most weekends after 11.30pm when a DJ hits the turntables. Excellent range of beers including some from the Skovlyst Brewery north of the city which uses quirky ingredients such as nettles and beech syrup for flavouring.

BRUS

MAP P.88, POCKET MAP D5
Guldbergsgade 29 @ tapperietbrus.dk.
Launched by students of Copenhagen's top craft brewer Mikkeller, *BRUS* combines a brewery with a good-looking minimalist bar, a shop and restaurant. There are 25 rotating beers on tap, all from To Øl.

ØlBaren

MAP P.86, POCKET MAP D5
Elmgade 2 @ oelbaren.dk.
A small, bar run for and by beer nerds – and proud of it. Don't expect conversation to drift far from the favoured subject – brews from around the globe – and you'll be fine.

Pixie

MAP P.88, POCKET MAP F3
Løgstørgade 2 @ cafepixie.dk.
Facing a small playground on Bopa Plads, *Pixie* is an authentic neighbourhood café, popular with parents relaxing on the outdoor terrace. Occasional live music in the evenings.

Props Coffee Shop

MAP P.86, POCKET MAP D6
Blågårdsgade 5 @ propscoffeeshop.dk.
Quirky bar-cum-café with a slightly chaotic, laidback atmosphere. All of its rickety furniture is for sale.

Kaffesalonen by the Copenhagen Lakes

TAP10

MAP P.88, POCKET MAP E3
Østerbrogade 122 @ 61 72 44 87.
At the top end of Østerbrogade close to Bopa Plads, this trendy basement bar specializes in Nordic craft beers, with more Scandi-brews chalked up on the board than you could imagine, many of them on draught.

Vivant

MAP P.86, POCKET MAP D5
Elmgade 4 @ barvinvant.dk.
Youthful, ultra-friendly natural wine bar in the hipster heart of Nørrebro. Staff truly know their stuff and are always able to recommend the best glass to suit your mood. Also an excellent option for grabbing a bottle to go.

Music venue

Rust

MAP P.86, POCKET MAP D5
Guldbergsgade 8 @ rust.dk.
Three floors of live music with edgy, experimental as well as more mainstream acts and a kickass clubbing scene too. Named after Cold War aviator Mathias Rust.

Day-trips

An afternoon away from the big city is essential for getting to know a gentler, quieter Denmark. Copenhagen is just a short train ride or even cycle from some stellar destinations in greater Zealand. If you're staying in town for more than just a day or two, you'll definitely want to venture north on a train (and take your rented cycle with you if you like) for art museums, parklands and castles galore – including the very fortress that inspired Shakespeare's Elsinore Castle in *Hamlet*. South, meanwhile, you'll find beaches, quiet townships, more art and Scandinavia's biggest and best aquarium.

Dyrehaven and Bakken

MAP P.96

Bakken, Train station: Klampenborg Ⓦ bakken.dk. End of March to end of Aug daily 11am–11pm, free entry; charge for rides.

A short walk from Klampenborg S-Tog station, the largely forested **Dyrehaven** (Deer Park) was established in 1669 as a royal hunting ground, and is still home to some two thousand (fairly tame) red, sika and fallow deer. It's a picturesque spot, with the

Dyrehaven

ancient oak and beech woodland an atmospheric backdrop, particularly in the early morning mist. Poised on a hilltop in the middle of the park is the **Eremitageslotten** (Ermitage Palace), a grand hunting lodge built for Christian VI in 1736, though it's closed to the public.

Occupying part of the park's southern section, **Bakken** is supposedly the oldest still-functioning amusement park in the world, tracing its origins back to 1583 when entertainers first set up business next to Kirsten Piil's holy spring. It lacks the polish or refinement of Tivoli – but with 33 rides and almost as many places to drink, there's plenty of fun to be had, not least at weekends when the place can be heaving.

Louisiana

MAP P.96

Humlebæk train station, from which it's a 10min walk (follow the signs) Ⓦ louisiana. dk. Tues–Fri 11am–10pm, Sat & Sun 11am–6pm, charge.

A perfect fusion of art, architecture and landscape, **Louisiana Museum of Modern Art** – with good reason Denmark's most visited art gallery – has a setting nearly as magical as the museum itself. Overlooking the Øresund strait, the museum began life in 1958, when a series of interconnecting glass pavilions was

Rocking Roskilde

The carnivalesque **Roskilde Festival** (ⓦroskilde-festival.com) might be Europe's single best open-air event, commonly drawing some 100,000 people. At the end of June, throngs of Danish teens, kidults and ageing hipsters descend on a Roskilde farm to hear more than 150 Scandinavian and international acts take to the eight stages. Kendrick Lamar and Rosalía were recent performers, but Roskilde is best for lesser-known acts. Logistically it's surprisingly efficient, with free camping next to the festival site and shuttle buses from the train station. Tickets regularly sell out, so plan in advance.

Roskilde (30min by train from Copenhagen) was thus the obvious location for **Denmark's Rock Museum**, which is located in the vibrant Musicon district. Also worth a look is the **Viking Ship Museum** (daily 10am–4pm/5pm in summer; 110/150kr; ⓦvikingeskibsmuseet.dk), home to five well-preserved Viking longships. In summer you can row a modern version in the harbour. Not least, don't miss the chance to step inside the fascinating, UNESCO-listed Roskilde Cathedral, burial site of the Danish monarchs for over a thousand years.

built around a nineteenth-century villa, Louisiana (named after the original owner's three wives, each of whom, oddly enough, was called Louise) – the ensemble landscaped within an outdoor sculpture park. Louisiana's collection grew quickly and the museum is now home to over three thousand permanent works from around the globe, many world-class.

The entrance is in the main villa, from which – moving clockwise into the west wing – you first reach a light, open space primarily used for temporary shows; exhibitions in recent years have included Andy Warhol, David Hockney, Ai Weiwei and Emil Nolde. Next, housed in a purpose-built gallery, is an outstanding collection of **Giacometti**'s gaunt sculptures and drawings, which leads on to the museum's extensive and colourful collection of abstract works by **CoBrA** (see page 60). Major Danish artists such as Henrik Heerup and Asger Jorn – who has a special room dedicated to his art – are featured alongside.

From the museum café, with its outdoor terrace overlooking

Øresund, a subterranean section of graphic art leads onto another of the museum's highlights, the permanent exhibition in the museum's south wing, which focuses on **Constructivism** with works by the likes of Vasarely, Albers and Soto. **Nouveau Réalisme** is represented with pieces by Yves Klein, César and Raysse among others, while Lichtenstein, Rauschenberg, Warhol and Oldenburg lead the charge for **Pop Art** and **Minimalism** collections.

Outside, on the lawns sloping down towards the coast, the **sculpture garden** is home to around sixty works including Max Ernst, Henri Laurens, Miró and Henry Moore.

Frederiksborg Slot

MAP P.96

Hillerød, S-Tog line E to Hillerød, then bus #301 to Ullerød or #302 to Sophienlund ⓦdnm.dk. Daily April–Oct 10am–5pm; Nov–March 11am–3pm, charge.

Glorious **Frederiksborg Slot** lies decorously across three small islands within an artificial lake, and is set within magnificent Baroque gardens. It was originally the home of

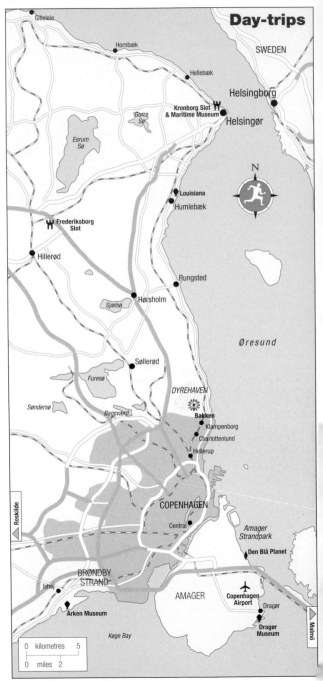

Day-trips

Gilleleje

Hornbæk

SWEDEN

Hellebæk

Helsingborg

Gurre Sø

Kronborg Slot
& Maritime Museum

Helsingør

Esrum Sø

N

Louisiana

Humlebæk

Frederiksborg Slot

Hillerød

Rungsted

Sjælsø

Hørsholm

Øresund

Søllerød

Furesø

Søndersø

DYREHAVEN

Bagsværd

Bakken

Klampenborg

Charlottenlund

Hellerup

Roskilde

COPENHAGEN

Central

Amager Strandpark

Den Blå Planet

BRØNDBY STRAND

Malmö

Ishøj

AMAGER

Copenhagen Airport

Dragør

Arken Museum

Dragør Museum

Køge Bay

0   kilometres   5

0   miles   2

Frederik II and birthplace of his son Christian IV, who, at the beginning of the seventeenth century, had it rebuilt in an unorthodox Dutch Renaissance style. It's the unusual aspects of the design – a prolific use of towers and spires, Gothic arches and flowery window ornamentation – that still stand out.

Since 1882, the interior has functioned as a **Museum of National History** with sixty-odd rooms charting Danish history since 1500. Many are surprisingly free of furniture and household objects, drawing attention instead to the ranks of portraits along the walls – a motley crew of flat-faced kings and thin consorts who between them ruled and misruled Denmark for centuries.

Kronborg Slot

MAP P.96

May–Oct daily 10am–5pm, Nov–April Tues–Sun 11am–4pm; guided tours of the royal chambers in English daily at 11am and 1.30pm; of the casemates daily at 12.30pm, charge ⓦ kronborg.dk. Helsingør train station, from which it's a 15min walk.

Tactically placed on a sandy curl of land extending seawards into

the Øresund some 45km north of Copenhagen in the city of Helsingør, **Kronborg Slot** is impossible to miss. It's known primarily – under the name of Elsinore Castle – as the setting for Shakespeare's *Hamlet*, though it's uncertain whether the playwright actually ever visited Helsingør.

Constructed in the fifteenth century by Erik of Pomerania, the original fortress of Krogen was for hundreds of years the key to control of the Øresund (Helsingborg on the other side of the strait was also under Danish rule), enabling the Danish monarchs to extract a toll from every ship that passed through it.

Maritime Museum of Denmark

MAP P.96

Ny Kronborgvej 1, Helsingør ⓦ mfs.dk. July & Aug daily 10am–6pm; Sept–June Tues–Sun 11am–5pm, charge.

This museum is set underground in the old dry docks next to Kronborg Castle. The structure comprises a continuous ramp looping around the dock walls, allowing for unobstructed views of the castle.

Maritime Museum of Denmark

Gruntvigs Kirke

Of Copenhagen's wealth of historic churches, one of the most striking is less than a century old: the gothic, yellow-brick **Gruntvigs Kirke** (POCKET MAP B1) is well worth the 20min bus ride northwest of the centre (take the 6A bus from Nørreport). Begun in 1921 on what was then a patch of rye, the cathedral was at last consecrated in 1940 in the nascent Copenhagen suburb of Bispebjerg. A rare and impressive example of the Expressionist style that briefly flourished in the early twentieth century, it was named for a Danish reformist pastor.

Many of the most unique elements of design on display are in fact a nod to Danish tradition, from the play on crow-stepped gables outside to the choice of handmade bricks sourced from New Zealand. The three-pointed, 49m (160 ft) tower faces onto the sprawling Bispebjerg Cemetery, brightened with cherry blossoms in spring. Still more impressive is the apparent vastness of the ribbed and vaulted aisles inside, particularly breath-taking for the sheer simplicity of design, with a near total lack of ornamentation. All but the roof, the baptismal font and a tiny carved crucifix adorning the altar is comprised of the same yellow bricks, totalling roughly 6 million in all. Also unusual is the lack of pews: arranged in rows up the nave are wicker-seat chairs in classic Danish style, designed by Kaare Klint, the architect's son.

Inside, informative and interactive exhibits span Viking, medieval and modern seafaring, exploration and merchant shipping (including a colossal Maersk freight container).

Amager Strandpark

MAP P.96
Katrup Søbad Ⓜ Øresund or bus #77 or #78. Mid-May–Aug daily 8am–10pm; Sept–mid-May Mon–Fri 6.30am–3pm, weekends 8am–10pm, free.

Just to the southeast of the centre of Copenhagen, beyond Christianshavn, is the large island of **Amager**. On its east coast, with fine views of the Øresunds Bridge, **Amager Strandpark** is one of the city's most popular summer getaways, with around 5km of beautiful, soft sandy beaches. The beautifully restored traditional wooden **Helgoland Søbadeanstalt**, where Øresundsvej meets Amager Strandvej, offers free changing facilities and showers (late June to end of Aug; free), while at the southern end you'll find **Kastrup**

Søbad, a ring-shaped wooden deck built over the water that serves as a wonderful spot to launch yourself into the water – there are changing rooms, showers and lockers available too.

Connected to "mainland" Amager by three short bridges is an artificial island some 2km long, with a shallow lagoon, popular for kitesurfing, windsurfing and kayaking and ideal for kids to paddle in. There are toilets and showers all along the beach, and at its southern end a couple of good places to eat (see page 100).

Den Blå Planet

MAP P.96
Amager Strandvej, Kastrup Ⓜ Kastrup Ⓦ denblaaplanet.dk. Mon 10am–9pm, Tues–Sun 10am–5pm, charge.

In a spectacular waterside position next to Kastrup marina, **Den Blå Planet** (The Blue Planet) is the state-of-the-art home for Denmark's National Aquarium – the largest in Northern Europe. All curves,

it's a remarkable structure, shaped
– when viewed from the air – like
a giant whirlpool, with five "arms"
radiating from the vortex centre, a
circular foyer. Each arm represents
a different environment: habitats
range from a sunken Amazon forest,
featuring Europe's largest school
of piranhas, to a Faroese bird cliff,
complete with puffins and divers.
Highlight for many, though, is
undoubtedly the walk through the
huge "ocean" aquarium tunnel, with
hammerhead sharks and manta rays
swimming above and below you and
inquisitive sea lions pressing up to
the glass. The building has already
won several design awards, and is
among the best spots in the city to
cut loose (and curry favour with)
the kids for an afternoon.

Arken Museum of Modern Art

MAP P.96

Skovvej 100, Ishøj Ⓜ Ishøj then bus #128
(10min), or a 20min walk Ⓦ arken.dk.
Tues & Thurs–Sun 10am–5pm, Wed
10am–9pm, charge.

Smaller and more manageable than
Louisiana or the Statens Museum
for Kunst, the **Arken Museum for
Moderne Kunst** (Arken Museum
of Modern Art), just outside the
coastal town of Ishøj about 20km
southwest of Copenhagen, is well
worth seeking out both for its
architecture and for its content.
Paying homage to its bleak position
in front of a windswept sandy
beach, architect Søren Robert Lund
designed the museum to resemble
a shipwreck, its prow thrusting
dramatically up from among the
dunes. The museum is known for
its excellent temporary exhibitions
– recent shows have covered eco
architect Hundertwasser and
Danish artist of the 1920s and
1930s, Gerda Wegener– though
these merely supplement a
permanent display that focuses on
contemporary art from the 1990s
wards and includes pieces by
mien Hirst, Antony Gormley,

Jeff Koons and Grayson Perry as
well as Danish artists Per Kirkeby
and Asger Jorn. Its café is also well
worth a visit (see page 100).

Dragør

MAP P.96

Museum, Tårnby Station, then bus #350S
to the end Ⓦ museumamager.dk. May &
Sept Sat & Sun noon–4pm; June & end Aug
Thurs–Sun noon–4pm; July to mid-Aug
Tues–Sun noon–4pm, charge.

South of Copenhagen Airport,
in the southeasternmost corner
of Amager, lies the atmospheric
cobblestoned fishing village of
Dragør, formerly the departure
point for ferries to Sweden. It now
mainly survives on tourism and the
high incomes of its city-commuting
inhabitants – properties in Dragør
do not come cheap. Apart from
meandering around the quaint
streets, and lazing on the peaceful
south coast beaches, while here
you could check out the **Dragør
Museum**, fully refurbished in
2020 and devoted to the maritime
history of the village from the
thirteenth-century herring trade to
the arrival of the Dutch in the early
sixteenth century.

Arken Museum of Modern Art

DAY-TRIPS

Cafés and restaurants

Arken Museum Café

Skovvej 100, Ishøj Ⓦ arken.dk.
Beautiful salmon platters and
sandwiches served in an elegant
café upstairs in the museum, with
sweeping views of marram-grass-
covered dunes and the deep blue
sea in the distance. Open for lunch
from Wednesday to Sunday, and
for dinner Thursday only (5.30–
8pm), serving a set two-course
meal. Reservations recommended
for Thursday evenings. €

Café Baaden

Havkajakvej 16, Amager Strandpark
Ⓦ cafebaaden.dk.
A modern houseboat in a fine
setting on Amager Strandpark,
serving scrumptious brunch
platters, spicy burgers and mixed
mezze. Enjoy a nice glass of
champagne on the rooftop deck
while looking out over the sea –
you may even see Sweden. €

Arken Café

Café Kystens Perle

Bryggergården 14, Kastrup
Ⓦ cafekystensperle.dk.
A short walk from Den Blå Planet,
this striking eighteenth-century
restaurant was once a brewery.
With its crooked walls and low
ceilings the "Pearl of the Coast" has
retained some of its old-fashioned
ambience while its front terrace
provides great coastal views. Food
is served throughout the day,
including brunch, a lunchtime
smørrebrød platter and burgers and
steak later in the day. €€

Café Sylten

Søndre Strandvej 50, Dragør Ⓦ sylten.dk.
Hidden away among the dunes a
stone's throw from the beach just
south of Dragør, this old dark-wood
cabin is a wonderful place to catch
the sunset on a summer evening.
Come for a drink on the terrace
(there's a small but select beer and
wine list) or to sample some hearty
meat dishes. At weekends there's a
brunch buffet. €€

Dragør Røgeri

Gammel Havn 6–8, Dragør
Ⓦ dragor-rogeri.dk.
Authentic smokehouse at Dragør
harbour that sells an enormous
array of freshly caught and freshly
smoked seafood, including
legendary smoked eel and herring.
They're suppliers to the main
restaurants in the city but you can
cut out the middleman and enjoy
their home-made *fiskefrikadeller og
remoulade* (fishcakes with tartare
sauce) or fried plaice and chips at
their harbourfront picnic table for
half the price. €

Peter Lieps Hus

Dyrehaven 8 Ⓦ peterliep.dk.
Quaint thatched restaurant on a
busy pedestrian junction at the
edge of Dyrehaven woods, not far
from the Bakken amusement park.
Lunch at *Peter Lieps* is a popular
weekend treat for busy city folk,
with a menu focusing primarily

Café Kystens Perle

on smørrebrød – with an extensive list of over twenty toppings – and classics such as krebinetter, a breaded fried meatball made from a blend of pork and veal. €

Kilden i Skoven

Dyrehaven 7, Klampenborg ⓦ kilden. kirstenpiils.dk.
Tucked away in Dyrehaven next to the famous holy spring of Kirsten Piil and overlooking a lake, this romantic log cabin is a great option for finding a hearty meal after a day in the woods. There is an excellent lunchtime menu featuring French onion tart and charcuterie from local producers, while for dinner there's just one item, "roast", served as a family-style meal. Just a ten-minute walk from Klampenborg station. €€

Spisestedet Leonora

Frederiksborg Slot, Møntportevej 2, Hillerød ⓦ leonora.dk.
Housed in one of Frederiksborg Slot's former stables, with seating outside in the palace courtyard in summertime, *Leonora* serves a traditional Danish lunch that's fit for a king. Lavishly presented

smørrebrød, tartlets overflowing with asparagus and chicken, fillets of plaice served with prawns and caviar, all reasonably priced. €€

Bar

Sukaiba

AC Hotel Bella Sky, Ørestaden ⓦ sukaiba.dk.
On the top floor of the extraordinary *AC Hotel Bella Sky*, a vast, 814-room complex, Japanese fusion restaurant and bar *Sukaiba* provides breathtaking views of the city skyline, all the way to Sweden. It's accessed via the super-cool aerial walkway that links the two twisting leaning towers. Justly earning the title of 'best hotel restaurant' in Denmark by the *World Culinary Awards 2023*, *Sukaiba* offers a world-class dining experience. Splash out on the seven-course tasting menu – "The Journey". Drinks are worth sampling, too: there's a good selection of cocktails; try the Pandemonium with gin, lime, basil and green tea or the smoky Slumdog Millionaire with whisky, lemon, garam masala, ginger and honey.

Malmö

Just a short hop across the water from Copenhagen, the Swedish city of Malmö makes for a tempting day-trip. Once part of Denmark (the Danes spell it "Malmø"), it was acquired by the Swedish King Karl X in 1658 along with Skåne (Scania), the surrounding province. Today Malmö is Sweden's third largest city, an attractive mix of chocolate-box medieval squares and striking modern architecture, most notably the Turning Torso skyscraper, Scandinavia's tallest building. You'll also find it a cosmopolitan, culturally diverse population – more than a hundred languages are spoken on its streets and Turkish and Thai food are as popular as meatballs and herring.

Stortorget and Lilla Torg

MAP P.103

The city's main square, **Stortorget** is as impressive today as it must have been when it was first laid out in the sixteenth century. It's flanked on one side by the imposing **Rådhus**, built in 1546 and covered with statuary and spiky accoutrements. To its rear stands the fine Gothic **St Petri Kyrka** (daily 10am–6pm; free) while to the south runs **Södergatan**,

Turning Torso

Malmö's main pedestrianized shopping street.

A late sixteenth-century spin-off from Stortorget, **Lilla Torg** is everyone's favourite part of the city. Lined with cafés and restaurants, it's usually pretty crowded at night, with drinkers kept warm under patio heaters and bars handing out free blankets.

Malmöhus Castle

MAP P.103

Malmöhusvägen Ⓦ malmo.se. Tues–Sun 11am–5pm, charge.

The princely **Malmöhus** is a low fortified castle defended by a wide moat and two circular keeps. Built by Danish King Christian III in 1536, the castle was later used for a time as a prison, but it now houses the **Malmö Museer**, a disparate but fascinating collection of exhibitions on everything from geology to photography – and an aquarium, too. The pleasant grounds, the **Kungsparken**, are peppered with small lakes and an old windmill.

Moderna Muséet

MAP P.103

Ola Billgrens plats 2–4
Ⓦ modernamuseet.se. Tues–Sun 11am–5pm; Thurs until 7pm, charge.

This branch of Stockholm's famous **modern art museum** hosts

Visiting Malmö

Frequent **trains** connect Copenhagen with Malmö, across the 16km Öresund Bridge/tunnel link. You arrive in the bowels of Malmö's rebuilt Central Station. **Malmö Airport** is located 30km to the east with frequent bus connections into the city as well as to Copenhagen. Small, private-owned infopoints are scattered across town, including a pair at the central station, offering maps and brochures. You can also download a free map from ⓦ malmotown.com. Many shops accept Danish kroner though at an uncompetitive 1–1 rate so it's usually best to convert to Swedish currency (SEK).

excellent temporary exhibitions. The building itself is worth a visit for the striking orange-red cube extension built on to what was the city's electricity works

The Turning Torso

MAP P.103

A good twenty-minute walk or five-minute cycle ride north of the station is Malmö's most iconic sight, the 190m **Turning Torso** skyscraper.

Built in 2005, it was Scandinavia's tallest building until 2022, when overtaken by Gothenburg's Karlatornet. A spiralling helix of glass and steel, the structure lords it over the sea towards Denmark. Heading coastwards takes you to a viewpoint of the 8km **Öresund Bridge**, the longest road-and-rail bridge in Europe. There's also access to the Ribban, Malmö's artificial sandy beach.

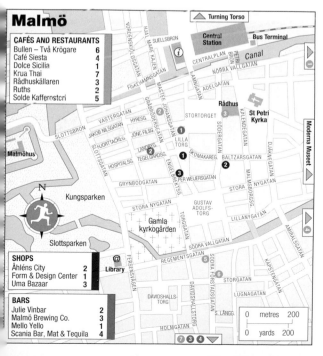

Malmö

CAFÉS AND RESTAURANTS
Bullen – Två Krögare — 6
Café Siesta — 4
Dolce Sicilia — 1
Krua Thai — 7
Rådhuskällaren — 3
Ruths — 2
Solde Kafferosteri — 5

SHOPS
Åhléns City — 2
Form & Design Center — 1
Uma Bazaar — 3

BARS
Julie Vinbar — 2
Malmö Brewing Co. — 3
Mello Yello — 1
Scania Bar, Mat & Tequila — 4

Shops

Åhléns City

MAP P.103
Södergatan 15 Ⓦ ahlens.se.
Malmö's glitziest department store, packed with Swedish designer labels including Acne and Nudie Jeans.

Form & Design Center

MAP P.103
Lilla Torg 9 Ⓦ formdesigncenter.com.
This gallery-café-shop has a lot to offer including a good selection of Scandinavian design knick-knacks, and some handmade items (tea cosies, candlestick holders and the like) by local artists.

Uma Bazaar

MAP P.103
Per Wijersgatan 9 Ⓦ umabazaar.se.
Fair Trade shop that sells everything from Indian pillows and African carpets to recycled jeans and wooden watches. Being Swedish it's all resolutely stylish, organic and sustainable.

Cafés and restaurants

Bullen – Två Krögare

MAP P.103
Storgatan 35 Ⓦ bullen.nu.
The décor has barely changed over the past century and a quarter at this Malmö landmark, in business since 1897. Packed with nostalgic charm, it remains the place to go for a traditional Swedish meal, with highlights include the fish soup and the veal meatballs with lingonberries. Worth booking ahead. €€

Café Siesta

MAP P.103

The Form & Design Center

Hjorttackegatan 1 ⓦ siesta.nu.
Terrific little café, popular for
brunch on weekends when you
can enjoy the likes of smoked
salmon smørrebrød and french
toast. Evening mains include sea
bass with zucchini and grilled
lemon. €€

Dolce Sicilia
MAP P.103
Drottningtorget 6 ⓦ dolcesicilia.se.
A proper Italian-run *gelateria* with
delicious organic ice cream made
fresh every day, as well as coffee
and ciabatta. Also a prime people-
watching spot. €

Krua Thai
MAP P.103
Mollevångstorget 12 ⓦ kruathai.se.
Affordable, authentic Thai
food just south of the centre on
Möllevångstorget. €

Rådhuskällaren
MAP P.103
Stortorget 2 ⓦ radhuskallareni.se.
Historic restaurant housed in the
vaulted cellar of the town hall,
serving a good-value lunch buffet
and an a la carte dinner menu
featuring delicious meaty mains
such as pork tenderloin or veal
schnitzel. €€

Ruths
MAP P.103
Mäster Johansgatan 11
ⓦ ruthsmalmo.se.
Set amid sleek, minimalist
surrounds, *Ruths* is a blend of
café, bakery and bistro with an
open kitchen at its centre, serving
inventive, Instagram-friendly
snacks, salads and meals; the
halibut crudo with cucumber,
sugar rush chilli, lemon and
capezzana is recommended. €€

Solde Kafferosteri
MAP P.103
Regementsgatan 2 ⓦ solde.se.
Lovely coffee bar that also sells
cakes, sandwiches and fresh

roasted beans. Perfectly poured,
ethically sourced and organic. €

Bars

Julie Vinbar
MAP P.103
Tegelgårdsgatan 9 ⓦ juliemalmo.se.
Winner of *Wine Bar of the Year*
and nominated for numerous
other awards, *Julie Vinbar* is a
popular drinking spot for both
locals and tourists alike. The
friendly and knowledgeable staff
members will pair your wine with
cheese and other snacks such as
meats and seafood for a delectable
combination of flavours. There are
14 wines on tap or you can choose
your tipple from the "wine room".
Walk ins only for the large dining
room but larger groups can reserve
the basement area.

Malmö Brewing Co. & Taproom
MAP P.103
Bergsgatan 33 ⓦ malmobrewing.com.
Sup pale ales, pilsners and porters
at the city's first microbrewery,
established in 2010, a ten-minute
walk south of the old centre.
The attached pub is open late
and on Fridays and Saturdays
you can take a tour of the
brewery itself.

Mello Yello
MAP P.103
Lilla Torg 1 ⓦ melloyello.se.
This stylish bar is the best of the
bunch on Lilla Torg. The long
cocktail list is supplemented by
good draught beers including
Brooklyn lager. Food ranges
from delicious small delicacies to
excellent seafood.

Scania Bar, Mat & Tequila
MAP P.103
Bergsgatan 18 ⓦ scaniabar.se.
Mexican and Korean restaurant
with six different kinds of
margaritas on the drinks menu.

ACCOMMODATION

Villa Copenhagen

Accommodation

Hotels do not come cheap in Copenhagen, hovering around 800–1800kr (£90–200/€110–140) per night for an average double room in high season (late June to early September). Those close to the sights of Tivoli and the Inner City (Indre By) are particularly expensive, while the Vesterbro area is the city's budget hotel district with Helgolandsgade in particular lined with more affordable options. Facilities offered at most places are ultra-modern, boasting fabulous design and eco-concious features in true Danish style.

Tivoli and Rådhuspladsen

CAB-INN CITY MAP P.25, POCKET MAP B14. Mitchellsgade 14 Ⓜ **København H** Ⓦ **cabinn.com**. Modern budget hotel around the corner from Central Station and a stone's throw from Tivoli, *Cab-Inn*'s main forte – apart from its compact and super-functional ferry-cabin-style rooms – is its central yet relatively quiet location away from the hubbub of Vesterbro. Rooms sleep up to three people. Part of a larger chain with hotels in Vesterbro (Arni Magnussons Gade 1), Frederiksberg (Vodroffsvej 55 and Danasvej 22) and Ørestaden (Arne Jakobsens Allé 2), the latter designed by Daniel Libeskind. **€**

H27 MAP P.25, POCKET MAP B13. Løngangstræde 27 Ⓜ **Rådhuspladsen** Ⓦ **hoteltwentyseven.net**. Good-value designer hotel slap bang in the city centre and a minute's walk from the Rådhus (whose bells toll every fifteen minutes until midnight and from 7am in the morning, so worth bearing in mind if you're a light sleeper). With spacious modern rooms and a popular courtyard where cocktails from the hotel's *Honey Ryder* cocktail bar can be devoured. **€€**

HOTEL NIMB MAP P.25, POCKET MAP A13. Bernstorffsgade 5 Ⓜ **København H** Ⓦ **hotel.nimb.dk**. Fairy-tale hotel located upstairs in Tivoli's Moorish-inspired Nimb building from 1909. With just fourteen individually decorated extravagant rooms this is Copenhagen's original boutique hotel. Features include open fireplaces, antique wooden furniture and sweeping views of the gardens. *Hotel Nimb*'s opulence encompasses in-room massage and a private chauffeur service. **€€€**

RADISSON BLU ROYAL HOTEL MAP P.25, POCKET MAP A13. Hammerichsgade 1 Ⓜ **København H** Ⓦ **radissonblu.com/**

Accommodation Price Codes

The prices listed below are based on two adults sharing the cheapest en-suite double room in high season inclusive of tax (25 percent). If breakfast costs extra, we have indicated this in the review. Online discounts and a shared bathroom can reduce prices significantly. We have opted for euros in the price codes in this guide as the Danish krone maintains a fixed exchange rate with the euro.

€ – 0–999kr
€€ – 1000–2999kr
€€€ – over 3000kr

Booking ahead

In order to get the lowest room rate book well in advance or try one of the many online booking sites. If you do arrive without a reservation the city tourist office should be able to help at their offices in the airport and on Vesterbrogade (see page 121) and online at ⓦ visitcopenhagen.com.

royalhotel-copenhagen. The *Royal Hotel* is an Arne Jakobsen masterpiece and a prominent example of Danish modernist architecture. A twenty-two-storey rectangular grey and green structure, the hotel is today graced with his furniture throughout, including the famous Swan, Egg, and Drop chairs which were designed specifically for the hotel. Although modern luxury abounds, the hotel today also has a funky time-warped feeling, not least as you step into the 1960s lobby. €€

SCANDIC PALACE HOTEL MAP P.25, POCKET MAP B12. Rådhuspladsen 57 ⓜ Rådhuspladsen ⓦ scandichotels.dk. Wonderful Art Nouveau hotel from 1910 located next door to the Rådhus. A recent refurbishment has reinstated its original décor, featuring lovely details such as George Jensen silver door handles and abstract artwork on the walls. During its heyday many a Hollywood star stayed here including the likes of Audrey Hepburn and Gregory Peck. Although restored to their original appearance, rooms have been totally modernized with comfy beds and luxurious bathrooms. Breakfast included. €€

THE SQUARE MAP P.25, POCKET MAP A12. Rådhuspladsen 14 ⓜ Rådhuspladsen ⓦ thesquarecopenhagen.com. Stylish, smart hotel that is conveniently located for easy access to Tivoli and the downtown shopping district. Housed in a former office block, the minimalist rooms – spread over five floors – have been tastefully decorated and come with all of the required mod cons discreetly tucked away. The breakfast restaurant on the sixth floor offers some great views of the city. €€

VILLA COPENHAGEN MAP P.25, POCKET MAP A14. Tietgensgade 35–39 ⓜ København H ⓦ villacopenhagen. com. Immediately next door to the Hovedbanegården and housed in the former Post & Telegraph headquarters, this beautiful hotel opened its doors in 2020 with an all-Scandinavian aesthetic and all the mod cons plus a few – a heated pool, a stylish cocktail bar and a superlative breakfast among them. Great care was taken to preserve the historical décor of the building, which dates back to 1912. €€

Strøget and the Inner City

D'ANGLETERRE MAP P.32, POCKET MAP E11. Kongens Nytorv 34 ⓜ Kongens Nytorv ⓦ dangleterre.com. This prestigious hotel dating from 1755 is Copenhagen's answer to *The Ritz* in London; hotel of choice for anyone who's anyone, from rock stars to US presidents. Offering classic elegance, with modern Danish design kept to a minimum (although you will find Bang & Olufsen TV screens above the bath tubs), the hotel encompasses a five-hundred-square-metre luxurious spa and fitness centre, a grand restaurant, and a new champagne bar with over 160 different champagnes on the menu. €€

HOTEL SANKT PETRI MAP P.32, POCKET. MAP B11. Krystalgade 22 ⓜ Nørreport ⓦ sktpetri.com. Ultra-stylish design hotel housed in a former five-storey functionalistic department store. The spacious rooms have dark parquet flooring and sleek Scandinavian furniture such as the super-comfortable Jensen bed. The hotel is full of business travellers during the week; you can usually pick up competitive deals at weekends. €€

Nyhavn and Frederiksstaden

71 NYHAVN MAP P.50, POCKET MAP F11. Nyhavn 71 ⓜ Kongens Nytorv

ⓌⓌ**71nyhavnhotel.com**. Two interconnected converted warehouses overlooking Inderhavnen and next door to the city's new playhouse, *71 Nyhavn* is a charming place to stay. Although it is slightly on the small side, the hotel's magnificent location easily makes up for this slight shortfall. Superior rooms feature pretty French doors opening onto a balcony. Primarily a business hotel, there are some good deals to be had during summer. €€

ADMIRAL HOTEL MAP P.50, POCKET MAP F11. Toldbodgade 24 Ⓜ Kongens Nytorv Ⓦ **admiralhotel.dk**. Romantic waterfront hotel in a vast converted warehouse from 1787 with lots of its original features still intact such as vaulted brick ceilings and enormous wooden beams. There are 300 rooms spread over six floors, each with its own unique charm; a sea view will cost extra. Breakfast is served in the downstairs restaurant *Salt* which is also a good bet for other meals, or simply to hang out in its waterfront café section. €€

BABETTE GULDSMEDEN MAP P.50, POCKET MAP G6. Bredgade 78 Ⓜ Marmorkirken Ⓦ **guldsmedenhotels. com**. Formerly the *Hotel Esplanaden*, the Guldsmeden hotel group have added a touch of luxury to this old building, which overlooks Churchill Parken and Kastellet. There's a rooftop spa and brasserie for real indulgence. €€

HOTEL BETHEL MAP P.50, POCKET MAP F11. Nyhavn 22 Ⓜ Kongens Nytorv Ⓦ **hotel-bethel.dk**. A former hostel for Icelandic sailors, *Bethel*'s superb location overlooking Nyhavn Kanal and the bars and restaurants on the opposite bank can hardly be bettered. Bearing this in mind, the somewhat dated but perfectly comfortable, clean and tidy rooms are excellent value. Ask at reception for a tour of the sailor's church round the back if that's what floats your boat. €

Rosenborg and around

IBSENS HOTEL MAP P.60, POCKET MAP A10. Vendersgade 23 Ⓜ Nørreport Ⓦ **arthurhotels.dk/ibsens-hotel**. Arty hotel situated on a Nansensgade street corner

with bright and airy rooms spread over five floors in two interconnected nineteenth-century apartment buildings. Works by local artists (some for sale) are on display throughout the hotel. €€

Christianshavn and Holmen

CPH LIVING MAP P.70, POCKET MAP D14. Langebrogade 1C Ⓜ Christianshavn Ⓦ **cphliving.com**. Absolutely gorgeous hotel boat with twelve identical smartly furnished rooms all facing Christian IV's red-brick brew-house on the opposite bank. Reception is unstaffed and you need an access code to get in, which is given to you when you pay for the room. The reception area doubles as a help-yourself breakfast buffet, which you can eat on the sundeck while taking in the fine views and fresh sea air. Moored next to it is the restaurant boat *Viva* (see page 75). €€

Vesterbro and Frederiksberg

ABSALON MAP P.78, POCKET MAP D8. Helgolandsgade 15 Ⓜ København H Ⓦ **absalon-hotel.dk**. Large good-value family-run hotel that has recently been refurbished with en-suite facilities and a fresh, bright decor in the colourful rooms, some of which can accommodate families of up to four. €€

ANDERSEN MAP P.78, POCKET MAP D8. Helgolandsgade 12 Ⓜ København H Ⓦ **andersen-hotel.dk**. Boutique-on-a-budget hotel with chic, bright rooms and a daily (complimentary) wine hour in the lobby. Only a short walk from Central Train Station. €€

ANSGAR MAP P.78, POCKET MAP A14. Colbjørnsensgade 29 Ⓜ København H Ⓦ **ansgarhotel.dk**. Small, friendly recently renovated family hotel in what used to be the dodgy red-light district of Vesterbro. The no-frills tidy rooms are superb value and the price includes a lavish breakfast buffet which in summer is served on an outdoor terrace. €

CITY HOTEL NEBO MAP P.78, POCKET MAP D8. Istedgade 6 Ⓜ København H Ⓦ nebo.dk. Age-old Danish Mission hotel with rooms that are nothing to write home about but perfectly pleasant and clean, some with en-suite bathroom, others sharing shower and toilet in the corridor. €€

COPENHAGEN ISLAND MAP P.78, POCKET MAP D9. Kalvebod Brygge 53 Ⓜ Islands Brygge Ⓦ copenhagenisland. dk. The Kim Utzon-designed *Copenhagen Island* is as sleek as it gets. With wonderful large windows looking out to the Copencabana harbour pool just outside, you could be excused for thinking that you're on a seaside holiday. Inside the stylish rooms are beautifully furnished with modern Danish design and top of the range electronics. In the hotel basement there's a fitness centre with steam bath and sauna. €€

GULDSMEDEN AXEL MAP P.78, POCKET MAP D8. Helgolandsgade 8 Ⓜ København H Ⓦ hotelguldsmeden.com/axel. Among the city's most appealing boutique hotels with beautiful Balinese-inspired decor and superb attention to detail. This is where the supermodels come to stay and you're likely to feel like one of them after a couple of days, your every whim being catered for by the super-attentive staff. Given the level of pampering, all this comes at a very reasonable price. €

HOTEL CENTRAL & CAFÉ MAP P.78, POCKET MAP C8. Tullinsgade 1 Ⓜ Frederiksberg Allé Ⓦ centralhotelogcafe. dk. Set above an appropriately tiny (five-seat) coffeeshop and once inhabited by a cobbler, this one-room spot definitely earns its billing as "the smallest hotel in the world". A bed, bathroom and flat-screen TV are squeezed into the twelve-metre-square room that nevertheless beckons with some real attention to detail and olde-worlde charm. €€

SAGA HOTEL MAP P.78, POCKET MAP D8. Colbjørnsensgade 18–20 Ⓜ København H Ⓦ sagahotel.dk. In the once grotty red-light district of Vesterbro, family-run *Saga* is today one of the city's really good budget options and popular with backpackers who've had their fill of rowdy and impersonal hostels. The sparsely decorated rooms sleeping up to five mostly share facilities although there are also a few en-suite rooms. Filling breakfasts are served on the second floor in a cosy dining area. €

SCT THOMAS MAP P.78, POCKET MAP C8. Frederiksberg Allé 7 Ⓜ Frederiksberg Allé Ⓦ hotelsctthomas.dk. Popular small Frederiksberg hotel housed in a nineteenth-century apartment block not far from lively Værnedamsvej and offering simple uncluttered rooms. The buffet breakfast, served in the newly excavated basement, is one of the best in town. Free internet only in the lobby. €

WAKE UP COPENHAGEN MAP P.78, POCKET MAP D9. Carsten Niebuhrs Gade 11 Ⓜ København H Ⓦ wakeupcopenhagen. com. Super-efficient and slightly impersonal, this budget hotel on the edge of Vesterbro overlooks the railway line to one side and Inner Havnen to the other. Spread over nine floors, the 500-odd a/c rooms verge on the small side but feel perfectly adequate thanks to the clever design and layout created by architect Kim Utzon. Larger rooms and rooms with a better view cost more. €

ZLEEP HOTEL CENTRUM MAP P.78, POCKET MAP D8. Helgolandsgade 14 Ⓜ København H Ⓦ zleephotels.com. No-frills accommodation a stone's throw from Central Station, this really is as Spartan as it gets. Hence the very reasonable prices, particularly if you book far in advance. Part of a wider *Zleep* concept chain, the hotel provides largely self-service accommodation with food and drink available from vending machines – although the basic breakfast buffet (99kr) is manned. Rooms sleep up to four. €

Nørrebro and Østerbro

HOTEL RYE MAP P.88, POCKET MAP E4. Ryesgade 115 Ⓜ Trianglen Ⓦ rye115. com. Homely *Hotel Rye* is a brilliant option away from the city centre yet near the lively lake area of Østerbro and the tranquil

Our top places to stay

For a damn-the-cost weekend: *D'Angleterre* see page 109
For romance: *Hotel Central & Café* see page 111
For luxury on a budget: *Hotel Twentyseven* see page 108, *Guldsmeden Bertrams* see page 111
For peace and quiet: *Copenhagen Island* see page 111
For Danish design: *Radisson Blu Royal Hotel* see page 108
Location, location: *CPH Living* see page 110
Watching the pennies: *Wake Up* see page 111, *Copenhagen Downtown* see page 112

Fælledparken. Housed in a former care home, the sixteen highly individualized rooms are spread over the second and third floors of an apartment building. All have shared bathroom in the hall (you are provided with a kimono and slippers for nocturnal visits). Outside the back yard is equipped with a play area for kids, and in the cosy dining area freshly baked rolls are available with breakfast every morning. €

Hostels

Copenhagen has some excellent hostels that can often rival budget hotels in terms of value and style. Many offer private doubles, twins and triples as well as the usual dorm rooms. Be aware that the latter are often packed with rowdy Swedish students during the summer holidays and availability can be an issue at these times. Danhostel (Ⓦ danhostel.dk) which runs two of the hostels below charges a one-off membership fee of 70kr if you don't hold a Hostelling International card.

COPENHAGEN DOWNTOWN

MAP P.32, POCKET MAP C12.
Vandkunsten 5 Ⓜ Rådhuspladsen
Ⓦ copenhagendowntown.com. Though affiliated to Danhostel, *Copenhagen Downtown* has a hip, independent feel with guests sprawling on bean bags out onto the pavement, and a cool retro Scandinavian design. The location right next to some superb music venues and a plethora of watering holes is also hard to beat. Rooms are on the smallish side sleeping two to ten people in bunk beds, usually with shared bathroom, but everything is clean and tidy and the vibe energetic. €

DANHOSTEL CITY MAP P.25,

POCKET MAP C14. H.C Andersens
Boulevard 50 Ⓜ Rådhuspladsen
Ⓦ danhostelcopenhagencity.dk. Modern five-star hostel housed in Denmark's first high-rise building, dating from 1955. Encompassing over a thousand beds in four-, six-, eight- and ten-bed rooms spread over sixteen floors it offers wonderful views over Copenhagen. Add the interior design by GUBI and facilities such as a bar-café in the lobby and games room in the basement and you could be forgiven for thinking that you're staying at a modern hotel albeit one with bunk beds. €

GENERATOR MAP P.60, POCKET MAP

D10. Adelgade 5–7 Ⓜ Marmorkirken
Ⓦ generatorhostels.com. Part of a Europe-wide chain of funky hostels, this one is housed in an apartment block designed by Phillipe Starck. It's one of the best places to stay in town if you're young and adventurous, but like your creature comforts. All rooms come with en-suite bathrooms and range from twin-bed doubles to female dorms sleeping six and mixed dorms sleeping eight. The hostel also offers plenty of places to chill out including a large outdoor terrace and a spacious lounge/bar boasting an enormous TV. €€

STEEL HOUSE MAP P.78, POCKET MAP

D7. Herholdtsgade 6 Ⓜ København H
Ⓦ steelhousecopenhagen.com. The former headquarters of the Danish Metalworkers' Union has been transformed into this sleek,

prawling hostel in a central location. The great-value, en-suite private rooms are small – some veritably tiny – but spotless. orms are limited to six per room and ommon areas include a bar, a kitchen, a evoted work space, a small indoor pool nd even a basement arcade. **€**

URBAN HOUSE MAP P.78, POCKET MAP D8. Colbjørnsensgade 5–11 Ⓜ **København H** Ⓦ **urbanhouse.me.** This trendy hostel/hotel opened in 2015 with 950 beds in 225 rooms. Dorms and private rooms (sleep one to four people), plus an in-house bike shop and tattoo studio. **€**

HOSTELS

ESSENTIALS

Central train station in Copenhagen

Arrival

However you arrive in Copenhagen you'll find yourself within easy reach of the city centre. Copenhagen Airport is just a few kilometres to the southeast, on the edge of the island of Amager, while almost all trains and buses deposit you near the city's main transport hub, Central Station.

By air

Getting into the city from **Copenhagen Airport** (ⓦcph.dk), 11km from the city in the suburb of Kastrup, couldn't be easier: one of Europe's fastest airport-to-city rail lines runs directly to Central Station (roughly every 10min; 14min). In addition, the metro (every 4–6min during the day, every 15–20min midnight–7am) links the airport with Christianshavn (12min), Kongens Nytorv (13min) and Nørreport (15min) stations in the centre. Copenhagen Airport is in Zone 3. A taxi to the centre costs about 250–300kr – there's a rank outside the arrivals hall.

You can pick up free maps from the helpful information desk in sleek Terminal 3 (daily 6.10am—11pm). They also sell Copenhagen Cards (see page 117). The airport has two late-opening banks (daily 6am–10pm), lots of ATMs, free wi-fi throughout, 72-hour luggage storage lockers (see page 119), numerous car rental agencies and a post office. The stylish *Hilton Hotel*, connected to the airport by a pedestrian walkway, is a good place to kill some time – their lobby bar is equipped with arrival and departure screens.

Buses from small **Malmö Airport** in Sweden (ⓦswedavia.com/malmo; see page 103) are integrated with flight arrivals. Some 60km east of Copenhagen, it has retained its role as a hub for budget flights to the city. From Malmö Airport, take the bus (ⓦflygbussarna.se) to Malmö Central Train Station (40min); from here, the Öresundståg has frequent departures for Copenhagen throughout the day.

By bus and train

All buses and trains to Copenhagen arrive at or near **Central Station** (in Danish, Hovedbanegården or København H), the city's main transport hub, from where there are excellent connections to virtually every part of the city via bus, local train or the metro circular line. The station also has an array of shops, a foreign-exchange bureau (daily 8am–9pm), places to eat and, downstairs, left-luggage lockers (see page 119). The national train company, DSB, has a travel agency and information centre just inside the main entrance off Vesterbrogade (Mon–Fri 7am–8pm, Sat & Sun 8am–6pm; ⓦdsb.dk) and an easy-to-use ticket machine in the hallway (daily 4.30am–2.40am).

Flixbus coaches from around Europe and cities across Denmark stop behind the station on Ingerslevgade, across from DGI-byen. Buses from Malmö airport stop in front of *Plaza Hotel* next to the station.

Getting around

The best way to explore Copenhagen is either to walk or cycle: the inner city is compact, much of the central area pedestrianized, and there's a comprehensive network of excellent bike paths, perfect for exploring the city. For travelling further afield, there's an integrated network of buses, metros, S-Tog (urban rapid transit) and local trains.

Tickets

All city transport operates on a **zonal system** encompassing the metro, trains and buses. The city centre and immediate area, as you'd expect, are in zones 1 and 2. The cheapest ticket (**billet**) is valid for one hour's travel within any two zones, with unlimited transfers between buses and trains. The City Passes are excellent value: The City Pass Large has various time-limited options (24-hour, 48-hour, 72-hour, 96-hour and 120-hour passes are available) and is valid on all transport to as far away as Helsingør and Roskilde, as well as night buses and all public transport to and from the airport. For half the price of the City Pass Large, the City Pass Small includes only Copenhagen's city limits. Obtain City Passes or individual tickets through the DOT Billetter app (ⓦ dinoffentligetransport.dk). If you're planning on visiting lots of museums and attractions, the Copenhagen Card (see box) also includes free transport.

Tickets can be bought on board buses or at train stations, while 24-hour tickets are only available via the Dot Billetter app. Route maps can be picked up free at stations, and most free city maps include bus lines and a diagram of the S-Tog and metro network. For more information see ⓦ dinoffentligetransport.dk

The metro

The ever-expanding, driverless Copenhagen **metro system** (ⓦ m.dk) provides a fast and efficient link to most parts of the city. Of its four lines, the M3 is among the most useful: a circular route with stops at the Central Train Station (Hovedbanegården) as well as Nørrebro and Østerport. The M3 links the centrally-located Nørreport – also a hub for trains and buses – with Vanløse to the west and the airport to the southeast. Stops marked with an "S" on the metro-map cross the S-tog line – Copenhagen's commuter rail system. Metro stations are marked by a large red underlined "M" painted onto aluminium pillars.

S-Tog and regular trains

The **S-Tog** rapid transit service is laid out in a huge "U" shape and covers the whole Copenhagen metropolitan area. Six of its seven lines stop at Central Station, with the others circling the centre. Each line has a letter and is also colour-coded on route maps. Stations are marked by red hexagonal signs with a yellow "S" inside them.

Regular national trains are run by the **Danish State Railway** (DSB; ⓦ dsb.dk) and among other towns connect the city to Helsingør and Roskilde, calling at Østerport and Nørreport stations and some suburban destinations on the way.

Buses

The city's **bus** network (ⓦ moviatrafik.dk) is more

The Copenhagen Card

If you plan to do lots of sightseeing, you might want to buy a **Copenhagen Card**. Valid for 24, 48, 72 or 120 hours, it covers public transport (including Helsingør and Roskilde) and gives free (or discounted) entry to most museums. This can save a lot of money – especially since it can also give you twenty- to thirty percent off car rental, ferry rides and theatre tickets. The card is electronic only; it can be purchased after downloading the Copenhagen Card app (ⓦ copenhagencard.com).

comprehensive than the S-Tog system and can be a more convenient way to get around once you get the hang of finding the stops – marked by yellow placards on signposts – and as long as you avoid the rush hour (7–9am & 5–6pm). The vast majority stop at Rådhuspladsen next to Tivoli. Buses with an "S" suffix only make limited stops, offering a faster service – check they make the stop you require before you get on. Buses with an "CA" suffix indicate that the bus runs frequently. All buses have a small electronic board above the driver's seat displaying both the zone you're currently in and the time – so there's no excuse for not having a valid ticket. A skeletal **night-bus** (*natdrift*) runs once or twice an hour (fares remain the same). Night-bus numbers always end with "N".

Harbour buses

A cheaper way to experience Copenhagen from the waterfront than a canal tour, yellow **harbour "buses"** sail along the harbour between Nordre Toldbod (near the Little Mermaid) and the Royal Library, stopping six times and costing the same as a normal bus fare. Services (daily every 20min about 7am–7pm) are cancelled when the harbour is frozen.

Cycling

If the weather's good, the best way to see Copenhagen is to do as the locals do and get on your bike. The superb, city-wide cycle lanes make **cycling** very safe and bikes can be taken on S-Tog trains (free of charge) through any number of zones. Lights are mandatory at night (you'll be stopped and fined if the police catch you without them). Copenhageners generally take the rules of the bike lanes very seriously; never ride side-by-side with other bikers and make sure to signal when turning or stopping or else you may be told off. You can usually **rent bikes** through your hotel or hostel. Otherwise try Baisikeli, Ingerslevsgade 103 (ⓦ baisikeli.dk). Alternatively, rent on a per-minute basis by setting up an account with Donkey Republic (ⓦ donkey.bike), allowing you to make use of the ubiquitous orange bikes.

Taxis

Taxis are plentiful, but with a flat starting fare of 39kr, then 10kr per kilometre and 7kr per minute, they're only worth taking in a group. There's a handy rank outside Central Station; you can also book with Taxa (ⓣ 35 35 35 35) or hail one in the street – the green "Fri" sign on top shows it's available.

Directory A–Z

Accessible travel

Copenhagen is a model city for travellers with disabilities: wheelchair access, facilities and help are generally available at hotels, hostels, museums and public places. To see whether a place caters for travellers with disabilities, check the website ⓦ godadgang. dk or contact the tourist office at ⓦ visitcopenhagen.com.

Addresses

The street name is always written before the house number, which is followed by the apartment number o floor the apartment is on, followed by the side the apartment is at (t.h. – to the right as you come up the stairs; t.v. – to the left; and m.f. the middle). So, Læssøesgade t.h., means the third-floor apa to the right, in building num n Læssøesgade. The city is divided into postal districts consisting of four igits followed by the area so Indre y is Kbh K preceded by a four-digit umber; Østerbro is Kbh Ø, Nørrebro Kbh N, Vesterbro Kbh V, Amager Kbh and Frederiksberg Fred. After the ompletion of the bridge across to weden the city of Malmö is jokingly alled Kbh M.

Cinema

nternational blockbusters are screened at Imperial (Ved Vesterport , ⓦnfbio.dk/imperial). More alternative films are shown at *Grand Teatret* (Mikkel Bryggersgade 8, ⓦgrandteatret.dk) and Vester Vov Vov Absalonsgade 5, ⓦvestervovvov.dk).

Crime

Copenhagen has an extremely low crime rate. Keep an eye on your cash and passport and you should have little reason to visit the **police**. If you do, you'll find them courteous and usually able to speak English. The central police station is at Polititorvet 14 (ⓣ33 14 88 88).

Electricity

The Danish electricity supply runs at 220–240V, 50Hz AC; sockets generally require a two-pin plug. Visitors from the UK will need an adaptor; visitors from outside the EU may need a transformer.

Embassies and consulates

Australia Dampfærgevej 26, 2nd floor ⓣ70 26 36 76; **Canada** Kristen Bernikowsgade 1 ⓣ33 48 32 00; **Ireland** Østbanegade 21 ⓣ35 47 32 00; **South Africa** Gammel Vartov 8, Hellerup ⓣ39 18 01 85; UK Kastelsvej

36–40 ⓣ35 44 52 00; **US** Dag Hammerskjölds Allé 24 ⓣ33 41 71 00.

Health

There are **24-hour emergency departments** at Bispebjerg Hospital, Bispebjerg Bakke 23 (ⓣ38 63 50 00) and Hvidovre Hospital, Kettegårds Alle 30 (ⓣ38 62 38 62). Call 1813 for any medical emergencies. For **dental emergencies**, contact Tandlægevagten, Oslo Plads 14 ⓣ70 25 00 41 (Mon–Fri 8–9.30pm, Sat & Sun 10am–noon, 8–9.30pm).

The city centre's only 24-hour **pharmacy** is Steno Apotek, Vesterbrogade 6C in front of Central Station (ⓣ33 14 82 66), while Sønderbro Apotek, Amagerbrogade 158, Amager (ⓣ32 58 01 40), is open until midnight.

Internet

Copenhagen has plenty of wireless hubs in cafés and bars and on trains. Most hotels and hostels – and even some campsites – offer wi-fi (most for free), and access is also available and **free** at libraries.

Left luggage

The DSB Garderobe office downstairs in Central Station **stores luggage** and is priced per item per day. There are also lockers (Mon–Sat 5.30am–1am, Sun 6am–1am). Copenhagen airport's left-luggage facility, in Parking House P4 across the road from terminal 2 (open 24hr), has small and large lockers for hire from anywhere between 4 hours to 7 days.

LGBTQ+ travellers

Copenhagen is one of the world's top **LGBTQ+** destinations. Attitudes

Emergency numbers

Dial ⓣ112 for police, fire or ambulance.

Public holidays

Denmark observes most religious holidays and moveable feasts. On the following days, expect all banks and most shops to be closed, and check the websites of attractions. Easter is a five-day holiday, followed by a number of single religious holidays up until Whitsuntide.

December 31 New Year; **January 1** New Year's Day; Maundy Thursday; Good Friday; Easter Sunday; Easter Monday; Ascension Day (6th Thurs after Easter); Whitsun (Sun & Mon, 7 weeks after Easter); **December 24** Christmas Eve; **December 25** Christmas Day; **December 26** Boxing Day.

are very tolerant and there is a lively scene which is enjoyed by many straight people, too. The Copenhagen Pride festival (see page 122) is a particularly great time to experience Copenhagen. Check out Ⓦ copenhagen.gaycities.com to see what's on.

Lost property

The police department's **lost-property** office is at Politigården ☏ 38 74 88 22. For items lost on a bus (including a habour bus), train or metro, go to Ⓦ dinoffentligetransport. dk and navigate to "Customer Service" then "Lost items" to find the relevant phone number depending on the company servicing your particular line. There's a lost luggage office at Central Station (Mon–Fri 8am–8pm, Sat & Sun 10am–5pm); for lost property at Copenhagen Airport go to Terminal 3 or look online at Ⓦ missingx.com.

Money

The Danish currency is the **krone** (plural kroner), made up of 100 øre, and comes in notes of 1000kr, 500kr, 200kr, 100kr and 50kr, and coins of 20kr, 10kr, 5kr, 2kr, 1kr, 50øre. At the time of writing, the exchange rate was approximately 8.70kr to the pound, 7.45kr to the euro and 6.95kr to the US dollar. For the latest rates, go to Ⓦ xe.com.

Opening hours

Shops tend to open Mon–Thurs 10am–6pm, Fri 10am–7pm, Sat 10am–4pm, Sun noon–4pm but shops in the centre of town tend to have longer hours. Most offices are open Mon–Fri 9am–4/4.30pm.

Phones

You should be able to use your **mobile phone** though it may be cheaper to buy a Danish SIM card or e-SIM. For around 99kr, you'll get a Danish number plus about forty minutes of domestic calls. The most commonly used network is TDC, but coverage with Telemore, Telenor and others is just as good. SIM cards and credit can be bought in supermarkets, kiosks and phone shops.

Calling Denmark from abroad, the **international code** is ☏ 45.

Post

It can be hard to find a post office these days, but you will find the classic red postboxes all around town. You can buy stamps from most newsagents.

Smoking

Smoking is banned in all public buildings and restaurants as well as on station concourses and platforms. Bars and cafés under forty square metres which do not serve fresh food may still allow smoking.

Price codes

We have used euros for the price codes in this guide as the krone maintains a fixed exchange rate with the euro.

For cafés and restaurants, the following price codes are based on a two-course meal and a drink:

€ – 0–249kr
€€ – 250–799kr
€€€ – over 800kr

Time

Denmark is one hour ahead of GMT, six hours ahead of US Eastern Standard Time, and nine ahead of US Pacific Standard Time.

Tipping

Service is included on all restaurant, hotel and taxi bills in Copenhagen, so unless you feel you've been given exceptionally good service, tipping is not necessary.

Tourist information

The Copenhagen Visitor Centre (Mon–Fri 9am–4pm, Sat & Sun 9am–4pm; Ⓦ visitcopenhagen.com), across the road from the Central Station at Vesterbrogade 4A, offers maps, general information and accommodation reservations, along with free accommodation-booking terminals.

Travelling with children

Copenhagen is a very child-friendly city with reserved children's pram areas on buses and trains, and children's menus and high seats available at most restaurants. The low level of traffic and many pedestrianized streets also make for a stress-free visit with kids.

Guided Tours

As well as the operators below, the Copenhagen Visitor Centre on Vesterbrogade (see above) has a long list of English-language guided walking tours - many of which are free.

Bike Copenhagen with Mike Ⓦ bikecopenhagenwithmike. dk. Cycle tours to Vesterbro, Amalienborg, the Little Mermaid, Christiania and much more, led by the knowledgeable and charismatic Mike. Book online.

Copenhagen Food Tours Ⓦ copenhagen.foodtours.eu. Three-hour and four-hour walking tours sampling tasters from the latest movers and shakers on the Danish food scene. The tasters along the way add up to a full-blown meal, so best to arrive hungry. Tours start and end at Torvehallerne.

Copenhagen Sightseeing Tours Ⓦ sightseeing.dk. A variety of bus tours (including hop-on hop-off routes which cover stretches by canal boat) with multilingual headphone commentary.

Kajak Republic Ⓦ kayakrepublic.dk. Kayak tours offering a view of the city from water level, with several departures each day during the summer. All necessary equipment provided. Evening tours include a glass of bubbly on the water.

Netto-Bådene Ⓦ havnerundfart.dk. Excellent-value one-hour canal tours departing from Holmens Kirke and taking in Nyhavn, Holmen, Nyholm, Amalienborg Palace and the Little Mermaid.

Festivals and events

Copenhagen Carnival

Whitsun weekend ⓦ karneval-kbh.dk
A mini Rio of samba and colourful costumes along Strøget and Købmagergade which culminates in all-night partying at Fælledparken supposedly allowing you to see the Whitsun sun "dance" as it rises in the early hours of the morning.

Sankt Hans Aften

Midsummer's eve
ⓦ visitcopenhagen.com
Bonfires and traditional Danish folksongs at various locations along the Copenhagen coast. Check the tourist board website for locations and times.

Roskilde Festival

Last week of June or first week of July (see page 95) ⓦ roskilde-festival.dk
Four-day Glastonbury-style music festival in the outskirts of Roskilde preceded by four days' warm-up in the camping area.

Copenhagen Jazz Festival

First or second week of July ⓦ jazz.dk
Local and international jazz stars – young and old – take over the city's music stages and venues, as well as many outside spaces, making it Europe's biggest jazz event. With loads of free gigs the entire city seems to be swinging to all sorts of jazz imaginable.

Copenhagen Pride

One week in July or August
ⓦ copenhagenpride.dk

Superb week of queer events focused on the area around Frederiksholms Kanal and culminating in the flamboyant and colourful Gay Pride Parade which makes its way through the centre of town on the Saturday.

Copenhagen Cooking

Last ten days of August
ⓦ copenhagencooking.dk
Riding on the Nordic cuisine popularity wave, over one hundred events across the city hosted by many of the city's famous chefs give you an opportunity to sample some of the amazing creations.

CPH Fashion Week

Biannually in January/February and in August ⓦ copenhagenfashionweek.com
Copenhagen brims with tastemakers and those eager to be seen as fashion shows are held around town. Many are invite-only, but whether invited or not, people-watching in the city during this week can be a little more fun than usual.

Christmas and New Years

Leading up to Christmas – which is celebrated Christmas Eve – the city is aglow with festive lights and decorations, and *gløgg* and *æbleskiver* (a version of mulled wine and dough balls with apple inside) is sold everywhere. On New Year's Eve Rådhuspladsen is the scene of a massive fireworks fest and champagne drinking.

Danish

In general, English is widely understood throughout Denmark, and young people especially often speak fluently. However, even with little need to resort to Danish, learning a few phrases will surprise and delight any Danes you meet. If you can speak Swedish or Norwegian, then you should

ave little problem making yourself
nderstood – all three languages share
e same root.

There is no single word in the Danish
anguage for "please". So when a Dane
oesn't say "please" when speaking to
ou in English, it's not because they're
ude – the word just doesn't come
aturally. Danes are also renowned for
eing direct – if they want something
ey say "Give me..." – which can,
correctly, be interpreted as impolite.

An idea of pronunciation for key
hrases is given in brackets below.

asic words and phrases

aler de engelsk? (tayla dee ENgellsg) Do
ou speak English?

a (ya) Yes

ej (nye) No

eg forstår det ikke (yai fus TO day igge) I
on't understand

ær så venlig (verso venli) Please (or the
earest thing to)

ak (tak) Thank you

ndskyld (unsgul) Excuse me

i (hye) Hello/Hi

odmorgen (goMORN) Good morning

oddag (goDA) Good afternoon

odnat (goNAT) Goodnight

arvel (faVELL) Goodbye

vor er? (voa ea?) Where is?

vad koster det? (ve kosta day?) How much
oes it cost?

eg vil gerne ha... (yai vil GERne hae) I'd
ke...

vor er toiletterne? (voa ea toaLETTaneh?)
Where are the toilets?

Et bord til ... (et boa te...) A table for...

Må jeg bede om regningen? (moah yai bee
uhm RYningan?) Can I have the bill/check,
please?

Billet (billed) Ticket

Food and drink basics

Brød Bread

Det kolde bord Help-yourself cold buffet

Is Ice cream

Ostebord Cheese board

Peber Pepper

Pølser Frankfurters/sausages

Rugbrød Rye bread

Salt Salt

Sildebord A selection of spiced and pickled
herring

Kylling Chicken

Oksekød Beef

Svinekød Pork

Kartofler Potatoes

Fisk Fish

Smør Butter

Smørrebrød Open sandwiches

Sukker Sugar

Wienerbrød "Danish" pastry

Øl Beer

Fadøl Draught beer

Guldøl Strong beer

Vin Wine

Husets vin House wine

Hvidvin White wine

Rødvin Red wine

Mineralvand Mineral water

Chokolade (varm) Chocolate (hot)

Kærnemælk Buttermilk

Kaffe (med fløde) Coffee (with cream)

Mælk Milk

Te Tea

Vand Water

Chronology

1043 The name "Havn" appears in the
Knýtlinga Saga, described as the place
Norwegian king Magnus sought cover
after being defeated at sea.

1160 Bishop Absalon is given control
over "Havn" by his foster brother King
Valdemar. Recent excavations have

shown that Copenhagen at the time was
a significant fishing village – Kongens
Nytorv largely built on fish bones – and
its residents unusually tall.

1167 Bishop Absalon completes the
construction of fortified Københavns
Slot on present day's Slotholmen

Island. Its aim is to protect the town's fishermen and traders from Wendish pirates.

1238 The construction of the town's first monastery commences – today's Helligåndshus.

1249 The earliest recorded attack and plunder of the town by a Hanseatic fleet from Lübeck.

1334 With 5000 inhabitants Copenhagen is Scandinavia's largest settlement.

1369 The town is attacked and briefly occupied by Hanseatic forces who systematically dismantle Københavns Slot.

1417 King Eric of Pomerania makes the newly reconstructed Københavns Slot his seat of power and residence of the royal family.

1443 Copenhagen replaces Roskilde as Denmark's capital.

1479 Copenhagen University, the first in Scandinavia, is established in today's Latin Quarter.

1536 Protestant Reformation takes hold with the arrest of the Catholic Bishop of Copenhagen.

1588 Christian IV aka "The Builder King" is born. After taking the throne at the age of ten he begins a lifelong programme of works. Among his many feats are the neighbourhood of Christianshavn, the city's defensive ring of moats, ramparts and Kastellet, Rosenborg Slot and Rundetårn.

1657 Skåne is ceded to Sweden at the Treaty of Roskilde, Denmark's second most important town Malmö thereby becoming Swedish.

1659 After three years' siege, the city is stormed by Swedish troops.

1660 Absolute monarchy is introduce

1711 Plague epidemic kills at least 22,000.

1728 The first "great fire" of Copenhagen destroys over a thousand buildings.

1730 Christian VI decides to have Københavns Slot torn down and a much grander Louis XIV Rococo-style palace - renamed Christiansborg – is erected in its stead. It burns to the ground 28 year after its completion in 1766. Only the stables and riding ground survive.

1795 The second great fire of Copenhagen burns Christiansborg to the ground.

1801 British and Danish ships engage at the Battle of Copenhagen. Horatio Nelson famously turns a blind eye to Admiral Sir Hyde Parker's orders to retreat.

1807 Fearing the Danes may side with Napoleon, the Royal Navy shells Copenhagen. After three nights of bombardment, large parts of the city lie in ruins. The Danish-Norwegian navy is surrendered to the British.

1828 A new Romanesque-style Christiansborg is completed.

1836 Hans Christian Andersen's *The Little Mermaid* is published.

1838 Sculptor Bertel Thorvaldsen returns to Copenhagen after forty years in Rome.

1843 George Carstensen's brainchild Tivoli opens in the former rampart area.

1843 Father of Existentialism Søren Kierkegaard's *Either/Or* is published.

1847 J.C. Jacobsen founds the Carlsberg brewery.

1884 The second Christiansborg is burnt to the ground leaving only Christiansborgs Slotskirke standing.

1897 The Ny Carlsberg Glyptotek is opened by philanthropic brewing magnate Carl Jacobsen, son of J.C.

1911 The National Romantic Central Station stands completed.

1913 The Little Mermaid statue by Edvard Eriksen (and paid for by Carl Jacobsen) is unveiled.

1928 The current neo-Baroque Christiansborg is completed.

1940 In the early hours of April 9, Copenhagen is occupied by German forces with barely a shot fired.

1943–1945 Most of Denmark's Jewish population is smuggled successfully across to Sweden in fishing boats.

1971 First Roskilde festival.

1971 Christiania is founded in disused military barracks on Christianshavn.

1972 Queen Margrethe II ascends the throne.

1973 Denmark joins the EU.

1992 The Danish football team beat Germany to win the European Cup, receiving a heroes' welcome on their return home.

2000 The Øresunds link to Sweden is opened.

2005 Crown Prince Frederik marries his Tasmanian bride Mary.

2007 Copenhagen-based crime drama *The Killing* becomes an international hit (along with its woolly jumpers).

2010 Copenhagen's *Noma* is rated as the world's best restaurant.

2012 Copenhagen's first official bicycle super highway opens.

2014 Copenhagen hosts the Eurovision Song Contest in a former shipyard on Papirøen, spending three times its budget.

2016 Copenhagen reaches a milestone, there are officially more bicycles than cars in the city.

2019 The new City Circle Line (M3) opens, marking the largest construction project in Copenhagen in the last 400 years.

2023 Outrage over Quran burnings outside Copenhagen embassies leads to the state's proposal to criminalize 'indecent' expression, sparking further uproar.

SMALL PRINT

Publishing Information
Fifth edition 2024

Distribution
UK, Ireland and Europe
Apa Publications (UK) Ltd; sales@roughguides.com
United States and Canada
Ingram Publisher Services; ips@ingramcontent.com
Australia and New Zealand
Booktopia; retailer@booktopia.com.au
Worldwide
Apa Publications (UK) Ltd; sales@roughguides.com

Special Sales, Content Licensing and CoPublishing
Rough Guides can be purchased in bulk quantities at discounted prices. We can create special editions, personalised jackets and corporate imprints tailored to your needs. sales@roughguides.com.
roughguides.com

Printed in Czech Republic

This book was produced using **Typefi** automated publishing software.

A catalogue record for this book is available from the British Library

The publishers and authors have done their best to ensure the accuracy and currency of all the information in **Pocket Rough Guide Copenhagen**, however, they can accept no responsibility for any loss, injury, or inconvenience sustained by any traveller as a result of information or advice contained in the guide.

Rough Guide Credits
Editor: Lizzie Horrocks
Author: Taraneh Ghajar Jerven
Copyeditor: Annie Warren
Updater: Anthon Jackson
Cartography: Katie Bennett
Picture Editor: Tom Smyth
Original design: Richard Czapnik
Head of DTP and Pre-Press: Rebeka Davies
Head of Publishing: Sarah Clark

Acknowledgements
Many thanks to Annie Warren for her excellent editing and to Lizzie Horrocks for reaching out in the first place; and thanks to my wife Joanna, whose insights

certainly enriched this book, for her sweeping introduction to Denmark, and for convincing me to call it home for the last decade or so.

Help us update

We've gone to a lot of effort to ensure that this edition of the **Pocket Rough Guide Copenhagen** is accurate and up-to-date. However, things change – places get "discovered", opening hours are notoriously fickle, restaurants and rooms raise prices or lower standards. If you feel we've got it wrong or left something out, we'd like to know, and if you can remember the address, the price, the hours, the phone number, so much the better.

Please send your comments with the subject line "**Pocket Rough Guide Copenhagen Update**" to mail@uk.roughguides.com. We'll credit all contributions and send a copy of the next edition (or any other Rough Guide if you prefer) for the very best emails.

SMALL PRINT

Photo Credits

(Key: T-top; C-centre; B-bottom; L-left; R-right)

Index

A

accommodation 108
  71 Nyhavn 109
  Absalon 110
  Admiral Hotel 110
  Andersen 110
  Ansgar 110
  Babette Guldsmeden 110
  Cab-Inn City 108
  City Hotel Nebo 111
  Copenhagen Island 111
  CPH Living 110
  D'Angleterre 109
  Guldsmeden Axel 111
  H27 108
  Hotel Bethel 110
  Hotel Central & Café 111
  Hotel Nimb 108
  Hotel Rye 111
  Hotel Sankt Petri 109
  Ibsens Hotel 110
  Radisson Blu Royal Hotel 108
  Saga Hotel 111
  Scandic Palace Hotel 109
  Sct Thomas 111
  The Square 109
  Villa Copenhagen 109
  Wake Up Copenhagen 111
  Zleep Hotel Centrum 111
addresses 118
Amager Strandpark 98
Amagertorv 33
Amalienborg 49
Arbejdermuseet 61
Arken Museum of Modern Art 99
arrival 116
Assistens Kirkegaard 87
A taste of Torvehallerne 62
Axeltorv Square 27

B

Bakken 94
bars
  1105 40
  Bang & Jensen 84
  Bibendum 66
  Blågård's Apotek 92
  Bo-Bi Bar 40
  Bopa 93
  BRUS 93
  Café Globen 67
  Charlie's Bar 40
  Curfew 85
  Den Vandrette 57
  Falernum 85
  Julie Vinbar 105
  Kalaset 67

Kayak Bar 47
  K-Bar 41
  Malmö Brewing Co. & Taproom 105
  Märkbar 77
  Mello Yello 105
  Mesteren & Lærlingen 85
  Mikkeller 85
  Nemoland 75
  ØlBaren 93
  Oscar Bar og Café 29
  Pixie 93
  Props Coffee Shop 93
  Ruby 41
  Salon 39 85
  Scania Bar, Mat & Tequila 105
  Søhesten 67
  Sukaiba 101
  TAP10 93
  The Barking Dog 92
  The Living Room 41
  Vinbaren Vesterbro Torv 85
  Vivant 93
bars (by area)
  Christianshavn and Holmen 75
  Day-trips 101
  Malmö 105
  Nørrebro and Østerbro 92
  Nyhavn and Frederiksstaden 57
  Rosenborg and around 66
  Slotsholmen 47
  Strøget and the Inner City 40
  Tivoli and Rådhuspladsen 29
  Vesterbro and Frederiksberg 84
Best places to explore on two wheels 5
Børsen 46
Botanisk Have 59
buses 117
by air 116
by bus and train 116

C

cafés and restaurants
  56° 73
  Aamanns 64
  Alchemist 73
  Ali Bageri 91
  Anarki 81
  Arken Museum Café 100
  Atlas Bar 37
  Bankeråt 65
  Bar'Vin 37
  Bento 82
  Bevar's 91
  Brasserie Nimb 29
  Buka Bakery 54

Bullen – Två Krögare 104
  Cafe 22 91
  Café and Ølhalle 65
  Café Baaden 100
  Café Kystens Perle 100
  Café Munk 65
  Café Oscar 55
  Café Oven Vande 73
  Café Siesta 104
  Café Sundet 91
  Café Sylten 100
  Café Viggo 82
  Cap Horn 55
  Chicky Grill Bar 82
  Christianshavns Bådudlejning 74
  Cofoco 82
  Conditori La Glace 37
  Den Franske Café 91
  Den Økologiske Pølsemand 37
  Det Lille Apotek 38
  Det Vide Hus 65
  Dolce Sicilia 105
  Dragør Røgeri 100
  Emmerys 55
  Europa 1989 38
  Famo 82
  Fischer 91
  Frk. Barners Kælder 82
  Glyptoteket 29
  Granola 82
  Grillen 91
  Grøften 29
  Hansens Gamle Familiehave 82
  Hija de Sanches Taqueria 82
  Høst 65
  Hyttefadet 55
  Kadeau 74
  Kafferiet 55
  Kaffesalonen 92
  KanalCafeen 29
  Kilden i Skoven 101
  Kødbyens Fiskebar 83
  Koefoed 65
  Kokkeriet 55
  Kong Hans Kælder 38
  Krebsegaarden 39
  Krogs Fiskerestaurant 39
  Krua Thai 105
  La Banchina 73
  La Galette 39
  Lagkagehuset 74
  Laundromat 92
  L'Éducation Nationale 39
  Lumskebugten 55
  Mad & Kaffe 83
  Madkartoteket 47
  Madklubben 55

Marchal 39
MASH 55
Maven 40
Mirabelle 92
Morgenstedet 74
Mormors 56
Mother 83
Nørrebro Bryghus 92
Nyhavn 17 56
Orangeriet 65
Paludan Bogcafé 40
Paté Paté 84
Peter Lieps Hus 100
Pilekælderen 40
Pintxos 66
Punk Royale 56
Rådhuskälleren 105
Ravelinen 75
Rebel 57
Reffen – Copenhagen Street
    Food 75
Riccos Kaffebar 84
Roast 75
Ruths 105
Sebastopol 92
Slotskælderen hos Gitte Kik 40
Slurp Ramen 66
Solde Kafferosteri 105
Søpromenaden 92
Spiseloppen 75
Spisestedet Leonora 101
Spuntino 84
Sticks'n'sushi 66, 84
Sult 40
Tårnet 47
Taste 57
Tivoli Food Hall 29
Torvehallerne 66
Un Mercato 65
Vandkunsten sandwich &
    salatbar 40
Vespa 57
cafés and restaurants (by area)
Christianshavn and Holmen 73
Day-trips 100
Malmö 104
Nørrebro and Østerbro 91
Nyhavn and Frederiksstaden 54
Rosenborg and around 64
Slotsholmen 47
Strøget and the Inner City 37
Tivoli and Rådhuspladsen 29
Vesterbro and Frederiksberg
    81
Carlsberg Visitor Centre 78
Central Station 26
Christiania 69, 71
Christiansborg Slotskirke
    (Palace Chapel) 44
Christianshavn and Holmen 68
Christianshavns Kanal 68
Christians Kirke 68

Chronology 123
cinema 119
Cisternerne 80
clubs
    Culture Box 67
clubs (by area)
    Rosenborg and around 67
Copenhagen Card 117
crime 119
cycling 118

D

Danish 122
Dansk Jødisk Museum 46
Davids Samling 62
Day-trips 94
Den Blå Planet 98
Den Sorte Diamant (The Black
    Diamond) 47
Designmuseum Danmark 52
Det Kongelige Teater 34
Dining with the Danes 63
directory A–Z 118
Dragør 99
drinking 7
Dyrehaven 94

E

eating 7
electricity 119
embassies and consulates 119
emergency numbers 119
ENIGMA 89
Experimentarium 89

F

Fælledparken 87
festivals and events 122
    Christmas 122
    Copenhagen Carnival 122
    Copenhagen Cooking 122
    Copenhagen Jazz Festival 122
    Copenhagen Pride 122
    CPH Fashion Week 122
    New Years 122
    Roskilde Festival 122
    Sankt Hans Aften 122
Folketing (Danish Parliament)
    42
Frederiksberg Have 79
Frederiksberg Slot 79
Frederiksborg Slot 95
Frihedsmuseet 52

G

getting around 116
Gruntvigs Kirke 98
guided tours 121

H

harbour buses 118
health 119
Helligåndskirken 31
Hirschsprungske Samling 60
Højbro Plads 33
hostels
    Copenhagen Downtown 112
    Danhostel City 112
    Generator 112
    Steel House 112
    Urban House 113

I

Islands Brygge 71
Israels Plads 62
Istedgade 76
itineraries 18

K

Kastellet 52
Købmagergade and around 34
Kødbyen 77
Kongens Nytorv 34
Krigsmuseet 45
Kronborg Slot 97
Kunsthal Charlottenborg 48

L

left luggage 119
LGBTQ+ Copenhagen 119
Lilla Torg 102
lost property 120
Louisiana 94

M

Malmö 102
Malmöhus Castle 102
maps
    Christianshavn and Holmen 70
    Copenhagen at a glance 8
    Day-trips 96
    Malmö 103
    Nørrebro 86
    Nyhavn and Frederiksstaden 50
    Østerbro 88
    Rosenborg and around 60
    Slotsholmen 46
    Strøget and the Inner City 32
    Tivoli and Rådhuspladsen 25
    Vesterbro and Frederiksberg 78
Maritime Museum of Denmark 97
Marmorkirken 51
Medicinsk Museion 53
Moderna Muséet 102
money 120
music venue
    Mojo 29

music venue (by area)
  Tivoli and Rådhuspladsen 29
music venues
  Den Grå Hal 75
  Drop Inn 41
  Islands Brygges Kulturhus 75
  Jazzhus Montmartre 41
  La Fontaine 41
  Loppen 75
  Musikcaféen 41
  Rust 93
  Vega 85
music venues (by area)
  Christianshavn and Holmen
    75
  Nørrebro and Østerbro 93
  Strøget and the Inner City 41
  Vesterbro and Frederiksberg
    85

N
Nationalmuseet 28
nightlife 7
Nørrebro and Østerbro 86
Nyboder 63
Ny Carlsberg Glyptotek 26
Nyhavn 48
Nyhavn and Frederiksstaden
  48

O
opening hours 120
Operaen 71

P
Park life 59
phones 120
post 120
public holidays 120

R
Ridebane (Royal Stables) 43
Rocking Roskilde 95
Rosenborg and around 58
Rosenborg Slot 58
Royal Reception Rooms 42
Royalty Danish style 43
Ruinerne Under Christiansborg
  43
Rundetårn 31

S
shopping 7
shops
  Accord 90
  Åhléns City 104
  Arnold Busck 35
  Bang & Olufsen 35
  By Malene Birger 35
  Christiania Cykler 73
  Decadent Copenhagen 35
  Designer Zoo 81
  DesignMuseum Danmark
    shop 54
  Donn Ya Doll 81
  Ecouture by Lund 35
  Enula 9 90
  Faraos Cigarer-Comics 35
  Form & Design Center 104
  Galerie Asbæk 54
  George Jensen 35
  Hay 35
  Henrik Vibskov 36
  Illums Bolighus 36
  Isoteket 90
  Karamelleriet 90
  Keramik og Glasværkstedet 64
  Lakor 90
  Lego 36
  Le Klint 36
  Løgismose 54
  Mads Nørgaard 36
  Magasin du Nord 36
  Meyers Bageri 81
  Munthe 36
  Nordatlantens Brygge 73
  Pegasus 64
  Peter Beier Chokolade 54
  Pour Quoi 90
  Prag 90
  Ravnsborggade Antique
    Stores 90
  Royal Copenhagen 36
  Samsøe og Samsøe 81
  Sögreni of Copenhagen 37
  Sømods Bolcher 37
  Spidsroden 90
  Stig P 81
  Summerbird 81
  Tranquebar 64
  Tutein & Koch 37
  Uma Bazaar 104
  Wilgart 91
shops (by area)
  Christianshavn and Holmen 73

Malmö 104
  Nørrebro and Østerbro 90
  Nyhavn and Frederiksstaden
    54
  Rosenborg and around 64
  Strøget and the Inner City 35
  Vesterbro and Frederiksberg 81
Skuespilhuset 51
Slotsholmen 42
smoking 120
Statens Museum for Kunst 59
S-Tog and regular trains 117
Stortorget 102
Strøget 30
Strøget and the Inner City 30

T
taxis 118
The Carlsberg Quarter 77
The Danish Resistance 53
The Latin Quarter 31
The Little Mermaid 53
the metro 117
The Rådhus 27
The Turning Torso 103
Thorvaldsens Museum 45
tickets 117
time 121
tipping 121
Tivoli 24
Tivoli and Rådhuspladsen 24
Torvehallerne 62
tourist information 121
travelling with children 121
Tycho Brahe Planetarium 77

V
Vesterbro and Frederiksberg 76
Vesterbrogade 76
Visiting Malmö 103
Vor Frelserskirke 68
Vor Frue Kirke 32

W
weather and climate 6
What lies beneath, digging up
  the town 25

Z
Zoologisk Have 80

NOTES

NOTES